ROD STEWART

Also by Stafford Hildred
(with David Gritten)

Tom Jones

ROD STEWART

A Biography

Tim Ewbank and Stafford Hildred

HEADLINE

Extracts from *True Britt* by Britt Ekland
appear by kind permission of Sphere Books

First published in 1991
by HEADLINE BOOK PUBLISHING PLC

10 9 8 7 6 5 4 3 2

British Library Cataloguing in Publication Data

Ewbank, Tim
  1. Great Britain. Rock music. Stewart, Rod *1945–*
I. Title   II. Hildred, Stafford
782.42166092

ISBN 0–7472–0345–8

Phototypeset by Intype, London

Printed and bound in Great Britain by
Richard Clay Ltd, Bungay, Suffolk

HEADLINE BOOK PUBLISHING PLC
Headline House
79 Great Titchfield Street
London W1P 7FN

To
Sarah, Emma and Oliver

and to
Janet, Claire and Rebecca

Contents

Chapter One
First Steps

'For goodness sake, don't bring him back home late' – Mrs Elsie Stewart.

Before the man who was to become a leading contender for the title of the world's greatest hellraiser was allowed out for the night which was to change his life, his mother had something to say.

Rod Stewart was just three days away from his nineteenth birthday when his forceful mother Elsie telephoned her son's newly found musical mentor Long John Baldry and firmly warned him to have her young son home in time for bed. Long John was surprised that the lusty youth still answered to his mum on matters of bedtime, but had already seen enough star potential to agree to this strange request.

That initial jam session in a dingy cellar in the depths of Soho was perhaps the real beginning of the musical education of Rod Stewart, the first step on the road to fully understanding the remarkable talents of the shy and nervous stand-in singer and harmonica player.

And more than once in the weeks and months afterwards, having been driven back across the city by Baldry to his humble North London home long after the deadline, Rod would stumble up the path to the sound of Elsie yelling: 'Is that you, Roddy? I'll pay you! I'll pay you!'

1

But the Rod Stewart story really began in January 1945, as the War in Europe was grinding to its grim conclusion and London was far from swinging. Huge areas had been devastated by the Luftwaffe; food was rationed and in desperately short supply; and the winter was bitterly cold. But there were still some warm celebrations long into the night of 10 January in the household of expatriate Scot Robert Stewart and his Cockney wife Elsie when they added a chubby young baby boy, one Roderick David Stewart, to their already chirpy brood of two sons and two daughters.

Just thirty minutes before Rod was born, an even bigger shock had hit the district in the shape of a German V2 rocket which made a direct hit on Highgate Police Station. Rod was to reflect, years later: 'I've always thought that I was very lucky because that bomb fell just a stone's throw from where I lived. I've sort of had a feeling that I nearly didn't make it.'

Robert Stewart came from King's Port in Edinburgh. He was just fourteen when he ran away to sea, but by the time he had reached his late teens he was washed up on dry land in London. He began his land-bound career as a plumber's apprentice but eventually worked his way up to become a master builder. Rod's mother, Elsie, came from Upper Holloway, North London. She fell for the fast-talking young Scot, the couple married in 1928 and the Stewart clan began to appear soon afterwards. Mary, Don, Bob and Peggy were born in quick succession and the happy family moved to 507 Archway Road, Highgate, where, after a gap of eight years, young Roderick was born.

Bob Senior retired from the building trade at sixty-five, but family funds were never large enough to make for a relaxed retirement, and so he opened a newsagent's shop when Rod was in his early teens.

Rod's earliest recollections are of a lively, laughing family. The main preoccupations of the male members were football and music, in that order. Now he says simply: 'I came from a very poor family, but I was extremely well fed and extremely happy. I was incredibly spoilt as the youngest of five kids. I had a fantastically happy childhood.' Perhaps because he now speaks from a personal perspective of immense wealth, Rod is inclined to exaggerate the 'poverty' of his childhood. Certainly the Stewarts were by no means well off but their small business selling sweets, cigarettes and tobacco and newspapers brought in enough to keep the large family in reasonable comfort.

Respect for his father, based on a very strong bond of love and founded in those early years, was to last Rod into his own middle age. 'The only thing I worry about,' he said, 'is my dad. If I upset my dad, then I'm really in trouble. He is nearer to me than anything.'

From his father, Rod also inherited a respect for loyalty and honesty. He always put that down to his 'good Scottish roots', and described his father as 'an interesting guy – rotund, about five foot ten, and he has got just one tooth because he doesn't believe in going to the dentist. A lot of Scots haven't got too many teeth; it's something to do with the water. He's very, very thoughtful, fairly puritanical and a quiet man. My mum's much more outgoing than Dad. She loved to get the family round and give them a drink and make everyone get up and sing a song. She was a very, very good mother.' Rod's own loyalty to his family has become legendary over the years as he has done his best to protect them from some of the more unpleasant and intrusive aspects of having a famous pop star for a son.

Rod's father and his two elder brothers were great soccer enthusiasts. Although his father was forty-two when Rod was born, he was still playing the game for a local amateur side. Rod remembers as a small child seeing his dad play a rather overenthusiastic game of football and break his leg as a result. 'He was playing a bit too tough, and he had to spend Christmas in hospital with his leg in plaster. An absolute

3

soccer nut,' he says with pride. And the stars of the Stewarts' spiritual home were their heroes. In spite of being born in London, both Don and Bob had their bedroom walls covered with pictures of Scottish football stars like George Young of Rangers and Hibernian's Gordon Smith. Rod's father ran the local Highgate Redwings club which at its height had three teams chasing all over North London every weekend. As amateur facilities were somewhat basic in those days this frequently meant anything up to thirty-three mud-splattered players using the house as a changing room on a Saturday afternoon.

Not surprisingly, a lifelong enthusiasm for football was instilled in Rod at a very early age and he was a keen supporter of local North London team Arsenal. Generally regarded as the most talented footballer in the family, even as a youngster he plunged into the game with enormous enthusiasm and with a style of play that relied as much on his considerable natural skill as on an almost reckless aggression.

At secondary school Rod's footballing skills were perhaps more highly regarded than his scholastic abilities. He rose through the junior teams to become school soccer captain and went on to play for Middlesex Schoolboys as centre half. As a useful all-rounder, he also became cricket captain, but football was always his real love.

After football the great enthusiasm of the Stewart family was music, which generally expressed itself as a good old-fashioned house party with assorted inebriated relations, much singing around the piano, and good times being enjoyed by all. 'We are a very close family,' said Bob Stewart in a rare interview in 1977. 'If you hurt one of us you hurt the lot. We never heard Rod singing at home, you know. Only when he was helping out in my shop.'

Rod fondly recalls the warmth and laughter of those family parties. His favourite moments were spent as a young boy

4

curled up underneath the piano wondering which of his older brothers would be the first to drop a sixpence on the floor in front of his Uncle John, just to find out exactly what a Scotsman did wear under his kilt.

Al Jolson, whose most famous line was 'You Ain't Seen Nothing Yet', was the family favourite. Rod still has a great affection for the legendary entertainer, even going so far as to cite Jolson as one of his early musical influences. 'My brother Don is a natural entertainer – the finest impersonator of Al Jolson I've ever seen. As far back as I can remember, when I was about three or four, my father was an Al Jolson fanatic. Every Saturday night, he'd come back from the pub singing Al Jolson songs.' Don's huge collection of Jolson 78s were a constant source of inspiration to the young Rod. When he was taken to see the two Larry Parkes films *The Jolson Story* and *Jolson Sings Again*, Rod was completely bowled over. 'It's incredible that he had no mike and could reach an audience of 2,000,' says the man who now regularly plays to packed stadiums of 20,000 and more, aided by all the latest sound equipment that modern technology can provide. Later, following in big brother Don's footsteps, he started listening to Little Richard records, which provided his introduction to rock 'n' roll. But that, as they say, is another story.

As a schoolboy, Rod's finer moments were clearly spent on the sports field. After failing to distinguish himself at Highgate Primary School, he was still surprised to fail the Elevenplus. When he moved on to William Grimshaw Secondary Modern School in Hornsey, known locally as Billy Grim, also numbered among the pupils and alongside Rod in the football team were the brothers Davies, Ray and Dave, and Pete Quaife – later to achieve fame and fortune as the Kinks. Whilst academic accolades passed him by, Rod did rise to become a prefect but the honour was summarily removed shortly afterwards following an incident involving the somewhat unnecessary discharge of a fire extinguisher.

Of course, when he was a schoolboy, Rod's famous spikey hairstyle had still to evolve but even then he was always very concerned about its appearance. He waged a constant battle against the hair at the back of his head, which, despite his best efforts, insisted on standing up. 'My mother used to spit on her hand and try to make it lie flat, but it still stood up. A cowlick, that's what you call it.' At the age of fourteen, strongly influenced by an American film he had seen at the cinema ('something to do with test pilots') he ceded temporary honourable defeat by opting for a crew cut, with mixed results: 'I looked terrible, all nose and ears.' It wasn't until he reached his late teens that, necessity being the mother of invention, he cultivated the famous 'Rod the Mod' hairstyle that he still sports in an updated form.

Rod's first experience with a musical instrument was no more encouraging. As an alternative to ordinary woodwork lessons an enlightened teacher coached Rod and a group of other boys in the specialised skills of guitar making. Rod's instrument looked highly promising until he put on the strings. Then it snapped in two. Partly as compensation and partly, perhaps, because he somehow felt there lurked untapped musical potential within his youngest child, Rod's indulgent father splashed out the then considerable sum of eight pounds fifteen shillings (£8.75) for a replacement.

The gift might have been remembered as one of the first significant musical moments in Rod's young life. Instead, Rod recalls: 'When I was fourteen, I remember I had a model railway and I asked my dad to buy me a station. Instead, he went and bought me a guitar, for no apparent reason. I think this was my first personal encounter with music. So what I do now is all my dad's fault.

'I didn't ask for it and I hardly used it. At first I wasn't really interested and I hated music at school – there was this teacher called Mr Wainwright who seemed to be always picking on me to sing in front of the class. Awful.'

As a youngster Rod displayed little or no indication of his musical potential. The first record he bought, at the age of thirteen, was, in spite of his enthusiasm for Al Jolson, Eddie Cochran's 'C'mon Everybody'. In his early teens he was much more interested in model railways, locking himself in his bedroom to make tiny carriages and scaled-down scenery by hand with painstaking care.

'When I was still at school I had no musical inclination whatsoever,' says Rod. 'And I was very shy to sing. Very, very shy.' But gradually, nurtured by his brothers and sisters, Rod's interest in music developed. He even picked up his guitar and, aged fourteen, joined his first schoolboy group.

'I used to strum around a bit,' he says, 'and gradually I got involved. It was an old Zenith guitar. The first thing I learned on it was "It Takes a Worried Man" in the key of E.' And so Rod's nascent musical abilities were stirred. Soon afterwards, he joined his first proper band, the Kool Kats, on guitar in 1960. Rock 'n' roll having barely reached Britain's shores, they played a lot of skiffle music, made hugely popular at the time by Lonnie Donegan. The Kool Kats consisted of eight guitarists, all strumming like mad, and their repertoire contained such classics as 'Freight Train, Freight Train' and 'Does Your Chewing Gum Lose Its Flavour on the Bedpost Overnight?' It was a beginning.

Rod's bedroom, however, was still dominated by his train set. It was laid out all around his bed and Rod had constructed an elaborate tunnel going in and out of one window. If the train came off the tracks in the tunnel Rod had to climb out through his bedroom window and on to the scullery roof to get it back on the rails. One of Rod's teenage pals, a would-be guitarist and future Rolling Stone named Ronnie 'Woody' Wood, stayed round at Rod's one night. The next morning, a little groggy from the night before, Woody jumped up in the morning and cracked his head on the tunnel almost knocking himself out.

Leaving school at fifteen, Rod took a job as a silk screen printer at the Framery in Muswell Hill, just down the road from his parents' home. He had shown some promise during art lessons at William Grimshaw and, despite his lack of formal qualifications, had nurtured a brief hankering to become a designer. But at the time football was still the only activity for which Rod could muster anything approaching real enthusiasm. Father Bob thought that at last he had produced a real footballer: 'All the boys played, but Roddy was the best. I'd really hoped to see him playing at Wembley.' He believed Rod had the ability to make the grade. West London professional side Brentford thought so too. And so, soon after he started his first job, he dropped his artistic ambitions to sign to them as an apprentice.

But while Rod loved playing football there were aspects of life as an aspiring pro that he found hard to cope with. He hated getting up at seven o'clock in the morning to travel to Brentford FC's training ground. And he was even less enthusiastic about the opening task of the day – cleaning the First Team's boots. The physical side of the game was also difficult for Rod in those days as he found it hard to cope with the club's intensive training routines. When he was seventeen Rod was five feet eleven inches tall, but he weighed only nine stone. Often he pushed himself so hard in training that he was sick at the side of the pitch.

And so, although he played in two months of pre-season fixtures as a lively but lightweight centre half, Rod Stewart decided he was not going to hang around for a whole season while the middle-aged men who ran the club made up their minds as to whether he had a future in the game.

Rod's decision naturally came as a great disappointment to his father. 'It was my dad's great dream that I would make it as a professional footballer.' Although good amateurs, neither of Rod's elder brothers had been quite special enough to make the grade as professionals. Bob Stewart had therefore pinned his hopes on his youngest – and most talented – son. But while maybe Rod had the ability, he himself admits that he did not have the necessary dedication. 'I had the skill but not the enthusiasm.'

Luckily for him, he had a choice, as the musical side of his life was beginning to develop promisingly at the same time. 'There wasn't ever a really conscious decision to go either way. Music and football, it's two ways to get out out of the streets. I was lucky because I had a shot at both ways,' he says now.

Weighing up the options, Rod decided that a professional musician had a lifestyle far better suited to him than that of a professional footballer. As he put it, 'I thought, well, a musician's life is a lot easier and I can also get drunk and make music, and I can't do that and play football. I plumped for music . . . They're the only things I can do, really, play football and sing.'

However, Rod's greatest asset, whether he wanted to become a footballer or a musician, was his insuperable belief in himself, fostered, perhaps, by his position as the youngest child in a loving and devoted family. He might not have been ready for fame – and in those early days he was unprepared to work for his future – but he most certainly wanted to make it, somehow or other.

Rod frequently insisted he had no ambition, except one day to become famous. Even when he left school he was convinced he was going to be famous for something. It didn't matter what – medicine, jumping off the Eiffel Tower, anything . . . he just had to be famous. Rod later reflected that the most important thing to have was the belief in yourself: that you are going to make it sooner or later. He said: 'If it's a half-hearted effort you'll fail. I always wanted to be the centre of attention. It's in my make-up. When I was at school I wanted to be the centre of attention in everything. Some of us are like that and some of us are not.

9

I don't think I've ever been ordinary.'

But, like so many seventeen-year-olds, Rod had no real clue about his future. After walking out of Brentford he used a small amount of money his father had given him to make his first trip abroad to Paris. He hitch-hiked to Dover and from Calais on to Paris. But he stayed only a couple of nights, sleeping on the Left Bank and wandering around. The language barrier and an acute shortage of money sent him scuttling home to Mum and Dad. But it was a first taste of the wide world outside North London and he was to return.

When not playing in the band, Rod worked in the family shop, doing odd jobs and ordering stock. Less successfully he attempted early morning newspaper deliveries. Rod's mother recalls that she would often go to wake him at seven only to find that he was still fast asleep an hour later. Rod remembers being press-ganged into an early morning round when one of the regular boys did not turn up one morning. 'I was seventeen at the time. My dad dragged me up at six in the morning. I was a humiliating sight. All those kids were up to my knees and he pushed me out into the snow and made me deliver papers. I threw them over the railway and went back to bed.'

Soon afterwards, he took up his most well-known job outside the music business, that of gravedigger. It was comfortably the oddest job he has ever had. He worked for a few weeks only at Highgate Cemetery, last resting place of Karl Marx. But he had a reason for taking the job other than the minimal financial rewards. As a boy and as a young man Rod Stewart had always felt an almost irrational fear of dying. He had suffered nightmares about death from a very early age and so thought, as an impressionable teenager, that perhaps by getting as close as he could to death, actually digging out holes to be filled by real bodies, he could rid himself of that fear. It was also the only job he could get at the time as, by now, he had grown his recalcitrant locks right the way down his back.

Rod perhaps got closer to experiencing death than he had initially anticipated. 'One experience that scared the shit out of me was when I first went on the job. What happens when you start is that the other guys who work in the cemetery sort of christen you when you get the job by putting you inside a coffin and closing the lid, which is a very, very frightening experience. It doesn't sound like it, but once you get in there and they close the lid on you, you wonder if they'll just leave you in there. That was the initiation.'

But it seemed that working as a gravedigger did calm some of those teenage tantrums. 'It's like when you fall off a horse you've got to get right back on or you might not ride again because your fears can grow to be too intense. So I thought in my case the best way of beating my fear of death was to confront it, to get as close to it as possible. And I've never had any problems with it since.'

By now, and by his own none-too-modest admission Rod was 'getting pretty good on the guitar' and so, with his brother Don, he set off for Tin Pan Alley, the street in London's West End where Rod fondly imagined all great guitarists of the future went for their instruments. The guitar Rod chose was priced at £40 which was roughly £40 more than he had to spend. However, Don indulgently signed on the dotted line as guarantor of Rod's hire purchase agreement – an act of generosity he was to regret when one of Rod's long adventures away from home caused him to forget to make the payments. Don was forced to pay up.

Rod learned very early in life that the music business could be hard and disappointing. He was just sixteen when he was asked to sing a one-off with a group called the Raiders. The band were to record a horror rock instrumental number entitled 'Night of the Vampire' but Rod went along to the studio to sing some extra tracks. The unpredictable producer,

Joe Meek, who was overseeing the session, brought it to an early close in typically dramatic fashion. After ten minutes of rasping youthfully around in a bid to get adjusted to his new colleagues, Rod was alarmed to experience Joe's considered opinion. Meek burst into the studio and blew a giant raspberry in Rod's direction. Rod's first recording opportunity came to nothing.

As he became more heavily involved in music, new influences were having their effect on the impressionable youngster. He recalls: 'I was listening to Woody Guthrie and Jack Elliot, and turning into a leftist Marxist type. You name it, I'd ban it. I skipped across Europe with just a guitar singing songs like "Cocaine All Around My Brain". Dylan came out with his first album and that was a turning point. I knew every song from that album – "Fixin' To Die", "The Cost Of Sorrow" – a great album. From there on I decided I'd become a beatnik, hair right down the back, radical left-wing type. Did that for a couple of years.'

Three decades on it is hard to recall the heady idealism of the new wave of thought that swept the young of the early sixties. Jack Kerouac's *On the Road* philosophy was handed earnestly on from teenager to teenager: they hadn't necessarily read the book, but they still received the rootless message of the new freedom. The poetry of Allen Ginsberg was spouted by nodding duffel-coated devotees in smoky coffee bars. The word 'beatnik' entered the language and battalions of rebels were launched in relentless search of a cause. The leading candidate was the threat of nuclear war. CND, the Campaign for Nuclear Disarmament, was formed under the leadership of intellectual leaders like Bertrand Russell and Marghanita Laski.

Those high-idealled thinkers at the head of the Easter 'Ban the Bomb' marches to Aldermaston were followed by waves of supporting youths. Among them in 1961, 1962 and 1963 was the slightly less than totally dedicated Rod Stewart.

'It was the fashionable thing to do at the time. I did four marches,' recalls Rod. 'We did feel strongly about the bomb, but we had a lot of fun, too. There used to be an awful lot of hanky-panky going on. I remember I was going on a march with a girl, but before we went, I took her home and we had it away under the rug underneath the piano. Few people used to get any sleep on those marches – they turned into mass orgies. Not that I did too much marching. I had another guitar by then and I was in a band – we used to ride in a Land-Rover.'

Although he jokes about the seriousness of his feelings, Rod was committed enough to the cause to get himself arrested on three different occasions at sit-in protests in Trafalgar Square and Whitehall. The passive resistance tactics had hundreds of CND members carried none too gently to the cells by the men of the Metropolitan Police. This was followed in Rod's case by a brief court appearance and a fine to be paid, inevitably, by Rod's father. The Stewarts may not have completely understood or even approved of what their youngest son was doing but, as with his model railways and his music, they indulged him.

On the annual march Rod, by then proficient on harmonica as well as guitar, recalls CND leader Bertrand Russell walking all the way ('Poor old sod') without too strong a twinge of conscience. He was more interested in the appeal of available sex and plentiful supplies of alcohol which made banning the bomb a not totally unpleasant experience.

Rod's memories of his sexual initiation are, perhaps not unsurprisingly, vague. On different occasions he has recalled the loss of his virginity as occurring under the family piano and under a grubby blanket at the 1960 Beaulieu Jazz Festival with an older woman. He has remembered the latter coupling ending rather prematurely on his part with consequent irritation on the part of his instructress. That evening had got off to a somewhat difficult start when Rod and his group of

13

friends were refused entry to the festival on grounds of being too scruffy – something of an achievement at an outdoor jazz festival. A friendly farmer suggested they used an underground route via some old sewers, which had them happily emerging close to the beer tent.

However Rod's sexual education began, it is clear that once he became interested in matters carnal he was an eager pupil. Perhaps his first serious relationship was with a 17-year-old girl from Bristol, whom he met on a march.

Rod was a year older and deeply attracted by the young lady who was very much in the mould of female that has become so strongly associated with Rod Stewart – long legs, blonde hair, shapely figure. They were beatniks together and everything about the relationship was wonderful for young Rod, apart from her gradually growing enthusiasm for marriage. This was certainly not on Rod's schedule. He was not at all sure what he wanted to do with his life, but his plans most definitely did not include settling down and taking a wife, however attractive the obvious candidate for the role might be. She tried hard to persuade Rod to meet her parents but he seemed to find the 120 miles an insuperable obstacle.

The relationship took a dramatic turn when she announced to Rod that she was pregnant with his baby and then went on to confront Rod's mother with the news. According to Rod, his mother was underwhelmed by the information and by no means about to force him to do what was then fashionably known as the decent thing. Perhaps the lowest point in this by now increasingly fractious affair came on the beach at Brighton where Rod and his girlfriend were taking a weekend to try to resolve their situation. His bluntly bachelor attitude to their baby so enraged her that she picked up his guitar, which he had been idly strumming, and crashed the instrument down on some rocks.

The distraught girl did have the baby but she no longer had Rod – although he did go to the hospital, with one of her closest friends, Chrissie Shrimpton, the night the child was born. In fact, while they waited for news of the birth, Chrissie, sister of top Sixties model Jean Shrimpton, told Rod about a promising young singer called Mick Jagger who had a band called the Rolling Stones . . . Rod's daughter was adopted and Rod later reflected that his tough stance on the baby was hard on the young mother but in the long term best for them both. He was simply not ready for family life.

As they drifted further apart after this unhappy interlude Rod also found himself moving through the beatnik phase and towards the way he is popularly remembered. The metamorphosis into 'Rod the Mod' was underway. Girls had certainly entered his life in a big way by this stage and young Rod had many different ways of attracting friendly females. Surely the most bizarre and least successful was impersonating jet-setting airline staff in the hope of lifting off a new romance. Rod recalled years later: 'Me and my mate used to dress up as airline pilots to get birds – the whole outfit, with the epaulettes, the hat, the little bag with all the maps in it, and wander around Heathrow trying to pull – it didn't work as the accent gave us away.'

One of the reasons why Rod was easing himself out of the beatnik movement was that he resented the way it was gradually being taken over by the less committed, the weekend beats, sneeringly dubbed the 'day trippers' by full-time drop-outs. Day trippers had respectable jobs, careers even, during the week and then reached for their joss sticks and duffel-coats on Friday nights, whereas Rod's only formal employment at the time extended to the occasional foray into his father's shop to help out.

Rod now moved for a brief period out of the family home to the South Coast. He was among a group of twenty beatniks dossing down in a derelict houseboat at Shoreham, Sussex. They had actually attempted a clean-up job on the sad craft and a sympathetic observer might have described it as almost habitable. But the locals thought it, and the people who lived on board, were an eyesore. Again Rod fell foul of the forces of law and order. He recalled: 'All the greybeards in the area didn't like the idea of us all not working so they got the police to drive us out with hoses of cold water. Then they towed the boat away and sank it so we wouldn't be able to go back, which was just as well really because the boat filled up with water every time the tide came in.'

Unfortunately, some of Rod's pals decided not to leave without a battle and scuffles broke out. A particularly reluctant evictee was a bearded individual known as John the Road. He happened to possess an historic firearm, a musket, which he fired off at the police. John the Road was probably in more danger from the gun than anyone else, but the police were not to know that. For a time all hell broke loose and locals cheered as most of their unwelcome visitors were hosed into the drink. This incident made page one news in both the *Daily Mirror* and the now-defunct *Daily Sketch*.

Rod did not last too long as a 'beatnik'. Cord trousers, baggy sweaters and sandals was never going to be his uniform for long. He was too conscious of his looks – the bright and sharp mod outfits that were coming into fashion were far more his natural style. In fact, clothes have always played an important part in his life. He frequently recalls what he was wearing along with significant moments in his life. For instance, he recalls: 'I got my first leather overcoat the day President Kennedy was shot,' and 'I went on holiday to Bognor Regis when I was fifteen and I had a little grey jacket that came to just above me backside.'

The rest of the Stewart family were delighted to see the back of the beatnik look. His mother decided to make it an irrevocable fashion change. 'Eventually I returned home with my tail between my legs. I was really smelly and I remember my mum burned all my bloody clothes, all my beatnik clothes. You know how long it takes to get our Levi's perfect? I mean,

I think I cried. And then me dad told told me I had to get me hair cut.'

The posturing, almost effeminate, 'Mod' style of dress could almost have been invented for Rod Stewart. The long hair was swiftly replaced by the forerunner of the spiky style that has become his trademark. He borrowed his sisters' hair lacquer and became known for what was always called in Cockney rhyming slang a 'great Barnet' (from Barnet Fair – hair). Rod then threw himself enthusiastically into the Mod style. One of his first new outfits was a collarless leather Beatles jacket and a polo-necked sweater from the newly opened John Michael shop. This was followed by matelot shirts, washed-out denims and leather jackets in an attempt to look French.

'I used to have my hair like Dusty Springfield,' said Rod. 'It stood six inches above my head. Bottles of hair lacquer: it was like a rock when you touched it. We used to hold our hair on the Underground platforms so the bouffant wouldn't get blown down when the trains came through.'

The transformation from Rod the Beatnik to Rod the Mod was well under way. And, with his ever-indulgent parents to support him in his endeavours, he was now ready to make his mark on the world. His formal education had made little impression but his musical education was about to begin.

Chapter Two
Rod the Mod

'Rod was always different. There was always something about him. Even then he used to wear outrageous gear and instead of underpants he used to wear ladies' knickers. Not because he was bent but because he had to do something different.' Jimmy Powell.

A motley crew of musicians influenced the young Rod Stewart. Brummie blues singer Jimmy Powell gave him a start in his Five Dimensions; Long John Baldry saw the raw talent; Brian Auger provided some hard lessons on life on the road; and Jeff Beck found himself upstaged in his own band.

But first there was Raymond 'Wizz' Jones.

Raymond had earned the nickname Wizz at school because he fancied himself as a bit of a magician. He welcomed the tag. It was far better than boring Raymond, he decided, and it all helped towards trying to establish an interesting identity from out of his somewhat mundane working-class roots in Croydon.

Like millions of youngsters in America and Britain in the Fifties, Wizz was influenced by Bill Haley. Before he ever picked up a guitar, Wizz bought himself a black plastic jacket, painted 'See You Later Alligator' on the back, and went to see Bill Haley at the cinema and got thrown out every night of the week.

But he managed to see enough to know that he wanted to play guitar and when the Soho jazz scene gave way to skiffle and then encompassed folk music, Wizz determined to be a part of it. He began busking round Soho and one day he found the 17-year-old Rod Stewart beside him joining in. Days later, he was sitting in a pub called Finch's in Goodge Street idly strumming a few chords when suddenly Rod was there again. He whipped his harmonica out of his pocket and the two began playing together before setting off in the general direction of Leicester Square to busk in the streets.

Rod's enthusiasm for the harmonica had been sparked by veteran American Blues singer Sonny Boy Williamson who used the instrument to such haunting effect on his 1963 tour of Britain. He found it easier to play than the guitar, especially after copying a young rival on the music scene, Mick Jagger. Rod said afterwards: 'An important thing I learned at that time was how to play the harmonica properly. That was through watching Mick do it. I realised I had been sucking when I should have been blowing and vice versa.'

Buskers were still something of a novelty in London's West End and Wizz and Rod certainly had curiosity value. It was not every day that you would find a scruffy Bohemian from Croydon and a snappily dressed Scot from Highgate singing 'San Francisco Bay Blues' in the middle of Leicester Square.

'We'd get an enormous crowd,' recalls Wizz, 'and we'd work it like a circus with people looking out for the police. I often spent the night in the nick for busking and Rod must have done too. You have to be quite extrovert to work the streets. I could turn that on but in the beginning Rod was shy in front of an audience.'

Wizz's great dream was to open a club in London to emulate the Blues club run at the Roundhouse by Cyril Davies and Alexis Korner. Eventually, he found a room upstairs in a pub called the Porcupine in Leicester Square and one of Wizz's earliest recollections of Rod was an argument at the door about Rod's unwillingness to pay to get in. 'Then he stood at the back and heckled,' Wizz recalls.

It was Wizz who first showed Rod the have-guitar-will-travel nomadic life of a musician and invited him on 'raves', as Wizz called them, to Brighton. Rod, Wizz and their pals would all turn out of the Soho coffee bars and walk some three miles to Waterloo station where they would catch the milk train to Brighton and arrive at six in the morning ready to hit the town. 'It was before the Mods and Rockers fights,' Wizz stresses. 'We were more gentle. We just wanted to be noticed.'

After the Shoreham escapade, Rod had decided to ease himself out of the beatnik scene and so he and Wizz headed for France, taking with them two ten-guinea Spanish guitars fitted with the steel strings they could bend more easily to suit their Bluesy styles. They hitched to Dover, caught a ferry over the English Channel, and then thumbed a ride to Paris where Wizz taught Rod the essentials of busking on foreign soil.

Over a period of eighteen months, the pair went on several such trips. They would arrive in Paris, find a good hotel, then leave their passports with the concierge as security. Having done that, they would go off and busk. 'We could earn enough to live in a good hotel, have a couple of decent meals a day, and have enough to pay for taxis to get us from one pitch to another alongside the cinema queues,' Wizz proudly remembers. 'Sometimes we slept rough but generally it was a great life.'

When other buskers followed the same Paris trail and the market became over-crowded, Rod made off for Spain where he continued to busk but with less success. When his money ran out he took to sleeping under the arches of Barcelona's massive football stadium. Eventually, he was turfed out of the stadium by the Spanish police and, along with some other impecunious British nomads, was taken down to the police station. Finally, the British Consulate was asked to repatriate

Rod and he was flown home to London.

Back in Highgate and safe in the bosom of his family he was able to have his first proper bath in weeks while his father, disgusted at the filthy state of the clothes that Rod had been wearing for so long, insisted the garments could easily have walked back home of their own accord.

Wizz, meanwhile, ploughed his folkie furrow and the busking duo gradually grew apart. Wizz was surprised when Rod turned up in the Hoochie Coochie Men two years later and truly amazed at how much Rod had learned. He says: 'Everyone copied each other. I learned all my licks from Davy Graham [a seminal early sixties folkie] and Rod used to watch and learn from me. I'd never realised he was going to be such a great singer. He didn't have that wonderful rasp in his voice then – that must have come from singing on the streets where you really have to force your voice.'

At the time, partly because of his 'distinctive' hairstyle, Rod was regarded as a bit of a joker by his fellow musicians-on-the-make. However, as Wizz now ruefully accedes, 'When he came up with those solo albums I was knocked out because he had done what we had all been trying to do. Rod had been inspired by raw acoustic folk music and he had taken it, put it into a rock form, and come up with something new.'

Another singer to spot the untapped potential of the strange young man in Mod's clothing was an energetic if unsophisticated young Blues singer from Birmingham called Jimmy Powell. With his throaty renditions of Blues classics Jimmy had built up a big reputation on the Midlands circuit with his band, Jimmy Powell and the Detours, which then went on to become the Dimensions. He made something of a national impact when he hit the lower reaches of the charts in 1960 with the rasping 'Sugar Baby'. Jimmy had made enough trips down to London to sing on the same bills as better-known bands like Cyril Davies All-Stars to realise that the capital was the place to be.

London was just swinging into the sixties and places like the Crawdaddy, the Manor House, Johnny's Jazz Club, Eel Pie Island and the Marquee. 'It was a fantastic time for music,' says Jimmy. 'We didn't know then we were in on the start of a musical revolution. We just knew we were having a bloody good time. Every pub, every club needed music. If you were in a band you were in demand.'

Rod was then just another would-be musician. He played the guitar not too badly, blew an enthusiastic harmonica, or 'harp' as they then called it, and sang in a voice that still had a long way to develop into the rasping tones that have become his trademark. Rod joined in the many jam sessions and sang and played with different friends but he was not in a group. In between trips to the Continent he lived at home, worked in his brother's business painting signs and making picture frames for London shops. Jimmy Powell had decided that a harmonica player and occasional second singer would add yet another dimension to the Dimensions and so he asked the youngster to join. It was not a happy experience.

The received wisdom on Rod Stewart's spell with his first professional group is that Rod eventually left because Jimmy Powell would not let him sing. Jimmy does not remember it quite that way.

'When I first saw Rod Stewart he was sitting in the corner playing a 12-string guitar during our interval. He was always a bit different. We all had long hair down our backs but he already had the puffed-up Mod style . . . When we got to know him and heard him sing I knew he had a good voice but it was not the distinctive sound that it is today.' However, Powell decided it was good enough for his purposes.

'When I gave him the job I told him just to start playing some harmonica backing. Then I'd come play some harmonica and we'd have a bit of a war on stage. Then I told him to sing a couple of numbers and I'd come on and take over. He was hired as second singer. The idea was that after his numbers there'd be a big riff and it would be "Introducing Jimmy Powell" and I'd leap on and away we'd go.

'At first it worked great. We did very, very well. I remember we played Ken Collyer's Jazz Club in Newport Street. Ken booked us to do a Blues night every Tuesday. It went apeshit. We did an absolute stormer. Then he took on another band called the Rolling Stones to do Thursday nights and that went a stormer, and then he booked the Pretty Things to do Friday and that went a stormer.

'We all used to be mates and help each other out in those days. We all did the same circuit and then Georgie Fame came on the scene and Geno and the Ram Jam Band and Jimmy James and London at that time was just fantastic.

'But Rod was always somebody who was never going to finish up as the second singer. He wanted to be *the* singer. Even from the start he would want to play all the best numbers. And he would snatch the band when I wasn't around and rehearse the best numbers with them. Then he would stick two or three more numbers on to the end of his spot and I would be stuck there waiting like a lemon to come on and he wouldn't come off.

'He would go on and do three or four or five more numbers. We would have rows but he didn't change. Rod was totally demanding, a very demanding person. He wanted everything he wanted doing when he wanted it. Of course, at that time he never got away with that because I was top of the band and that was that.'

As time went on, though, Rod's spell with Jimmy Powell and the Five Dimensions became more and more fraught. Jimmy recognised Rod's undoubted talents as a singer but he was not going to step down from his own band to ease Rod's path. In the end he did not have to.

'In one paper years later Rod said he left Jimmy Powell because I would not let him sing,' says Jimmy. 'But that was just his offbeat comment. I wouldn't let him sing all night because they were booking me and he didn't like that.

'He was very, very disruptive. He was so fucking disruptive. He just wanted to be the star of stage, screen and music hall. All the time.

'In the end he nicked my band. He wanted to go on his own. We were approached by the agency that was bringing over Chuck Berry. I didn't know about it at the time but from what I can gather Rod and some of the lads got hold of the approach, cottoned on to it, spoke to this guy and they were offering megabucks to back this tour. Rod saw it as an opportunity to snaffle the band and get away from me and snatch it for himself, which he did. But he didn't last with the band that long after that. After the Chuck Berry tour, that was it, and it was a pretty disastrous tour. It was the time when Chuck was shouting abuse to people all over the country – the thing closed down short of where it should have done.'

And so Jimmy Powell and the Five Dimensions dissolved into sorry disarray.

Before that stage, Powell claims to have had his difficulties with Rod, who frequently simply refused to do as he was told. On one occasion, Powell recalls that they turned up to play at a rockers' club called the 69 Club. Rod would not go on. Powell insisted. They ended up having a stand-up row in the dressing room.

Jimmy Powell was, though, an early witness to the rapid development of both Rod's idiosyncratic clothes sense and his 'star quality'. He remembers how, even then, Rod used to wear outrageous gear, including ladies' knickers instead of underpants, 'not because he was bent but because he had to do something different'. And, despite the acrimony of their final parting, Powell recognised Rod's talent: 'Rod was always different . . . I knew he had something. He was a very determined lad. He would set his mind on something and go for it . . . He was a fucking nightmare of a bloke to manage, but

25

having said that he did have a skill and he did have a talent. I could see that.'

Now, mellowed by age, Jimmy Powell can look back on his days with Rod Stewart with a certain wry distance. As he puts it, 'Rod Stewart was just one bad experience in a great life for me. I knew I'd never have his fame or his life but I wouldn't want it. Music took me from a council house in the back streets of Birmingham to all sorts of amazing experiences.'

Not surprisingly, Rod remembers his time with the Dimensions slightly differently. 'I joined the Dimensions,' he says, 'before Jimmy Powell had joined. I was the *bona fide* harmonica player *cum* singer in me tweed trousers and leather jacket. It was never put down officially that it was Jimmy Powell's Dimensions. I remember every time we went along to try to get a recording contract everybody would frown on me for not being clean cut. When I was singing with the Dimensions I was an amateur singer. I was not being paid too many pennies for doing so.'

Whatever the truth of the matter, it is generally regarded that Rod made his first appearance on record during his time with Jimmy Powell and the Five Dimensions – playing the harmonica on the 1964 hit 'My Boy Lollipop' by Jamaica's Millie Small, which reached Number Two in the British charts on 12 March. However, Jimmy Powell insists that this is just one of the many myths about Rod Stewart. Jimmy recalls: 'Everybody gives Rod the OK for playing but that is not strictly true. I did it. I played the harmonica with Millie because at that time I was recording for Chris Blackwell at Island Records [Millie's record label.] Rod was with my band at that time but I played the harmonica.

'I guess that because Rod was with me at the time and because he went on to become the known name that Chris forgot and thought it was maybe Rod Stewart but it wasn't . . . Chris just said come and play the harmonica one night and I did.'

* * *
26

Rod's first big break came in 1964, when he met Blues singer Long John Baldry. Not too many Blues singers come out of Haddon in Derbyshire but Baldry was a young man who would have stood out in any crowd. He was a towering six feet seven inches tall and, with his fair hair and lanky, boyish features, he was a natural front man for the wide range of groups he gigged with in the Soho pubs and coffee bars in the mid-Fifties.

Baldry loved to sing the Blues and he started to build up a following from the moment he got up to sing with Alexis Korner and Cyril Davies at their folk-Blues club, the Round-house. By 1961 Baldry had joined Korner's first permanent line-up Blues Incorporated, regularly appearing at the Craw-daddy Club in Ealing and at the Marquee, where they secured a residency leading a 'Blues Evening' on Tuesdays.

Towards the end of 1962 Davies left to form Cyril Davies All-Stars and when Baldry joined him in 1963, the group quickly became a major attraction on the London club scene. They made two singles that year and appeared to be going places but, unknown to Baldry, Davies was desperately ill with leukemia. It was his sudden death that was to pave the way for Rod Stewart.

The band's last gigs with Davies were at Eel Pie Island, a club situated on an island in the middle of the river Thames at Richmond on the outskirts of London. On 7 January 1964, the contented crowd of r'n'b followers who drifted away from the club after an All-Stars gig included Rod, harmonica in pocket as usual, and currently not attached to any band in particular. He made his way to Twickenham station to catch the train home, settled himself on a bench on the platform, and blew a few wailing notes from his harmonica into the chill night air.

Also waiting to catch a train home was Baldry who had hurried away from the club. 'Suddenly down the platform I heard this harmonica riff from "Smokestack Lightning". It

27

was coming from this figure wearing a Mod-style belted black leather coat huddled up in a mass of scarves. It was Rod.' They got chatting. Baldry was always looking for new talent and so he asked Rod if he'd like to come along to a jam session the following Wednesday. Rod said he'd love to.

Until that moment the thought of earning his living full time as a professional musician had never seriously crossed Rod's mind. 'If I hadn't been so drunk I would probably have turned the offer down flat,' he reflected. 'I was singing loudly on Platform Four and he was on Platform Six. And he hollered across to me, "Young man, it sounds as if you've got a good voice there for singing r'n'b." '

Before Rod set off for the jam session, Baldry was surprised to get a call from Rod's mother, asking him to make sure he didn't bring her son home late. Baldry was surprised at the request as Rod was then approaching his nineteenth birthday and was well able to look after himself. However, Baldry was living in South Hill Park, South Hampstead, at the time, not far from where Rod's family lived, and so in fact it was no big deal for him to drop the Prodigal Son off on his way home. It was to become a regular event. Once or twice, they came back later than expected and as Rod went stumbling up the path, Elsie would yell: 'Is that you, Roddy? I'll pay you! I'll pay you!'

Baldry gained the impression that at the time Rod's parents were fairly set against him pursuing a singing career. He had been in and out of so many things in his teenage years, they must have been thinking, 'Oh God, what's he going to do now?' But after Rod had worked with Baldry for a while, they saw that he was happier than he had ever been in a nine to five job and that it was not just a frivolous way of life, so they began to come to terms with the idea.

Rod's impact on that first jam session with Baldry was less than memorable. 'He did "Bright Lights, Big City" and didn't go down too well,' Baldry remembers. But just days later

Cyril Davies died from a form of leukaemia at the age of thirty-two.

His tragic death spelled the end of the All-Stars and was a devastating blow for Baldry. It was another five months before he formed a new band called the Hoochie Coochie Men. The line-up was fluid but Rod was enlisted as a permanent member on harmonica and back-up vocals.

At Rod's debut at Manchester University, he was almost sick with nerves. He knew only one number, 'Night Time is the Right Time', and he had had just the one rehearsal.

'Don't worry, just get up there and sing,' said Baldry and, as further encouragement, one of the band gave Rod a Black Bomber pill promising him it would do wonders for his first-night nerves. Rod knew absolutely nothing about drugs and gulped down the pill.

It certainly had the desired effect. To the amazement of the university students Rod leaped out on stage and somehow managed to make 'Night Time is the Right Time' last for fully forty-five minutes by singing the first two verses over and over again.

The audience didn't know whether to laugh or cry. There was a smattering of sympathetic applause, but Rod was so disheartened that he would have happily given up there and then. But Baldry admired Rod's spirit and at subsequent rehearsals in Soho cellars he was pleasantly surprised to find he could successfully duet with Rod. Rod's place in the Hoochie Coochie Men was assured.

Baldry struck a deal with Rod that he would pay him ten percent of everything the band earned. At that time the band could command between £30 and £40 a night but by doubling up and sometimes trebling their nightly gigs, Rod's wages worked out at around £25 a week. It was hardly a fortune, Rod felt, but it was a tidy sum for singing a handful of songs a few nights a week. Better still, it all helped towards the £300 he was desperately trying to save up to buy the bird-pulling Austin-Healey Sprite sports car he had set his heart on.

'Rod was a frugal person even back then,' Baldry remembers. 'Before he got involved with banks he put all his money into the Post Office and his only main expense was clothes. He didn't smoke and he didn't drink that much. If it was free he'd indulge but I can only recall Rod being out of it drunk two or three times in all the time he worked for me.' Later, of course, when the Faces were on the road it was a different matter, but in his early days Rod was the very picture of self-restraint.

From the outset it was clear that Baldry, with his already sizeable following, was always going to be the lead vocalist. But, as Rod grew in confidence, Baldry generously allowed him more prominence at gigs. 'He was an impressive singer from the word go,' Baldry stresses. 'His voice was higher-pitched then but there was a bit of Sam Cooke in there even in the early days. After a while he got fed up with just playing harmonica and so he just sang and didn't even bother to bring the harmonica along any more. We used to do a lot of the Muddy Waters catalogue and Jimmy Witherspoon-type songs and we duetted on quite a few numbers. But there was no rivalry between us and Rod was very different from me. He had his hair backcombed up with spray as if seeing who could get the highest beehive. In many cases, club owners would bill us as Long John Baldry and The Hoochie Coochie Men with Rod 'The Mod' Stewart. Lots of people used to say to me: "How can you let him take the spotlight? It's your show." But I've never been greedy for the limelight.'

On stage, though, Rod would hide in corners or behind the amps. Sometimes, despite Baldry's chastisement, he would sing with his back to the audience. According to Baldry, Rod was an extremely shy performer and an extremely shy individual, 'apart from when he was tracking down tarts – he wasn't so shy then'.

But even then there were distractions. Rod's old pal Rod Sopp was one. Sopp recalls fondly: 'Many times Rod and I would meet up in a pub, have a drink, then go off in my car. We always seemed to finish up forgetting the time so Rod would be very late for the gig and Baldry would go mad.'

Baldry's long apprenticeship on the Blues and r'n'b scene ensured that the Hoochie Coochie Men got off to a reasonable start in London. In the audience at Eel Pie Island to see one of Rod' early appearances was a budding young keyboard player called Ian 'Mac' McLagan. Mac was none too impressed with Rod's vocals. He thought he screamed rather than sang and the screams tended to be either very sharp or very flat. But he felt Rod had some kind of presence and considerable courage for getting up on stage in a three-button hand-me-down suit and a bouffant hairdo. The girls, Mac noted, seemed to go for Rod.

In fact, quite unknown to each other, Mac and Rod, later to team up in the Faces, were then sharing more than an interest in music that night at Eel Pie Island. A pretty girl called Linda was dividing her amorous favours equally between them. They only found out years later when, at a Faces rehearsal, Rod was talking about some girl called Linda he had gone out with. Slowly the penny dropped. Mac said: 'Did she have a safety pin in her bra?' Rod said, 'Yeah, that's the one.' They eventually worked it out.

As word began to spread about the Hoochie Coochie Men, the band found themselves being booked seven nights a week, with as many as three gigs a night at weekends. They were especially popular in the north of England, which involved a lot of travelling for the band. However, Rod's first taste of life on the road was hardly in the style to which he was later to become accustomed. The chauffeur-driven stretch-limos and the private jets were still a world away. As one of the Hoochie Coochie Men, Rod had to travel in the back of a yellow ex-Bovril truck that Baldry had bought to cart the group's gear around.

Baldry paid £40 for the truck, which looked like an old-fashioned removal van, and spent a few extra pounds having windows cut in the side, the interior lined with tongue-and-groove cladding, and old aircraft seats installed in the back. It offered little in the way of comfort, especially on the long winter hauls to and from the northern clubs and dance halls.

As Rod lived in Highgate, North London, he was usually the last member of the band to be picked up as the Hoochie Coochie Men headed towards the M1. He would clamber into the van and settle down among the amps and speakers, occasionally getting up to move closer to its only form of heating, an old tubular open paraffin stove tied to the floor with ropes. 'It was a death trap,' Baldry concedes. 'Can you imagine what would have happened if we had had any kind of an accident?'

Rod and the rest of the band also had to come to terms with the terrifying antics at the wheel of their driver, Mad Harry. An eccentric former RAF fighter pilot, Mad Harry's other main duty was to announce the band on stage at each gig while dressed in 1930s tails with his service medals pinned proudly to his chest and to ask the crowd to show their appreciation at the end.

Mad Harry treated Baldry's beloved ex-Bovril truck as though it really was an aeroplane. He had the dashboard fitted out with altimeters and an array of other aircraft dials and would climb behind the wheel wearing his leather flying helmet. When it was 'chocks away', he propelled the truck to the next gig at heart-stopping speed. His favourite manoeuvre on the way to Eel Pie Island was to career round a corner and nearly pull the truck over on its side into the Thames, a terrifying spin at the best of times, but bordering on a death-wish with an oil-fuelled stove perched precariously in the back.

Baldry soon became disenchanted with that trick and

caught the train whenever possible. Pianist Ian Armit, a Scot who now lives in Switzerland, was so terrified that he could stand it no longer and went out and bought a car. But for Rod it was all a new and exciting adventure.

Much to Mad Harry's chagrin, the truck eventually died the death in Newcastle. Rod and the rest of the band were forced to make an ignominious arrival at their Newcastle University gig on the back of a tow truck.

As the months went by, Rod and Baldry forged a strong friendship that was to last throughout the sixties. Baldry's family also took a liking to Rod, especially his Great Aunt Polly who was in her nineties and developed a great affection for him.

Rod's only major set-to with Baldry in all the years they worked together was born out of Rod's jealousy when Baldry was called in to appear as a guest star on a Beatles TV show called *Around the Beatles*. The show occupied a considerable amount of Baldry's time during the month of May, 1964, and one night Baldry was unable to travel with the rest of the band to a gig in Portsmouth because he was required at the TV studios. Instead, he decided to follow on later by train but arrived late to find the band were already on and Rod having a tough job holding things together on his own. Baldry: 'He got very annoyed and called me out from the stage screaming something to the effect "I don't know why the fuck you bothered to show up." I got furious at him publicly insulting me like that. We had a big shouting match backstage afterwards.' However, they rapidly patched up their differences.

Indeed, Rod and Baldry became such good pals that some suspected they might be more than that, especially when the following graffiti was daubed on the walls of the gents toilets at Eel Pie Island: 'Next week: Ada Baldry and her Hoochie Coochie Ladies featuring Phyllis Stewart'. 'I don't know whether it was Ginger Baker who wrote it on the wall but it was Ginger who coined the phrase,' says Baldry. 'To this day Ginger still refers to me as Ada.'

Rod and Baldry just laughed at the rumours but there was one night, however, when the two men found themselves sharing a bed in a Birmingham hotel after a late-night gig. The band arrived at the hotel in the early hours of the morning only to discover the place appeared to be almost derelict. Exhausted and bleary-eyed they banged on the door which was warily opened by an old woman who explained that there had clearly been a dreadful mix-up over the reservations because the hotel was due to be demolished and work had already started.

The look of confusion on the faces of Rod and the other band members quickly gave way to desperation. At that hour there was no question of them being able to find alternative accommodation. Finally, the woman took pity and agreed that they could come in and put their heads down for what was left of the night. At least it would be a roof over their heads.

Any hopes the band had that the remnants of the hotel would rate even one star in any accommodation guide quickly faded as they stepped inside. What was left of the premises was primitive in the extreme and pretty filthy. Rod and Baldry were shown into a room with bare floorboards and grimy walls where the air was thick with dust. The room was empty except for a bed in one corner.

The two singers glanced at each other, thought about tossing a coin for it, then agreed that as it was now past four in the morning and they were both in need of some shut-eye, the only reasonable solution was for them to share the bed. Wearily, they slipped between the covers, turned their backs on each other and closed their eyes.

A few minutes later, Baldry was all but asleep when he became conscious of something furry rubbing against his backside. What the hell was going on, he wondered. More to the point, what the hell was Rod up to? Rousing himself from his soporific state, Baldry sat bolt upright in bed and turned to face Rod whom he found also sitting bolt upright with a similarly puzzled expression on his face. For a split second the two men looked accusingly at each other, then Baldry suddenly threw back the covers. There, nestling cosily between them and blinking up at the intrusion, was a huge fluffy cat.

The graffiti may have temporarily sown seeds of doubt in some minds about Rod's sexual preferences. But Rod was always one for the girls, as Baldry consistently discovered once he moved out of his Victorian mansion garden flat in Hampstead to a much more convenient home in central London. He was now to discover that his friendship regularly extended to letting Rod use his flat in which to entertain his ladies. (Rod was still living at home at the time.) The flat was in Reece Mews and ideally placed on two counts. It was close to the then fashionable nightclub the Cromwellian which had become a popular haunt for pop stars, actresses and models. It was also but a few steps from South Kensington Tube station from which an increasing number of mini-skirted dollybirds emerged clutching directions Rod had given them.

To accommodate them, Baldry obligingly took himself off to a pub or to see a movie, leaving Rod the run of the flat in which to explore the fruits of his burgeoning sex appeal. 'Rod was a great one for the girls,' Baldry remembers. 'He always had a tart in every port, as it were. And they weren't all blondes. I seem to recall quite a few black-haired witches as well. He was pretty active.'

Old drinking pal Rod Sopp recalls: 'He was always very gentlemanly with girls. Even then when he was in his teens he would always open doors for females and pull chairs out for them.

'I don't think he and I ever pulled a pair of birds together except once when we got hold of a couple of grippers together in Belsize Park. We went to their bloody awful flat and there was a lot of grunting going on but he was missing out and so was I.'

Long John Baldry was good for Rod musically. In 1965, Rod made his very first recording when he was featured on Sister Rosetta Tharpe's song 'Up Above My Head', which formed the B side of Baldry's single 'You'll be Mine'. Baldry also included Rod on his album *Long John's Blues* of the same year, even if it was only singing the chorus with P. J. Proby on 'Got My Mojo Working'.

On 3 September 1964, Rod arrived at Decca's Number Two studio in Broadhurst Gardens, West Hampstead (now the home of the English National Opera) to record several tracks from which one would be chosen to be released as his debut single. Among the session musicians hired for £35 to provide the backing was John Paul Jones, later to find fame on bass with Led Zeppelin. Unfortunately in his enthusiasm Rod had mixed up the dates. He was precisely one week early. Cursing his mistake he trudged home with instructions to return in seven days' time.

On 10 September 1964, even more unfortunately, he overslept.

Studio time means money and there were some anxious faces at Decca when there was no sign of Rod at 11 a.m. – the time the recording session was due to begin. When he still had not appeared after the best part of an hour, a call was put through to his parents' shop where Rod's mother revealed that her Roddy was still in bed. When Rod came to the phone he was full of apologies, explaining that he had had a very late night. He was urged to jump in a cab and get down to the studio straight away but protested that he could not afford a taxi. 'Just get a taxi and we'll pay this end,' Rod was told.

Finally he arrived, the cabbie was paid, and it appeared that the day had been saved. Then Rod revealed that he had not learned the songs that had been orchestrated because he did not like them. He felt they were too commercial. By now tempers were becoming somewhat frayed in the studio and Rod was asked which songs he would like to record. When he said he had had heard some numbers he liked on Sonny Boy Williamson's new LP, the question that naturally followed was: 'Have you got the music with you?'

Sheepishly, Rod had to admit that he did not have the music with him but he had seen a copy of the LP in a record shop on his way to the studio. He volunteered to go and buy it so that the session musicians could listen to it and pick up the chord progressions to reproduce for his recording. The LP was duly played into the studio over the speakers by the Decca sound engineers and the musicians put together an arrangement to suit Rod's vocals. Which was how Rod's first single, 'Good Morning, Little Schoolgirl' came to end up on vinyl. The B side was 'I am Gonna Move to the Outskirts of Town', from the same Sonny Boy Williamson LP.

'By the time I'd finished recording "Good Morning, Little Schoolgirl", the Yardbirds had done the same song,' says Rod ruefully. 'Of course, mine went down the toilet and theirs became a Top Twenty hit.'

Rod's version was issued with the press release in which he was quoted thus: 'A white person can sing the Blues with just as much conviction as a negro. All these coloured singers singing about "walking down the railroad" . . . they've never walked down a railroad in their lives. Nor have I. You've got more to sing the Blues about in the Archway Road near my home than on any railroad track I know.'

The public were not the only ones unimpressed by Rod's version of 'Good Morning, Little Schoolgirl'. It was his only single for Decca. They already had what they considered to be a potentially popular white Blues singer by the name of Michael Phillip Jagger, who fronted a band called the Rolling Stones, and they did not need another.

That first single did, however, precipitate two important events on Rod Stewart's bumpy road to rock-stardom: his first television appearance and the appointment of his first manager. The television appearance, on *Ready, Steady Go!*, the ITV show that had been launched to cash in on the beat boom, was not, perhaps, his finest hour. He was so excited and nervous at the prospect of appearing on television that he tanked himself up in the pub beforehand, an unwise move since the programme's set required him to climb down a ladder and then walk towards the camera. The Dutch courage he had taken in the pub prompted Rod to stumble and fall down the ladder – although he did manage to make it to the camera.

Now two enterprising business men called John Rowlands and Geoff Wright had spotted Rod singing with the Hoochie Coochie Men, saw his solo potential and offered to manage him. Rod was concerned initially because he did not want to offend Baldry or jeopardise his financial arrangement with the group. Baldry, who had his own management, raised no objections and so Rod decided to sign to the duo. However, as he was still under the age of twenty-one, Rowlands and Wright were obliged to ask his parents' permission too. Once Bob and Elsie saw how keen Rod was on the idea, they quickly gave their blessing.

To celebrate, the managers and their new signing repaired to the Kensington Palace Hotel for dinner and champagne. After drinking to his rosy future, the man who was later to become famous as one of the world's most enthusiastic party-goers slumped quietly forward in his chair, fast asleep and dreaming of stardom.

Rod's elder brother Don, who was an accountant, checked the contract in which Rod shrewdly insisted that Wright and Rowlands should not receive any percentage of the money he was already earning as a regular member of Baldry's band.

Rod's soulmate in the band was keyboard-player Ian Armit.

Coming as he did from Kirkaldy in Fife, Armit was bound to be popular in Rod's eyes, as he was of course a fellow Scot and, although Armit was older than Rod, they shared the same musical tastes. However, just as the Hoochie Coochie Men had established themselves, the band suddenly broke up. 'I was just told the band was finished,' Armit recalls. 'The way I heard it, Rod and John were told they had to break up the band because there was an idea for another band. That, of course, was Steampacket.'

At this point, Wright and Rowlands wanted to launch Rod as a solo star with backing group. However, he was still none too sure of himself and so was very reluctant to become a leader. He felt much happier as just another group member. They did, though, persuade him to do one gig backed by a group called Ad Lib. Rod did not enjoy the experience. In the winter of 1965, he also appeared a few times backed by Southampton outfit the Soul Agents. Again Rod was unwilling to have the whole weight of an act resting on his shoulders. He still wanted to share the load and so Baldry's plans for a new band, Steampacket, suited him perfectly.

While working in Manchester, Baldry had been to a club called the Twisted Wheel where he had immediately been impressed by a young organist named Brian Auger. Soon afterwards, Auger was summoned to a meeting with Baldry and his management. Jointly they came up with the idea of an innovative group that was to have three singers – Baldry, Rod and a young girl called Julie Driscoll.

Auger at that time was being managed by the enterprising Giorgio Gomelski, who ran the Crawdaddy club where the Stones and the Yardbirds had first flourished. He also had Julie on his books and had given her a job as fan club secretary to the Yardbirds while he sought the right moment to launch her. Julie had real talent but what she really needed was to get out with a band and have the chance to perform in front of an audience.

'Here was the perfect time,' Auger recalls. 'So I suggested we had Julie. I said I could come on and do a couple of instrumentals and then Julie could come on and sing a couple of numbers. Then Rod could come on while we played and sang back-up for Rod and then finally we could bring on John and we could all back John. That way we could do all sorts of material – Tamla, Blues, soul – like a travelling package show.

'At that time the word for someone who played up a storm was 'a steamer' and because we had a package I came up with the name Steampacket.' The full line-up was Julie Driscoll, Long John Baldry and Rod Stewart on vocals, Brian Auger on keyboards, Rick Brown on bass, Mickey Waller on drums and Vic Briggs on guitar.

At the meeting it was made clear to Auger that he should run the band and take care of everything. He readily accepted. He also agreed to meet with the managers of all the various parties involved every Monday for a post-mortem of the previous week's performances.

Steampacket immediately became a major draw in the clubs and halls. They headed north and soon found they were playing to appreciative audiences of anything between five hundred and a thousand people who had flocked to hear such an interesting spectrum of music.

Invariably, Auger would kick off with a number by Jimmy McGriff or Jimmy Smith, then on came Julie to sing Tamla Motown, Aretha Franklin and Nina Simone favourites, winding up with the Martha and the Vandellas' classic 'Dancing in the Street'. Then it was Rod's turn to shine with Sam Cooke numbers like 'Another Saturday Night', the Drifters' favourite 'On Broadway', followed by a Howlin' Wolf or Muddy Waters Blues. Finally, Baldry took centre stage with his Blues and gospel songs. Auger knew Baldry's pedigree and was well aware of Julie's budding vocal talent. But Rod surprised him, not just by the way he delivered on stage but by his flair and showmanship. Rod's previous shyness was disappearing fast.

Says Auger: 'When we arrived for a gig Rod would immediately get out of the truck and instead of grabbing a drum or an amp he'd depart for the nearest mirror and backcomb his hair. He was very interested in image and dress. Then I noticed a lot of Roddys were turning up at the gigs. I remember specifically a Roddy standing in front of me, same haircut, same brown jacket, and I tapped the guy on the shoulder and said: "Come on, Rod, we're on now,' and the guy turned round and it wasn't Rod. It was weird.Baldry had a lot of fans but Rod suddenly had his own visible band of supporters.' Rod's confidence had grown as an equal partner in the band. Now he was also beginning to realise the effect he could have on audiences.

Rod Stewart thought he knew his effect on women. However, Julie Driscoll intrigued him – she was out of his usual ken. On the way to gigs he would sit in the back of the van and observe her as she either sat with her back straight practising yoga or tried to teach herself French with the help of a grammar book which she peered at under the little reading lamp she had had especially installed in the van.

They had a mild flirtation but Rod was much more interested in Julie's best friend, Jenny Ryland. 'He seemed to go for long-haired blondes,' says Julie, 'and Jenny was blonde and pretty. She was lovely. All Rod's girls seem to look like Jenny. I think she was probably in love with Rod and they had a steady relationship for quite a while.' After the romance finished Jenny Ryland fell for and later married another highly distinctive solo singer, Stevie Marriott of the Small Faces.

'I enjoyed working with Rod,' Julie recalls. 'Except that we used to like the same kind of songs and he always got the first pickings. But what I liked was that he always seemed to sing with such passion and, given the space, he would always be on the move jigging around, always on the go, always flamboyant. Our voices went well together and we duetted on things like "My Guy", the big Mary Wells hit.'

Their relationship was mostly a harmonious one, except on the night in the dressing room at the Klooks Kleek club at the Railway Hotel in West End Lane, Hampstead, when Julie flew into a fury at Rod. The explosive row that followed is still etched in Auger's and Baldry's memories.

Auger: 'It started by Rod making a nasty remark about Julie's legs. At that point she was a little heavy. She was a teenager and had some puppy fat she was immensely obsessed about, out of all proportion. There were all these guys lusting after Julie and she'd be running herself down. At a weak moment Rod attacked and scored a direct hit.

'He said something very nasty to Julie and she freaked out and it became a screaming kind of chaos. The balloon went up like you can never imagine. There was half an hour of hysterical shouting. Julie had a pint of beer and she threw it on the floor and it shattered and went all over Rod's shoes. She started to scream at Rod.'

Baldry takes up the story: 'Julie blew her top and thumped and punched Rod. She slapped him round the room and gave him a black eye. He was screaming "Get her off me!" He was screaming in terror.'

Auger, as MD of Steampacket, was relieved to find that this horrendous row was uncharacteristic and that the band was largely a happy bunch. Any excesses were usually down to booze or birds or both.

At an all-nighter at the Twisted Wheel, Steampacket had completed their early set and Rod and the rest of the band then hit the bars for two hours before assembling for their second set. All was fine on the second set until Rod finished off his spot and Auger started a slow blues to bring in Baldry.

Auger: 'When I came to the intro chord there was no John. So we went round again and the second time there was still no John. We went round a third time and John made it in. The line went: "Baby, baby, baby, what is wrong with me?" and in the pause for the chords to go through their cycle, guitarist Vic Briggs leaned over and said, loud enough for all of the audience to hear, "You're pissed, you c***." There was hysterical laughter.'

When a band had gone down well, club-owners would invariably stump up a bottle of whisky to help them unwind back at their hotel over a game of cards – Crazy Eights or Gin Rummy. It was a regular occurrence with Steampacket and the band gratefully consumed all that was on offer and more. However, drinking bouts were carefully excluded from the agenda when Auger made his Monday morning reports.

Perhaps Steampacket's most memorable appearance was when they were booked to play at a party for one of the Guinness heirs at a rambling English country estate near Leeds. Rod and the rest of the band knew this was to be no ordinary gig the moment their van swung through the gates up the drive and halted in front of a house of such splendour it took their breath away.

Rod, Baldry and Auger all dumped their gear in an upstairs room and then took up a flunkey's invitation to stroll over to the colourful marquee for a bite to eat. They were walking along the duckboards carefully laid out to make a path across the rolling, scrupulously manicured emerald lawns, when they passed two expensively dressed ladies in long evening gowns and fur shoulder-wraps, dripping with jewellery. As they passed Baldry, who had recently made several appearances on *Ready, Steady Go!*, one of them exclaimed in plummy, aristocratic vowels: 'Oh look, Agatha! It's that Big Jack Bradley!'

Rod and Auger were still smirking about this at Baldry's expense when they entered the marquee to find the biggest running buffet they had ever seen in their lives. The tables were groaning with food and drink and they needed no invitation to get stuck in. Suitably replenished, Auger began overseeing the setting up of the band's equipment, but later looked round to find no sign of Rod or Baldry.

Auger: 'Rod had disappeared with some redhead with gigantic knockers and then John disappeared. Later I decided to start the set and Julie came on but when I called for Rod he didn't appear. Frantically I signalled to our roadie, Eric Brooks, to go and find him. I said I thought he had gone upstairs. Rod had retired to some room opposite our dressing room.'

Some ten minutes later an agitated Eric reappeared:

Eric: 'He's not coming down.'

Auger: 'You must be joking!'

Eric: 'He's in this room with that bird. I banged on the door for ten minutes and told him he was on.'

Auger: 'What did he say?'

Eric: 'He told me to fuck off.'

Auger: 'Well get John, then, for Christ's sake!'

Eric duly disappeared to look for John and returned with an ashen face. 'Aug, John's had an accident.'

'Give me a break!' said Auger. 'How could he have had an accident here?'

Eric: 'Well, he had a few this afternoon and went to our dressing room and lay down on the bed and some geezer came in and, without putting the light on, threw his suitcase on to the bed and it hit John in the balls. He can't come down.'

That was the end of it. Neither Rod nor Baldry appeared, although Auger does recall a rowdy Rod surfacing in time for the firework display screaming at the top of his voice 'On the blue, eighty-two!' while suave young men elegantly dressed in smoking jackets tut-tutted aloud: 'Who are these people? Who invited them?'

As Eric had consumed too much alcohol, to complete his dismal evening Auger was forced to drive the merry band back to London that Saturday night. At the Monday morning post-mortem the management greeted him with the news that they had received a telegram. It read: 'Due to the band's cavalier behaviour, the fee for Saturday's booking will not be forwarded.'

There is no doubt, however, that when Steampacket were fired up they were a fine band. Their live performances and several appearance on *Ready, Steady Go!* were beginning to earn then a good reputation. But Auger, in particular, began to realise that they were never going to take off in a big way for one simple reason – there were too many managers involved. He and Julie had the same manager, Baldry had his manager, and Rod had his own representation. Inevitably there were arguments among the management, especially when it came to determining which company would release any Steampacket records. Rod was now signed to Immediate, Baldry to Pye, and Auger and Julie Driscoll to Columbia.

'Popular as it was, I knew the band was never going to go anywhere because it looked as though we were never going to get any records cut,' says Auger. 'Finally things went into auto-destruct.'

Whilst still trying to pursue a solo career, Rod did in fact record some messy demos with Steampacket, plus two singles, 'The Day Will Come' and 'Shake', for which Brian Auger did some arrangements. However, they were met with popular and critical indifference. Still there was no hint of the hits to come.

At the end of an exhausting tour, Auger was feeling the pace. As well as looking after the band, he drove one of the two vans, which often meant him getting home two hours after everyone else by the time he had dropped Rod off in Highgate, John in Kensington and Julie in Vauxhall, South London, before heading for his own home in Shepherd's Bush. He shouldered all the musical responsibilities and had the Monday morning meetings to contend with as well.

'We had a lot of fun but it got rather wearing in the end,' he says. 'Also, I thought Rod was fairly parsimonious in that at one point he left London for a ten-day tour of Scotland and England with £1 and would constantly be at the bar saying: "Buy us a drink, will you?" '

As the summer of 1966 approached, Auger was desperately tired and in need of a break. But he was also conscious of the need for Steampacket to keep working and so he begged Gomelski to try to fix up the band with a summer season residency somewhere. That way, he figured, they would all stay put for a month or so instead of slogging round the country, a different venue each night. It would be like a working holiday.

Rod could hardly contain his excitement when Steampacket were subsequently offered a four-week engagement at the Papaguyo Club at St Tropez in the south of France. The very mention of St Tropez was enough to send his senses spinning in anticipation.

St Tropez had been a simple French fishing port until it provided the backdrop for *And God Created Woman*, the controversial movie which launched Brigitte Bardot to stardom. The opening scene has Brigitte rolling naked in the surf in her role as a freewheeling, highly sexed teenager who casually shares her amorous favours among her husband, her brother-in-law and a much older yachtsman. When Brigitte later bought a holiday home in St Tropez and was constantly photographed frolicking with her lovers or sunbathing naked on her private beach, she unwittingly changed the town into a public playground for the rich and a resort famed for its nude and topless beaches. If St Tropez was the place where the famous Bardot body beautiful was acquiring an all-over tan, then St Tropez was the place for the jet set-to-be.

In the summer of 1966 the little harbour was over-run with expensive yachts and floating gin palaces, each one seemingly more grand than the next. As for the beaches, they sported rows of lithe, bronzed young girls stretched out on the sand often wearing nothing more than a glistening film of suntan oil and a lazy smile. For Rod, the alluring prospect lay ahead of four weeks of strolling along these sun-kissed Mediterranean shores taking his pick of the bunch. But the fun-loving, pleasure-seeking girls who flocked to St Tropez that year never got to meet future superstar Rod Stewart. His midsummer's dream was rudely shattered when he was suddenly fired from Steampacket – and it was all down to money.

Although the St Tropez gigs promised to provide the band with a working holiday in an inviting location, there was one vital snag. The financial terms of the four-week engagement matched the swimsuits of the St Tropez beach girls – they were barely adequate.

A meeting was called at which Baldry, Auger and the three managers were present where it was decided that, in view of the poor financial offer, one of the band would have to stay behind in England. As Steampacket could not function without its musicians and as Baldry was clearly the number one singer, it came down to a straight choice between Rod and Julie.

'I voted to take Julie,' says Auger. 'Julie was in my office and was managed by my manager. Also, we had a male singer in John. The myth has gone on that I fired Rod. I would love to have had the dubious distinction of having fired Rod Stewart. But I didn't. It wasn't a vote to get Rod out of the band.

'At that meeting I could have been over-ruled by John or by John's manager. John was the big name and whatever he had wanted would have gone. It was his band. I was simply one of the five people who didn't vote for Rod.'

The decision reduced both Rod and Julie to tears. Rod was devastated. Julie says: 'I didn't think it was fair and it upset me. I never really quite understood why it happened.'

Twenty-five years, on Baldry still has a twinge of conscience about Rod's sacking. 'It was a sad business. Brian wasn't totally happy about the financial rewards he was getting and persuaded me to be party to asking Rod to find other things to do. Rod was disappointed that I didn't stand up to Brian and I look back on it and think it was a very wrong thing for me to do. I should have stood up to Brian.'

Salt was rubbed into Rod's wounds when the rest of the band headed for the club on the Côte d'Azur. 'When we eventually got there,' says Auger, 'we walked in to find Brigitte Bardot standing at the bar.'

Steampacket played four half-hour sets a night, seven nights a week for a month. The huge Papaguyo disco really jumped to their music. But by then Auger was already planning to leave the band and form a new outfit bridging rock and jazz. When they came back from St Tropez the band fulfilled their existing commitments of a few gigs already booked, then split up. A recording contract was not a realistic possibility because of all the managers and record labels involved. Auger went on to form the Trinity, heavily aided by Miss Driscoll. Baldry went on to form Bluesology with Elton John and Rod joined Shotgun Express where he recorded another flop single called 'I Could Turn The World Around'.

Auger suspects that Rod still believes, wrongly, that he fired him from Steampacket. More than ten years later, by which time Rod was a huge star, Auger found himself on the same bill as Rod at Maryland University. 'I left him an album and a note in the band room,' he says. 'But he never came to our band room even though ours was just ten yards from his.'

Julie has no doubts that Rod blamed Auger. 'I used to bump into him occasionally and he'd always say: "Are you making any money yet or is Brian taking it all? You ought to be making more money." He'd give me a ticking off as though

I shouldn't be so involved with just the music but I ought to make some money as well. But I never wanted to be rich.'

For Rod, his years with the Hoochie Coochie Men and Steampacket were all part of an invaluable learning process in all manner of ways. When Steampacket backed the Rolling Stones, opening their show at the Palladium, Rod saw mass fan-hysteria close up for the first time. He saw how a young Mick Jagger had teenage girls frenziedly fighting their way to the front of the stage at his sexual showmanship. Rod also learned a lot from Baldry. One piece of advice he took to heart was never to keep his legs together while singing. 'It sounds funny but it's absolutely true,' Rod agrees. 'It looks daft.'

Baldry says: 'I still recognise little nuances in Rod as a performer on stage, on TV, or even on record. I know there are little bits of Baldry in there – the movements of the hands, the leg movements, the stumbling motions.'

But Baldry also learned a lesson from Rod. It helps to have luck on your side as well as talent. Baldry notes: 'Rod was very lucky – he always has been in his life. He wasn't hungry for stardom then in the way that Elton John was, for instance. Rod lucked out into many situations . . . He didn't have to work at it. It just dropped in his lap. He just jumped straight out of the Steampacket situation into Shotgun Express with Beryl Marsden and Peter Green, which was basically the fore-runner of Fleetwood Mac.'

Rod never bore Baldry a grudge for casting his vote against him and, after Baldry spent a couple of uncomfortable years on the cabaret circuit following his 1967 chart-topping ballad 'Let the Heartaches Begin', Rod helped produce a new album for him called *Everything Stops for Tea*, Baldry's attempt to get back nearer his musical roots.

'By then Rod was a very good acoustic guitar player in the Jack Elliott-Woody Guthrie mould and he also played fairly decent five-string banjo. He duetted with me on a track called

'Mother Ain't Dead' with him playing banjo and me on guitar.'

Former Hoochie Coochie man Ian Armit was also called in to play on the album and was impressed at the musical authority Rod had gained since they had last played together. 'As a record producer I thought he was very good. He had a really fine feel for the Blues, a good ear, and he knew what he wanted. At one point Rod decided he wanted an electric harpsichord on 'Mother Ain't Dead'. I hadn't even heard of such a thing. The argument against it was that it would cost a fortune to rent and it would take hours of tuning in the studio. But Rod got his way.' And, according to Armit, Rod was right.

He was also fun to be with in the studio. 'He was the opposite of a hard task-master. There was a bar at the studios and we'd go out and have a quick one and then come back again. It was all very laid-back.' He also generously gave his old pal Armit a brief moment of glory when a sixty-second gap needed filling at the end of the album. Armit: 'Rod told me to put down something, anything, on the piano. So I did and they recorded it straight away. Then nobody could think of a title until Rod said: "I know. Let's call it 'Armit's Trousers'." And that is how it ended up on the album.'

Baldry himself believes that a later LP of his, *It Ain't Easy*, had a strong influence on the album that was eventually to take Rod to superstardom. '*It Ain't Easy* was in many ways like a blueprint, a rehearsal for Rod's album *Every Picture Tells A Story* which was recorded a few months later. Most of the musicians we used were on Rod's record too. That album broke the mould for Rod. I had seen his songwriting talent coming from the folkie angle rather than the heavyweight, bashing, rock 'n' roll variety.'

Between the break-up of Steampacket and *Every Picture Tells A Story*, however, Rod still had five more years of paying his dues. And his first taste of America and the big time came with the Jeff Beck Group.

Jeff Beck had established enough of a reputation as a hot guitarist during his time with the Yardbirds to try and form his own band. He recruited Ron 'Woody' Wood on bass and Rod as singer. 'The original line-up,' Rod says, 'was going to be Viv Prince, Jet Harris, Ronnie Wood and a couple of other people I'd never heard of. It was a stupid band.

'We just rehearsed once over the top of a pub and I think Jeff thought that this wasn't the best band in the world so that was knocked on the head. Then we had an Australian bass player who was so bad we sent him back on the first flight to Australia.'

Rod finally made his debut with Beck on stage at the Finsbury Park Astoria on 3 March 1967. Recalls Rod, 'We all walked on stage in our band uniform. We all had white jackets and Jeff had a different one on because he was the leader of the group. We got through one number and the electric went off. Somebody had pulled the plug. We immediately blamed the Small Faces [who were headlining]. I always blamed Mac for doing it, or instructing someone to do it, because he thought we might steal the show. Beck decided this was the end of the show, he wasn't going to stand any more and walked off stage.

'I remember I wasn't too pleased because I looked down and saw I hadn't done my flies up. We'd been on stage for one and half minutes and the curtain came down and nearly knocked Woody over because it was so hefty. I caught him and he knocked it into me and sort of did a dance off the stage. We still had to find someone to take the blame. In the end we made the drummer take the blame.'

The Jeff Beck Band was remarkable for its turnover of drummers. They certainly had more drummers than hit records, as no fewer that six stickmen were employed in the outfit's short life, including Aynsley Dunbar, Roger Cooke and

Mickey Waller. In Rod's view, Waller was the most memorable, if only because he was so careful with his money that even Rod thought he was mean. Sightings of Waller buying a drink were allegedly as rare as those of Halley's Comet. When he did buy Rod a drink the singer celebrated not by drinking up but by encasing his glass in clingfilm and keeping it upright in his car with a little note on the side that read: 'This is the first drink that Mickey Waller ever bought me.'

The débâcle at Finsbury Park was enough for the band to abandon the tour. And it marked a new low point for Rod. He despondently wondered if he was ever going to make it. While contemporaries like the Yardbirds, the Rolling Stones and the Small Faces soared towards fame and stardom, he lurched from embarrassment to disaster.

Even when Beck notched up a Top Twenty hit with 'Hi Ho Silver Lining' in 1967, Rod who had had nothing to do with it, was musically appalled: 'For a guitar player like that to come out with a thing like "Hi Ho Silver Lining" was a crime.'

The band were treading water until they went to America for an eight-week tour in May 1968. It was Rod's first trip to the States and he was totally in awe of New York, so much so that on the opening night at the Fillmore East, Rod was consumed by a severe bout of stage fright. In England he had rarely sung in front of more than eight hundred people. Now he was having to go out and perform in front of a full house of three thousand people who had principally come to see the Grateful Dead, topping the bill.

First on were a band called Seventh Sons who were so abysmal they were pulled off in the middle of their set amid a chorus of deafening boos from the audience. Once the rumpus had subsided, the house-lights were dimmed once more and on walked Beck followed by Woody and Micky Waller with Rod barely visible at the back. Beck plugged in his guitar and stormed into the six-note intro to 'Ain't Superstitious', but nothing came from Rod's throat at all. The rest of the lads played on to cover up for him while Rod ran behind the amps to where he and Woody had stashed a small flask of brandy in a pouch for just such an emergency. Frantically he pulled open the pouch, took a slug from the flask and again tried, unsuccessfully, to coax some notes from his mouth. He stayed hidden behind the amps till the end of the number – a harkback to his early Long John Baldry days.

Fortunately, Beck's snarling guitar had such an impact on the audience that by the time 'Ain't Superstitious' had finished they were on their feet cheering and only then did Rod dare poke his bouffant-styled head above the amps and gingerly walk to the front of the stage. By the end of the set, the audience were so appreciative that they won two encores and were stamping their feet for a third when the band finally walked triumphantly off stage. After that, the Grateful Dead proved an anti-climax.

From the outset there was inevitable rivalry between Beck and Rod. It was the Jeff Beck Group, of course, but, much to Rod's amusement, some fans and even record company executives would come up to him and say: 'Great show, Jeff!' They automatically assumed that the band was named after the singer. Beck was not amused.

There was no doubt, however, as to who was top dog off-stage. Beck stayed at the Hilton in New York while Rod and Woody had to share a room at the considerably less luxurious Gorham Hotel. Woody remembers that on occasions they were so desperate they stole eggs from the automat.

The wheel came full circle in 1985, though, when Rod was a superstar. In spite of their differences, Rod retained enormous respect for Beck's musical abilities and invited him on tour. Beck was to have his own spot on the show. He was elated and on a Thames river boat party he revealed his plans to his good friend Keith Altham, one of the most respected public relations men in the rock business. Altham's comment was: 'You must be mad!' and promptly bet Beck £100 he would not last twelve dates on the tour. 'You're on,' said Beck.

By a quirk of fate, Altham received a call a month later from Rod's manager, Arnold Stiefel, asking him to come over and do some PR for Rod. Altham duly met Stiefel and agreed to take on some PR duties. His next step was to take a party of British journalists over to America to join Rod's tour. When they arrived, Altham decided immediately to seek out his old mate Jeff backstage at the gig in Philadelphia.

He recalls: 'I went backstage and passed a number one dressing room which was about the size of a suite in the Waldorf Hotel. It was wall-to-wall with flowers. It looked like a cross between a crematorium and an Interflora shop. Inside there were buckets of champagne everywhere and food piled up on the table.

'The next dressing room was the band's – half the size of Rod's with not so many flowers here, and only one bottle of champagne.

'Next was the crew's – no flowers and just a bottle of Southern Comfort.

'Right at the end of the corridor was a door with Jeff Beck's name on it.'

'I said, "Hello, Jeff." He looked up and without saying a word he proceeded to write me out a cheque for £100.' The roles had been reversed. Rod was now the unquestionable star. After seven shows Beck disappeared.

But back in 1968 the eight weeks Rod spent on tour with Beck put him on the road to stardom. He learned to fit his voice in with a guitar and the tour was a genuine success. Rod also contributed three songs for Beck's next album, *Truth*, which was put together, recorded and mixed in a matter of days. The emphasis on Beck's follow up LP *Beck-Ola*, however, was largely instrumental with a heavy metal flavour.

Luck again played a major part in Rod's career when the Jeff Beck Band were down to play at Woodstock, the great outdoor peace-and-love, hippie rock festival of August 1969. But Beck decided to pull out. Woodstock became one of pop music's great landmark events and there is no doubt that, had the Beck band played, with Rod and Woody in their supporting roles, they would have been launched internationally as that set-up and Rod's career would have taken a completely different course. 'Woody and I have often talked about that,' Rod said later with the benefit of hindsight. 'We think that was the best thing Jeff Beck ever did for us – not doing Woodstock.' Instead, Rod's road to recognition came through the impact he made on Beck's album *Truth* . It was enough for Lou Reizner of Mercury Records to approach Rod about a solo recording deal.

As head of Mercury, Reizner had helped to launch David Bowie to stardom with the release of *Space Oddity*. He had been impressed with Rod from the moment he first saw him singing with the Jeff Beck Group at the Shrine Auditorium in Los Angeles. Reizner happened to be staying at the same hotel as Rod, the Hyatt House Continental. They got chatting after the gig and Reizner raised the possibilities of Rod recording a solo album. They agreed to talk again back in London.

At the time the one thing Rod wanted most in the world was a Marcos build-it-yourself car kit. But it would cost £1,000 and Rod simply didn't have that kind of money. So, as a bait to persuade Rod to sign for Mercury, Reizner gave him the money for the Marcos and Rod duly signed the contract on 8 October 1968. His first album, *An Old Raincoat Won't Ever Let You Down*, was duly released on 13 February 1970. Made up mainly of folk-oriented songs, with two strong cover versions of established hits and four of Rod's own compositions, it sold 100,000 copies in America and Mercury pressed for a follow-up, anxious to strike while the iron was hot.

Reizner found Rod in typically tough negotiating form. The singer was determined not to miss out on any of his money – he had kept the master tapes of *An Old Raincoat* under his bed until his cash came through. When it came to doing a deal for his second LP, *Gasoline Alley*, Rod drove an even harder bargain. He took Reizner's much-loved, carefully restored pre-War Rolls Royce as an advance against royalties. The record producer reflects sadly: 'I have regretted that ever since. I really loved that car.'

The Beck band may have been the catalyst for Reizner signing Rod to a solo recording deal. But it also came about at a time when Rod's association with Beck on record had started to turn irrevocably sour.

The seeds of discontent were sewn when *Truth* was released with the album sleeve containing only the merest mention of the other members in small print. On the next album, *Beck-Ola*, Rod had an input on seven of the ten tracks and ensured his presence was noted by having himself listed on the album sleeve credits as Rod Stewart, vocalist extraordinaire.

When Beck later fired both Woody and Micky Waller, the group's disintegration was inevitable and led to first Woody, then Rod looking to join another band. That band was to be the Faces.

The take-off of Rod's solo career coincided with his joining the Faces, but not before another flop single, 'Little Miss Understood', written by Manfred Mann lead singer Mike D'Abo, had been released that same year, 1968, on Immediate. When it came to the recording, D'Abo kept telling Rod how to sing the song, saying: 'Can't you get rid of that frog in your throat?'

Rod's reply was: 'No, mate. That's the way I sing.'

Chapter Three
Faces

'It was the ultimate heavy-drinking band. Not because we had a mission in life to be a load of boozers. We were scared and we didn't think we were very good' – Rod Stewart.'

Whatever else he may be, John Peel is not a dancing man. And yet even today, the BBC disc jockey who has long been acknowledged as Britain's guru of avant-garde rock music still receives the odd letter from a fan reminding him of the night he was spotted dancing deliriously on stage at Newcastle City Hall with a bottle of Blue Nun in his hand.

The occasion was an appearance by Rod and the Faces on the night that Second Division football club Sunderland had done the seemingly impossible and beaten mighty First Division Arsenal in the semi-final of the FA Cup in 1973.

'Quite simply,' says Peel, 'it was the best gig I have ever been to in my entire life. The whole place was in ecstasy. Rod and the boys were, inevitably, as they always were, an hour late coming on stage but they were just tremendous. It was an incredible night.'

Peel, an early convert to the brash brand of rock that characterised the Faces, introduced them to a wider audience through his BBC radio shows. Of the several concert programmes they recorded for Peel, he says: 'I enjoyed their music so much I actually threw out someone who was heckling Rod – one of the few courageous acts of my life.

'When I'd first met the band I thought they were impossibly rowdy and vulgar people and then it occurred to me that possibly they were having a much better time than I was. I liked the noise they made and their attitude to it. I was so sad when Rod became a big celeb.'

The Faces may have had a reputation as a hard-drinking, wild, fun-loving band whose party trick was to all fall down in a heap, but there are other rock aficionados besides Peel, such as writer John Pigeon, who believe that between 1972 and 1975 there was no one to touch them as a live band. They behaved like lunatics and pulled ridiculous faces, they were rowdy, they trashed hotels, and they were womanisers, but during that time they rarely failed to put on a good show. As Rod kept telling his pal Rod Sopp: 'I'm sure we can be bigger than the Rolling Stones.' He was very nearly right.

It has to be remembered that the Faces came along at a time when British pop music was going through a stagnant period. Rock venues were largely presenting a procession of deadly earnest musicians in voluminous jeans and T-shirts who stood still and played lengthy, self-indulgent guitar solos. Introspective dirges were the order of the day. Even smiling was unfashionable for a time – so looking as though you were enjoying your music was unthinkable.

The Faces offered a complete contrast. Their clothes, their behaviour and their music were all loud. While other bands were performing on bareboard stages, the Faces were possibly the first group to go in for a complete look to the stage. They had mirrored panels laid down on the stage and gaffer-taped. On later tours they transported with them white vinyl flooring for the stage which was meticulously scrubbed clean by roadies after every show. Style was important. Mac may have had a pint of beer perched on top of his piano but there were candelabras there as well.

Above all, the Faces gig was an invitation to a wild rock

'n' roll party and everybody was encouraged to join in – even the singing. These days it's part of almost every performer's show to have at least one number where the audience can join in and sing along. But audiences at Faces gigs did not simply join in. They took over. On a number like 'Angel', for example, or 'Stay with Me', Rod would stop the band because the fans were simply too noisy, vociferously chanting the words of the song right back at him.

The Faces were nearly always late on stage (another trend now all too familiar to the long-suffering rock concert-goer) so that the crowds who flocked to see them were frequently over-excited and often swelled way beyond capacity by late comers who had joined the crush. When the band finally did appear they would be dressed up in handmade shirts and flashy satin suits, brandishing bottles of beer and Mateus rosé which they passed from the stage to be circulated among the audience.

The moment Woody's guitar savagely snarled the first chords to launch a Faces gig was the signal for bedlam to break out around the front of the stage. There was an unmistakable scent of danger in the air, of not knowing quite what was going to happen. Coupled with this, too, was a sense that everything could rapidly fall apart.

But it never quite did and the gig would finish with Rod feeding the fan fervour by kicking plastic footballs, thoughtfully provided by the record company's promotions man, from the stage into the audience.

The Faces also enjoyed that priceless – and saleable – quality of appealing to both sexes. They appealed most definitely to young girls but their boyfriends liked the band too. They thought the Faces were 'good lads' and Rod was 'one of the boys'. The band's blatant pursuit of booze, birds, football and having a good time struck a common chord with teenage boys. On the, admittedly rare, occasions when they troubled to listen to the words of the Faces songs, they found them chock full of male chauvinism. The females who featured in Faces songs were mostly randy, causing the men emotional aggravation, or getting in the way of the men having themselves a good time.

Crucially, the Faces captured Rod Stewart at a time when his ambition, energy, showmanship and creativity were becoming unstoppable. For much of his career as the Faces lead singer, Rod was a double attraction, for he was simultaneously pursuing a much more lucrative solo recording career – a situation which inevitably led to jealousy, bitterness, and a break-up with repercussions that have lasted to this day. However, to start with, it was seen as a bonus.

But Rod Stewart might never have got his big chance if Steve Marriott had not left the Small Faces. An East London outfit who epitomised the Mod culture with the centre-parting hairstyles and their Carnaby Street clothes, within ten weeks of their formation they had notched up their first hit with 'Whatcha Gonna Do About It' in September 1965. They went on to enjoy five Top Ten hits between February 1966 and April 1968 with numbers like 'Itchycoo Park', 'Sha La La La Lee' and 'All or Nothing', which even knocked the Beatles off the top of the British charts.

But Marriott was rapidly tiring of being screamed at by hysterical young girls. A former child actor who had gone on to play parts in films and on TV, he felt that he had more to offer if he sought new rock pastures and so left to form a new band called Humble Pie.

When lead vocalist and guitarist Marriott left, the remnants of the Small Faces were like a ship without a rudder. But Ian 'Mac' McLagan, who played piano and organ, drummer Kenny Jones, who had worked in a musical instrument shop, and bassist Ronnie Lane, who had started work in a fairground, all wanted somehow to carry on. They felt their nucleus was strong enough to go on to other things.

They continued to rehearse unsatisfactorily as a three-piece.

Soon afterwards, though, they were joined on lead guitar by old friend Ronnie Wood, who had just been fired as bassist from Jeff Beck's group. Woody in turn encouraged Rod to come along to listen to them going through a few numbers at rehearsal rooms in Bermondsey lent to them by the Rolling Stones. Rod agreed, but first he wanted to hear for himself what he might be letting himself in for. He stood unseen at the top of the stairs listening to the combined efforts of Woody, Mac, Kenny and Ronnie Lane. What he heard were mainly instrumentals, so he knew how much they needed him before he breezed through the door. But for the first few minutes he simply sat and eyed them all.

'We were jamming on a Blues when Rod joined in singing and all of a sudden we sounded like a band,' remembers Mac. 'But I didn't want Rod in. Not another bloody lead singer, I thought to myself. I had been kinda relieved when Steve had left because he was very domineering. I was against the idea of having another lead vocalist because I figured there would be an ego to go with it – and I was right. Also, I'd seen Rod sing with Beck and he'd sung behind the amps. He would just stand there singing with a frown on his face. He could sing very well but I felt he just didn't have the stage presentation.'

One aspect of Rod that Mac did approve of, however, and also envied, was his extraordinary rooster-style hair. 'He always had a great Barnet. Woody did too. Woody used to cut his own and put coffee, butter, anything on it to keep it sticking up. Rod always had hairdressers.'

Ronnie Lane also had grave reservations about Rod. Ronnie harboured his own ambitions to be the lead singer but recognised his own vocal limitations. He realised that if they were to become a group to be reckoned with and pick up where Steve Marriott left off, then they needed a strong front man. Rod, with his husky voice and his spiky-haired Mod looks was certainly different and could possibly fit the bill.

61

It was Kenny Jones who formally asked Rod to join the band over a drink at the Spaniard Inn near Hampstead Heath. Rod needed no convincing and together they drove off to a rehearsal to tell the others. 'I just bit my tongue,' says Mac. 'I thought it would have to do.'

Mac had other reservations about Rod. 'We'd go out for a drink socially or we'd walk into a pub and Rod would invariably be a gentleman and open the door for you. We soon worked out why.

'We'd go in and be first to the bar and if you're first to the bar you pay. Rod was very shrewd with his money, very tight. Sometimes we'd drive to a pub in five cars and there would be a lot of checking the car locks so as not to be first to the bar.'

Rod's appointment as lead singer was officially announced in the music press on 18 October 1969 and, because he towered over Mac and Ronnie, it was decided to drop the title Small Faces and for the group to become simply the Faces.

They quickly gained a manager and a recording contract thanks to a series of introductions, each involving Jimmy Horowitz, a musician who had played in Baldry's band Bluesology and was now writing songs and producing records as well.

Horowitz was friends with Billy Gaff, an Irish Jew who had a reputation as a tough businessman. Together they shared a small, gloomy basement apartment in Warwick Way near Victoria Station and became business partners when he and Gaff formed a management-publishing-record company, Gaff Management.

The partners worked desperately hard. Initially, as they could not afford to take clients out to dinner, Horowitz even learned to cook so they could entertain them at home in their flat's long ugly hall which they converted into a dining-room when the occasion demanded. Later, when Horowitz got married and moved out, they bought a long lease on offices at 90 Wardour Street. Appropriately, they were opposite the famous rock venue the Marquee.

Here they threw themselves so hard into their work that Horowitz would regularly double up as an accountant in the office from eleven until five and then go off and make albums in the evening. On several recording sessions Horowitz was using Kenny Jones as a backing musician and one night they walked round to the Speakeasy, a trendy club frequented by rock stars, where Horowitz introduced Kenny to Gaff. Kenny in turn introduced Gaff to Rod and the Faces. They were impressed by Gaff's directness and quick mind from the start. They needed someone they could trust to watch their corner in all the increasingly complex deals that were now beginning to come their way. Gaff measured up. He was roughly their age and he spoke their language rather than the bewildering business-speak of accountants and record company executives. And so, Rod's association with Wright and Rowland, having by now come to an end, Gaff became the Faces' manager.

'He managed Rod and the Faces for 5 per cent and no contract,' says Horowitz. 'Then with a recording contract he upped it to 10 per cent and then when Rod left the Faces he upped it to 15 per cent. Most of the time Billy was managing Rod, he did a wonderful job. He was very protective of Rod and wouldn't let anyone screw around with him. He was very protective about Rod's work and his art.'

With Gaff as manager, all the Faces needed now was a recording contract. 'I also introduced Billy to Ian Samwell who was kind of the house hippie at Warner Brothers,' continues Horowitz. 'Warner Brothers didn't have much of an A and R department then, so they hired Samwell who was one of those happening people, a finger-on-the-pulse kind of a guy. He was very enamoured of Rod and the Faces and that's how a deal was signed with Warner Brothers.'

The recording contract was signed on 1 November, just

weeks after Rod had officially joined. It was achieved on the strength of six demo discs from the band which Warner Brothers thought showed sufficient promise for them to pay the Faces a £30,000 advance. The deal allowed Rod to continue to make solo records for Mercury.

The band's first appearance was a try-out under the name Quiet Melon at a Cambridge University Ball with barely adequate equipment and with scant attention to rehearsal. Ronnie, Kenny and Mac's initial misgivings about Rod having completely disappeared by this stage, they, Rod and Woody set about giving a whole new definition to the word rehearsal. For them it was a chance to get together and get drunk. They would meet at the pub for a liquid lunch and stay there drinking shorts till closing time before running through a few numbers in the afternoon. Then it was all back to the pub again.

John Pigeon, who was then acting roadie on one of the Faces tours, later witnessed one such rehearsal at Wood Green at the start of a British tour. 'They turned up late and they did a stupid version of "Crazy Horses" by the Osmonds – pretending to be the Osmonds – and that was about the extent of the rehearsal. They wrote out a set list and that was it! Then I was sent down to Marks and Spencer to see if I could change a $100 note and they all went off to the pub.

'We all then went up to Dundee and the night before the first show there I made the mistake of opening my hotel door to a knock and various members of the crew came in with fire extinguishers and all my bedding went out of the window.'

Rod has always explained away the band's boozing habits as a reaction to fear. 'When we started nobody wanted to listen to us,' he said. 'Nobody had taken us very seriously and so we decided to go round to the pub beforehand. Call it Dutch courage, if you want. That's what it was down to – we were just lacking in confidence. It wasn't a conscious thing. We weren't trying to be different from every other band. That's just the way it came out.'

By February of 1970, the Faces with Rod as lead singer had released their debut album, *First Step*, to which Rod contributed three songs with one each from Mac, Woody and Ronnie. It managed to reach number 45 in the LP charts but disappeared after just one week. The same month saw the release of Rod's first solo album, *An Old Raincoat Won't Ever Let You Down*, which failed to register at all in the British charts. In America, however, where it was released as *The Rod Stewart Album*, and where he was now rather better known as a result of his tour with Jeff Beck, it caused a lot of interest for its wide range of musical tastes.

For many, the stand-out track was another Mike D'Abo composition, 'Handbags and Gladrags', on which Rod sang with all the anguished bluesy feel he could muster to what was predominantly a piano accompaniment. This was the track chosen for release as a single but yet again Rod failed to make a dent in the charts. The album also included a gutsy attempt at covering the Jagger-Richard number 'Street Fighting Man'. The traditional 'Man of Constant Sorrow' and Ewan McColl's chestnut 'Dirty Old Town' provided echoes of Rod's folkie roots.

In addition, there were four of Rod's own compositions. Melodically the best of the four was 'I Wouldn't Ever Change A Thing', in which the lyrics have Rod seemingly recalling his beatnik days when he would sit for hours drinking and talking with friends about how they would put the world to rights.

The lyrics of 'Cindy's Lament' had Rod bewailing the fact that he has a girlfriend whose family do not approve of him romancing their daughter. But Rod has the last laugh by wondering in the final lines how they would feel if they knew she had already spent the night with him. The title track, 'An Old Raincoat Will Never Let You Down', and 'Blind Prayer' also pick up on the theme of rejection.

It was during the making of this album that Rod began writing songs for the first time and he was able to evolve a method of composing which has continued down the years. He would have an idea, sometimes only just a glimmer, and convey it to guitarists Woody and Martin Quittenton in the studio who would develop it before laying down a basic track. Then he would take the tapes home and work out the lyrics.

Rod has since described his first solo album as 'naive'. Nevertheless, it started to put him on the map in America. And that's where the Faces, too, had to look for a first glimpse of recognition.

British rock fans were initially aghast at the band's sloppy stage antics, their raw approach and their nonchalant attitude to their plentiful mistakes. 'There was a general smile whenever we played a dodgy note,' Rod concedes. Audiences were also bemused at the band's tendency to all fall down in an undignified heap giggling to themselves while they tried to carry on playing. As for Rod, who on earth was this strutting peacock? Who did he think he was running around all over the stage, jumping up on the drum riser and hurling an aluminium microphone up into the air? To British rock fans waiting to see their idols, the singer with the support group must have seemed like a demented drum major on speed.

But in America, and for some reason Detroit in particular, it was a totally different story. On their first tour in April of 1970, the Faces started at the bottom of the bill but the sheer energy with which Rod conducted the continual party atmosphere was just what the American kids required.

They had been dealt a surfeit of self-proclaimed fret kings conjuring up ever more pained expressions as their fingers stretched for even higher notes on the upper reaches of the guitar neck. What Rod gave them was unashamed, no-nonsense, down-to-earth rock music and they welcomed him with open arms.

At first Rod was wracked with the usual nerves before

every concert. He had more responsibility now than when he was with Beck's band and it frightened him. But once he took the stage, helped by the warm response he received, the worries melted away and the adrenalin flowed. As the tour progressed he visibly grew in confidence with every appearance and the Stewart stage trademarks began to evolve.

While other vocalists stood right up to the microphone, Rod would stand leaning two or three feet away from the mike, put his head back, and project his voice with awesome power and clarity. He was never still for long, darting from one side of the stage to the other or strutting in time to the beat. Then suddenly he would strike a mid-stride pose, pick up the mike stand and straddle it across one thigh like a naughty girl he was about to spank. The crowd went wild. And always there was that distinctive husky vocal.

Even in a country as vast as America, it does not take long for word to spread and the message on the teenage pop grapevine was that the Faces were not just hot, they were really cooking. Suddenly they became a huge draw. The tour gathered irresistible momentum and, when it was finished, the American promoters quickly took the opportunity to book them again. If Britain was not yet ready for them, America was only too willing to welcome the Faces back. They returned to the US in the autumn for a further twenty-eight dates, mostly headlining, by which time Rod's second solo album, *Gasoline Alley*, was starting to make waves.

Gasoline Alley was again a mixed musical bag of songs. Woody provided the melody and Rod the lyrics for the title track but the album was largely very different from what the Faces were producing, even though Rod was using them as backing musicians. There was a strong selection of ballads and acoustic guitar work and Rod demonstrated again a quality that was to hold him consistently in good stead – a shrewd selection of other writers' songs which he felt suited his voice. For the *Gasoline Alley* LP he chose to record the Elton John-

Bernie Taupin number 'Country Comfort', Dylan's 'Only a Hobo' and Bobby and Shirley Womack's 'It's All Over Now'. There was also a creditable version of 'Cut Across Shorty' by one of Rod's early idols, Eddie Cochran – even though there was a line missed out from the song. Rod later blamed Woody for the mistake, saying he forgot one change when they were laying the track down. The album received critical acclaim in America and spurred still more interest in the Faces.

When they reached Detroit the Faces blew Savoy Brown, whom they were supporting, off the stage and Rod was able to look down in triumph for the first time at an audience where girls were going crazy for him. Several showed Rod their appreciation by dancing topless, brazenly jiggling their breasts in front of him in time to the music. In their exuberance they had peeled off their T-shirts, unhooked their bras and hurled them at Rod's feet.

In New Jersey there was almost a riot when the concert promoter informed the Faces that as the show was overrunning they would not be called upon to play. Rod sorted out that little problem by leading the Faces on stage where, suitably fortified by liberal amounts of alcohol, as usual, they proceeded to forcibly relieve Savoy Brown of their instruments and started playing. That caused another near-riot. In Chicago Rod almost literally managed to bring the roof down when he hurled the microphone stand through the ceiling of a club.

After generating such excitement among American audiences, it was difficult for Rod and the band to return to England where, unable to capitalise on the success of the Small Faces, interest in them was still barely lukewarm.

They jumped from playing to 20,000 frenzied fans in huge American arenas like the Los Angeles Forum to performing in pubs for a hundred people or, as on one occasion, at Dudley Zoo below the bill to T Rex and Edgar Broughton. The comparison was brought home when Broughton openly dubbed the band that America was taking to its heart as 'a bunch of drunken East End yobs'.

Only the hotels in America reserved a less than enthusiastic welcome for Rod and the Faces, and with every good reason. On their travels the band perfected a new sport – trashing hotels. They discovered that 're-arranging' or, in some cases, demolishing hotel rooms proved the perfect antidote to the hours of boredom, loneliness, exhaustion, frustration and isolation they were now coming to experience on the road as they criss-crossed the States. Besides, the Faces were a party band. Parties meant booze and girls, and with the Faces there were always large quantities of both freely available. All they needed was somewhere to party and the obvious place was back at the hotel.

'In those days we were staying in Holiday Inns all the time,' Mac recalls. 'We weren't going home, we were going back to the same room no matter what city we were in – so basic and so mind-numbing it was like listening to Musak. So we had to break out of it. We had all this energy after a show and there we were back in this miserable-looking hotel every night in a town we didn't know and where we knew nobody. So we partied, and we trashed a lot of hotels.

'We'd knock on Billy Gaff's door and we'd invite thirty people into his room. Billy would open the door and he'd have his business papers out, his briefcases open, and he'd be on the phone. But none of us would give a damn. We'd pile in there, take our clothes off, and fall over and we'd be feeling up girls' tits and there would be this maelstrom of faces and legs and bodies and all of a sudden I'd come across Rod and he'd be pulling stupid faces and making silly noises and everyone would join in although they didn't know why they were doing it.

'Rod was the real instigator of all that. We were all raving loonies and crazy. It was endless crazy chicks all the time – the corridors would be full of them. These girls would be waiting to be brought into the rooms one at a time. Some of the girls were just fans of the music. They weren't there for sex or drugs but hopefully they had friends who were. We were there for two things – music and fucking.'

The pranks were mostly played on people for whom the band had some affection – which was why Billy Gaff came in for more than his fair share. His room was frequently attacked while he was asleep after spare keys had been purloined from the hotel reception. Rounding up complete strangers, Rod, Woody and Mac would burst into Gaff's room shouting at the tops of their voices, tip him out of bed on to the floor, then turn the bed over on top of him. While Gaff was being unceremoniously debagged, other members of the invading party hurled furniture out of the windows and disconnected the lights while still more havoc was being created in the bathroom with the flooding of basin and bathtub.

Then they would all rush out of the room as noisily and as suddenly as they had arrived, leaving Gaff to gingerly squelch his way round a darkened room that was ominously filling up with water. It was lucky the Faces were earning big bucks because the bill for the damage was always considerable and it always had to be paid.

The catalogue of outrageous misbehaviour reached its peak of destruction in Tucson, Arizona, where the band happened to arrive at their hotel on a public holiday to find the bar temporarily closed. At that time the Faces considered there was no greater torture possible than to be denied a drink. There was only one way to vent their anger – take it out on the hotel. But first they were determined to get drunk and when a paltry two cans of beer were produced they proceeded to employ a technique they had perfected for just such dry occasions.

All that was required was a twelve-ounce can of beer, one-shot glasses for everyone and synchronised watches. As the second hand hit twelve, each member of the Faces filled his glass up to the line – just one ounce – and put the bottle down. Then they waited sixty seconds before knocking back the glass. They refilled and waited another sixty seconds before repeating the process.

'We did that regularly every minute on the button,' recalls Mac. 'If you can get through two cans that way and not end up rolling on the floor, it's a miracle. Everyone started giggling and it was crazy because we were used to huge amounts of drink and even though we hadn't finished the second can we were rolling drunk.'

Suitably tanked up they were now all set to extract violent revenge from the hotel and the first target was to be an enchanting railway that ran all the way round the hotel grounds. It was a miniature railway large enough to take children on joy-rides and certainly not designed to accommodate inebriated fully-grown adults. The Faces thought it looked fun and soon had the train in motion. It rumbled along the tracks to the point where they had engineered an unscheduled derailment which caused the engine to jump from the rails and thunder down a hill, a trail of carriages snaking crazily behind it, before ending its journey in a shattering pile-up. Mac: 'I was very drunk but I do remember we then wrecked several rooms. Billy's room was on the second floor and we threw all his furniture out of the window and set it all up again in the grassy area. We had everything working including the television set and the lamp by the bed! Billy was screaming at this point.'

Somewhat appropriately, Mac's high spirits were heightened even further by a telephone call he put through to England to the beautiful Kim Moon. Kim was the ex-wife of Keith Moon whose crazed destruction of cars, hotels and airports had earned him the nickname Moon the Loon and the title of pop's undisputed King of Havoc.

Mac, who has now been married to Kim for thirteen years, recalls: 'I phoned Kim from my room and asked her to come

71

over and she said she would. I felt great I'd had such a great telephone conversation with her so we wrecked several rooms.

'At six the next morning I was awoken by the sound of a helicopter and then there was a bang on the door. I said: "Fuck off, whoever you are." Back came the reply: "Open the door or I'll shoot!" It was the cops. We paid for the damage.

'Rod loved all that and next time we were due in Tucson we couldn't get into any hotel, of course. Not Tucson, I thought to myself. Helicopters, police, shooters. Where were we going to stay? But Rod got round this – we checked in as Fleetwood Mac. And what was the first thing we did when we got there? That's right, we derailed the train again.'

February of 1971 saw the Faces back in America for a third tour and the band's second album *Long Player* was released the following month to excited American reviews.

The extraordinary comparison between Britain and America's view of Rod and the Faces can be summed up by the night Rod invited his old pal Rod Sopp round to his house to look at some home movies. 'He showed me this film *Los Angeles Welcomes Rod Stewart and the Faces*,' Sopp says, 'and there was an advertisement on it for Coke or Pepsi and Rod said he wanted to do one of those. I said: "Whaaaat?" and he said: "Oh yes. Joni Mitchell's done one and I've sold more records than her." I had no idea. I didn't realise they were doing as well as they were – they were still playing the Greyhound, Croydon, for £100 in their hands.'

But, as so often happens, what America likes today, Britain likes tomorrow. Faces fever was starting to build back home as winter was nudging the spring of 1971. The remarkable Rod Stewart explosion marked by the LP *Every Picture Tells a Story* was now but a few months away.

The detonator was 'Maggie May', a fine song and a classic example of Rod's unique gift for rocking a ballad. Rod wrote it with guitarist Martin Quittenton who had worked on Rod's first two solo albums as a musician but not as a composer.

Martin had been playing in a band called Steamhammer and Rod first spotted his talents when Mickey Waller persuaded him to go and listen to the band at the 100 Club in Oxford Street.

Rod was then in the process of choosing musicians to back him on his first solo album and Martin's classical training immediately appealed to him. Martin hailed from Sussex and was in many ways the complete opposite to Rod. He wasn't interested in fast cars and fast blondes and he had an uncomplicated approach to life. 'Rod rather liked my simplicity and non-hardnosed attitude,' Martin recalls. 'We offset each other and he knew there was no side to me and he could relax with me.' Rod also admired his musical creativity. 'He's got such beautiful chords in his head,' he said.

When recording dates were set for *Every Picture Tells a Story*, Rod invited Martin to come up and stay at his house in Highgate and played the perfect host. From the moment Martin was shown into the third bedroom Rod thereafter referred to it as 'Martin's room'. Martin was touched to find that Rod had thoughtfully provided in his room a music stand in case he wanted to practise.

'One night we were in Rod's sitting-room, I was on the settee and Rod was sitting in a chair, and he just asked me if I had any ideas for any songs,' Martin recalls. 'We started messing around with a few chords and up came "Maggie May". I thought up the 12-string guitar introduction to the song while I was on the Tube on the way to the studio and I borrowed Rod's 12-string to play it when I got there.

'When Maggie May became a big hit I couldn't, at the time, see what the fuss was about. It took me a long while to realise it was actually a very good popular song.'

But for the record to become an international hit it needed two waves of the magic wand from Lady Luck whom Long

John Baldry believes is seated so firmly on Rod's shoulder.

Firstly, 'Maggie May' was so nearly omitted from the album. Rod played the song to a friend who ventured the opinion that it had nothing to offer melodically. Fortunately for Rod, this crushing sentiment was delivered too late for the song to be excluded from the LP – quite simply there were no other tracks available. 'Maggie May', by its sheer existence, was in.

When it came to selecting a single from the album, the vote came down in favour of 'Reason to Believe', Rod's version of a gentle ballad by American singer-songwriter Tim Hardin, and 'Maggie May' was chosen as the B side. However, a disc jockey in Cleveland, Ohio, turned the record over and played 'Maggie May' as the A side. Six weeks later, on 2 October 1971, 'Maggie May' was a Number One smash in America.

Rod had to wait only a further seven days before 'Maggie May' also stood at the top of the British singles charts. By then, *Every Picture Tells a Story* was also the Number One LP on both sides of the Atlantic. It was an unprecedented feat in the history of pop music. Not even Elvis Presley or the Beatles had managed to achieve top-selling singles and LPs in both Britain and America simultaneously.

Down at the BBC's TV studios in west London there was mounting excitement at *Top of the Pops* when it looked as though Rod was about to hit Number One, thus completing the Anglo-American double. But with the Faces by now enjoying a well-founded notoriety as a wild, boozing band, their appearance on the programme was also greeted with no little trepidation. There were edicts issued that the band simply must behave while on the BBC's premises and desperate prayers were offered in the offices of the high-ups in the BBC's Light Entertainment department that Rod and the Faces would not arrive awash with alcohol.

Naturally, Rod and the band had a drink or four but they arrived in good humour and their search for fun at the BBC centred more on their other two main pleasures – football and girls. John Peel, who was to figure controversially in the show that evening, remembers a violent game of football ensuing in the corridors of Television Centre with the pop group Slade as willing and determined opponents.

There was also an attempt to burrow into the dressing room of Pan's People, the troupe of nubile liquid-limbed Top of the Pops dancers, at the precise moment the girls were expected to be slipping into their stockings and suspenders. But it was a failure, foiled by the difficulty of locating the exact room in such a rabbit warren of offices.

Then, a very different problem arose. Rod and the Faces wanted their old mentor John Peel to join them on the Top of the Pops studio set and have him pretend to play the brief mandolin solo which features so distinctively at the end of 'Maggie May'. They felt it would be a nice gesture to the man who had done so much to 'break' the band in Britain. The unions rang the alarm bells at this suggestion but after a discussion it was decided that it was permissible as long as Peel did not actually pluck or strum the mandolin or produce any musical note from the instrument. He was allowed merely to look as though he was doing so. 'I had to swear a terrible oath that I wouldn't play,' Peel recalls. 'But even so they tried to keep me out of shot.'

The resulting showing on *Top of the Pops* on 13 October 1971 was a curious compromise, with Peel perched on a stool half-hidden behind Mac's keyboards while the cameras tried to make out as if he was not really there at all.

Rod chose a deep red velvet suit to wear on the show. But at the historic moment rock's new monarch should have been regally looking down at the rest of the pop field from his lofty trans-Atlantic Number One perch, Rod somehow contrived an extraordinary fall from grace when he went walkabout in the middle of the instrumental break. 'On the first take he got so carried away he actually fell off the back of the stage,'

Peel remembers. 'There was shrieking and shouting and he had to climb back up and start again.'

The final version had Woody going walkabout this time, jumping off the back of the stage and messing around with a football. The clip ended with the Faces maintaining their football fervour by kicking a ball around among themselves while Peel mimed deadpan to the sound of the mandolin. 'Maggie May' stayed at Number One for five weeks and remained Rod's signature tune until 'Da Ya Think I'm Sexy' some eight years later.

The success of 'Maggie May' as a single undoubtedly helped to keep *Every Picture Tells a Story* at the top of the LP charts. But one good song does not turn an album into a multi-million seller around the world. 'Maggie May' was only one of many outstanding tracks on an LP that was the culmination of Rod Stewart's efforts so far as singer, songwriter and producer. It was a wonderful mixed bag of musical styles – even if Rod discovered some coughing and spluttering on the tapes when he came to re-mix them years later!

By common consensus there are three, and arguably four, classic tracks on the album, notably Rod's own composition 'Mandolin Wind'. This is a stunning ballad about a frontier settler declaring his love for the woman who has stayed with him while the buffalo died around them during a freezing winter. Rod sprang a double surprise on this track. It was amazing that he managed to conjure up such startling imagery from Muswell Hill and he made every pop producer sit up and applaud his audacity for projecting the sound of the mandolin in such dominant fashion. 'I always thought the mandolin was such a romantic-sounding instrument,' he says.

Musically, the title track, 'Every Picture Tells a Story' is a mess – unbalanced and shoddily thrown together. But it is the vocals that pull the song out of trouble and, with Rod calling in his old friend John Baldry plus Maggie Bell to urge the harmonies along with infectious enthusiasm and energy, it all somehow ends up as a storming rock number.

Considering Rod was then only twenty-six, he demonstrated a remarkable breadth of vision as a record producer on Tim Hardin's 'Reason to Believe'. Hardin's own recording of the song had been simple in the extreme, relying mainly on finger-picking guitar and barely audible piano. For his own version, Rod took the song crisply up-tempo, cleverly used a blend of organ and piano to flesh out the musical arrangement, introduced a soaring fiddle break in the middle, then sang his heart out over the top of it all to make sure the gorgeous melody was fully delivered.

'Tomorrow is Such a Long Time' continued Rod's preference for covering the less obvious compositions by great songwriters. This one was Bob Dylan's, but Rod stamped his own vocal character all over it with double-tracked harmonies. '(I Know) I'm Losing You' was Rod's nod of appreciation to the Temptations.

On Side Two he also bravely included a rousing rendition of Arthur Crudup's 'That's All Right' which Elvis Presley had virtually made his own some fifteen years before. He followed that up with the traditional anthem 'Amazing Grace', sung just to a slide guitar. It was, in every sense, an album for everybody.

Martin Quittenton believes there were two other important factors that made *Every Picture Tells a Story* such a success.

'At that time there was a very good chemistry among all of us in the studio,' he says. 'That's why things didn't take very long to record. A couple of takes and that was it. Also, as a producer, Rod was very shrewd and tended to keep a slight edge to everything, a certain roughness and home-made quality – for instance, Mickey had the most basic drum kit borrowed off Charlie Watts. But that roughness and home-made quality of course got completely erased on Rod's later records by the American type of production.'

Every Picture Tells a Story was greeted with great critical acclaim, notably from John Mendelsohn in *Rolling Stone* magazine. He commented that Rod was the single most glamorous rock figure rolling and that there was no better backing band than the one Rod assembled for his solo recordings. He added: 'His are just about the finest lyrics currently being written, lyrics constructed solidly of strong, straightforward images that convey intense emotions. He's eloquent, literate, and moving – a superb writer.'

For Rod, the unparalleled success of *Every Picture Tells a Story* was a relief. At last he had the recognition where he craved it most – in Britain – and it was a complete vindication of all the hard work that had gone before. But most pleasing to Rod was the fact that the faith he had placed in himself to arrange, produce and write much of the album had paid off handsomely.

The album turned Rod into a superstar and it was the start of a golden period for him on record – his next five albums all topped the British LP charts.

In the summer of 1972 advance sales for *Never a Dull Moment*, the follow-up to *Every Picture Tells a Story*, topped one million in America alone and went high into the British LP charts within a week of its release on 21 July. But whereas *Every Picture* had been made in a matter of weeks, Rod spent four months putting *Never a Dull Moment* together. Success inevitably meant that Rod's recordings were bound to become more sophisticated.

The new album yielded another chart-topping single, 'You Wear It Well', also co-written with Martin Quittenton. It was somewhat derivative of 'Maggie May', but the fans did not seem to mind. There were three new Stewart-Wood compositions and three more examples of Rod's impeccable choice of covering other people's songs. These included a storming version of Sam Cooke's 'Twistin' the Night Away' and a rendering of Jimi Hendrix's 'Angel' in which Rod brought out and emphasised the melody which had been largely over-looked by Hendrix.

Rod personally felt the highlight of the album was 'I'd Rather Go Blind', a soulful version of a song which had been a minor hit for singer Christine Perfect and Chicken Shack. Deliberately choosing to record the song because he had never heard it sung by a man, Rod knocked it off in one take.

Never a Dull Moment quickly shot to the top of the LP charts and was helped on its way by Rod and the Faces using much of the album as the cornerstone of their live repertoire. Although it was a Rod Stewart album, it was the closest to where the Faces were on stage at that time.

But despite the worldwide acclaim Rod was enjoying, the phenomenal record sales he was generating and the wealth he was accumulating beyond his wildest dreams, there were times when Rod would happily have traded it all in for a chance to line up at Hampden Park in a Scottish jersey along-side his soccer idol Denis Law.

'I'll never forget,' says John Pigeon, 'the night I was stand-ing at the side of the stage when the Faces were playing Manchester. Rod was just waiting to go on and he dug me in the ribs and said: "Guess what I saw this afternoon? Denis Law's knob!" He was elated. He had obviously been in Law's team dressing room.

'I played football with Rod in north London when he was a big star. He's a good player, not one of those stars who dresses up in football kit and everyone passes the ball to him. Rod was in the thick of it and you knew that all those hard lads scrapping it out with him in midfield would happily have broken his legs. But he wouldn't hide or tell them to go easy on him because he had a tour to do. He played hard and gained everyone's respect. It was a brave thing to do and I always admired him for that.'

On another occasion, Rod's love of soccer came close to costing him his life. He arrived in Argentina to watch Scotland in the 1978 World Cup to be met off the plane by anxious record company executives warning him of the dangers of bandits.

Rod was advised that to minimise the risks he would be taken only to the most expensive restaurants which were deemed to be perfectly safe. He did not have long to wait to discover they were horribly wrong. 'We had only sat down for about five minutes,' he recalls, 'and in they came with guns shooting. They told everybody to put their hands on the table while they went around stealing everyone's watches.

'Then somebody in the back, one of the chefs, rang an emergency button that called the police. He got shot stone dead right in front of our eyes. Then the police came storming through about three minutes later and shouted to all of us to get down under the tables.

'I was pushed under the table with two great big security guards on top of me. The two bandits were shot dead, lying in the gutter.'

The gravity of the situation was comically defused when the restaurateur asked Rod to pay the bill. 'You must be kidding,' he protested. 'I'm not paying the bill. The restaurant has just got held up and I was nearly killed.'

It was a disastrous World Cup for Rod. His beloved Scotland were eliminated in the first stages of the finals.

If football managed, literally, to keep Rod's feet very much on the ground, the mass adulation he was receiving still apparently failed to scotch an insecurity inside him that close friends have pinpointed as one of his character traits.

One night at a gig in Los Angeles Bobby Womack and Mick Jagger dropped by and called in at the band's dressing room. Suddenly it dawned on everyone that here in the same room were three singers who had all recorded Womack's classic song 'It's All Over Now'. The opportunity was too good to miss.

'We started jamming on it,' recalls Mac, 'and Rod walked

out. He couldn't handle the competition. He was very insecure and always envied Mick. He was so pissed off when Woody joined the Stones because that was his Keith Richard.'

As Britt Ekland later revealed, Rod was jealous of Mick and there was, in any case, a running rivalry between the Faces and the Stones as they followed each other from venue to venue across America. Mick enjoyed stirring things up with sarcastic comments to Woody about Rod wearing the same sort of gear on stage that Mick himself had been wearing the year before.

And when Mick turned up to see the Faces at Roosevelt Stadium, New Jersey, he went so far as to stand behind an amp pulling funny faces at Rod and shouting out to Woody 'Look at the LV' (short for lead vocalist). If he had but known it, Mick would have made great play of the fact that the Faces sometimes warmed up backstage by listening to the Stones' live album *Get Yer Ya-Yas Out*.

Mac noted still more peculiar behaviour from Rod when David Ruffin from the Temptations dropped by to see the band. 'Ruffin was humbling himself sitting outside Rod's room and Rod wouldn't acknowledge him,' Mac recalls. 'He was very rude to people he idolised. He'd play nothing but Temptations records, he'd put his head back and sing like David Ruffin, but he couldn't handle meeting him.'

What cannot be denied was that Rod's solo success gave the Faces a tremendous boost, both as a live attraction and as a spur to record sales. The Faces, with Rod on lead vocal of course, followed 'Maggie May' into the charts for the first time, reaching Number Six with Rod and Woody's composition 'Stay with Me', a song that became a favourite anthem at every Faces gig.

And the band's album *A Nod's as Good as a Wink . . . To a Blind Horse* chased *Every Picture Tells a Story* so hard that it ended up at Number Two in the LP charts. 'That's really when we came good,' Rod says. 'The Faces as a band never surpassed *A Nod's as Good as a Wink*. Incredible album.' Few would disagree.

Now they travelled in specially chartered jets and chauffeur-driven limousines. And so what if they trashed a few hotel rooms along the way? They could afford to pay for the damage as they were now commanding up to $50,000 per show. Everywhere they went Rod and the Faces were a sell-out.

The standing joke the entire time the Faces were together was to greet any problem, especially a lack of booze, with 'Right, I'm leaving the band.' So Mac took no notice when Ronnie Lane sidled up to him in the dressing room in Chicago in May 1973 and said just that. Every one of them had heard it – and said it – over and over again. But this time Ronnie kept repeating it all the while until the band took the stage.

Mac: 'In the middle of a number he came up to me doing the Ronnie Lane glide and he looked at me and said: "Fuck off!" I got up from the piano and I kicked him so fucking hard he didn't know what had hit him.'

Ronnie Lane walked off. However, this time he was serious. According to Mac, 'Ronnie wanted to get Rod out of the group. He saw there was a power struggle and he thought if he said he was leaving that we would agree to throw Rod out and make him leader of the group. But he was wrong. The answer was: Fuck off, Ronnie.'

As Mac recalls: 'It wasn't the only time I kicked Ronnie. In 1976, when Rod had announced he was going solo, we decided to reform the Small Faces and we spent two days in Joe Brown's studio recording some tracks and writing together. Ronnie got very cantankerous. He'd drink Mateus but he wasn't a good drinker like the rest of us and he'd throw up a helluva lot, hopefully out of windows, but sometimes in cars. And if he drank brandy he'd fall down.

'This time he had a couple of brandies and he got very nasty, very bitter and very angry to the point where I physically kicked him up the arse and out of the studio and told him to fuck off and not come back. I didn't speak to him then for some years and of course it turned out that around that time he realised he had MS. He was very down and upset with life, angry and bitter because he couldn't see the future. It was very sad that we kicked him out but he never told us.'

With Ronnie's departure in June 1973, fittingly at the Edmonton Sundown, the Faces were never the same again and Rod knew it and privately admitted it. 'For me Lanie was the Faces,' he said frequently. 'Once he left, it took the ass out of it for me.'

Mac agrees: 'None of us was the greatest musicians but Ronnie was one of the finest bass players in that his approach was very fresh and melodic. Technically he wasn't the greatest bass player but he had some great ideas and he stuck to them and didn't over-develop them. That was the basis of the band – Ronnie and Kenny rock solid. Ronnie wrote a lot, too, and so the balance shifted when he left. Basically, things changed because Rod then did not have a foil so it became in his mind Rod Stewart and the Faces.

'Also, the strength of the band and what people loved about us was the comedy, the silliness, the drunken behaviour and the good fun which came from having a bunch of different personalities. When Ronnie left we missed his personality.'

The balance of power had shifted. Rod was now first among equals. He had more clout and there was one less voice to say 'Let's not do that'.

Examination of the Faces' albums shows that Rod and Woody wrote the rabble-rousing songs while the extremely poignant ballads that formed just as important a part of the band's repertoire were written by Ronnie Lane. Moreover, of all the band members, Ronnie was the most aware of just how much life had changed in a few short years. He had become thoroughly disillusioned with the life of limos, private jets and hotels and having to dress up on stage every night. If that was what the others wanted, then they were welcome to it, he decided, and headed off to recapture a simpler life.

Ronnie's replacement was Japanese bass-player Tetsu Yamauchi who was a genial character but spoke hardly any English, understood less, and largely did as he was told.

Further divisions appeared in the band when Rod brought in Jimmy Horowitz with a 12-piece string section for the final tour. Mac was furious and felt strings were simply not what the Faces music was all about. Often the string section comprised of different musicians every night which meant Horowitz continually had to rehearse them and the more there were, the more chance there was that they would be out of tune. For amplification they had pick-ups they were not used to. Mac was delighted when invariably one of the musicians would get fed up and pull off the pick-up which meant every one would get blown out. Mac took to openly ridiculing the string section when they came on.

Rod also brought in guitarist Jesse Ed Davis because he wanted a bit more power. So instead of it simply being the five Faces, the band now comprised a Japanese bass-player who could not communicate very well and was going through emotional problems plus an assortment of outside musicians.

The divisions boiled down to Rod, Kenny, the strings, Jimmy Horowitz and the managers on one side and Woody, Mac and Tetsu on the other. The two factions even ended up staying in separate hotels.

Another clear problem for the Faces was that the band had no records to put out. In America, a double live album, *Coast to Coast/Overtures and Beginners*, was released but it was so far below par that it severely damaged the Faces' reputation.

It wasn't only on tour that the cracks were beginning to widen. The tension was all too apparent when the Faces went into the studio to record a new LP called *Ooh-La-La*, released in April 1973.

'Rod didn't come into the studio for two weeks,' Mac recalls bitterly. 'Un-fucking-believable! We had all written songs and put a lot into it and for two weeks he wasn't even there. So we did all the tracks and when he came down to the studio we hoped he would like them. But it was a case of: Fuck it if he doesn't, because we've put in all the hard work. There was one song, "Ooh-La-La", Rod said he didn't like, didn't like the way it was done, and it was in the wrong key for him. I said: "Well, where the fuck were you? What key do you want it in?" He said he didn't know, he wasn't really interested.

'Eventually we got a key out of him and he went away and took the tapes with him to work at the words. So we cut it again with Ronnie doing the guide vocal and Rod came down again and said he didn't like it. So Woody then put a guide vocal on it and it sounded great and that's the way it stayed. We recorded it three times.

'Rod had two deals, two careers and every night he went on stage he was promoting both sets of records. We were promoting his solo albums so he should have been promoting ours.'

Jimmy Horowitz has a different view. 'One of the problems was that the Faces were undisciplined – Rod wasn't. They would book a session at a studio to cut a Faces album at six o'clock and Kenny Jones would be there with his kit at five-thirty ready to play and shortly after that Rod would turn up. Then Ronnie Lane would come in and then they'd start look-ing for Woody and Mac and they'd turn up about ten by which time Rod would say: "Fuck this, there's a football match on at eleven tonight and I'm going home for that." And he'd go and tell the guys to get on with it and that he'd come in and do the vocals when they'd cut the track.

'I know that Rod was very frustrated at trying to cut records with the Faces and they always complained that he saved his best songs for his own solo albums. But it wasn't so much that as the fact that he had more say in his own albums. He didn't like spending hours and hours in the recording studios. He liked to get in, get it done and go home. Also, if you listen to Rod's albums and compare them with what he was doing on the albums with the Faces, Rod's were so much more imaginative and interesting.'

The rift between Rod and the rest of the band became a chasm when, in an interview in *Melody Maker*, Rod described the new *Ooh-La-La* album as 'a bloody mess'. The rest of the Faces were understandably incensed.

Mac: 'The day the album came out we had a lot of press to do, all of us, but before we did any he had slagged the album off. There was no reason to do that. It was just bloody-minded. He had everything to gain from it being a success. He wrote some songs on it and we would be playing them every night.' In retrospect, *Ooh-La-La* had much to offer, notably the punchy rock number 'Borstal Boys' and Ronnie Lane's tuneful title track. But at the time Rod was not the only one to voice his criticism of the album.

Such was the popularity of the band in 1973 that despite Rod's outburst about *Ooh-La-La* the album got to Number One and a song taken from it called 'Cindy Incidentally' reached Number Two in the singles chart. The following year, *Overture for Beginners*, the sad attempt to capture on vinyl the excitement the Faces generated live, even got to Number Three in the album charts despite heavy criticism.

Ooh-La-La proved to be the final Faces studio album and the band was to discover, to its cost, over the next two and a half years that it was simply not enough just to be regarded as 'the best' on stage. They needed new material – and the new material was Rod's solo material. Inevitably, the Faces were left behind hanging on to Rod's flying coat-tails.

On stage there was still no doubting their pulling power. Their British tour of 1974 grossed over £100,000, the year's top-earning tour. But the betting was that the majority of fans were there primarily to see Rod. The following year, 1975, they toured America together twice but they all knew this was the end. By now Woody had been 'on loan' to the Rolling Stones for their American tour.

Woody had been asked to step in temporarily to replace Mick Taylor when he quit the Stones in December 1974. The rest of the Faces resented Woody for it and suspected, rightly, that he was set to join them full time. Rod was disappointed that his old friend saw his future away from the Faces. The band also resented the fact that they were increasingly being billed as Rod Stewart and the Faces. 'We were always on an even split in the Faces, albums, gigs, everything, even when Billy Gaff eventually billed us as Rod and the Faces,' says Mac. 'But I knew that was the end. I mean, it was never Mick Jagger and the Rolling Stones, was it?'

The answer to that argument is that Mick Jagger never had chart-topping solo hits and albums while he was with the Stones. It cannot have escaped Rod that the other Faces were increasingly trailing along behind him while he was flying to heights they were never going to reach. The fact was that the Faces had had just one Top Twenty hit in America, 'Stay With Me', which reached number 17 in 1972. For his part, Rod was becoming increasingly distant from the others and was having to field questions every day about whether he was leaving the Faces and going out on his own. He also had a new girlfriend, Britt Ekland, and his own personal publicist and assistant Tony Toon who was doing a fine job of keeping Rod's name firmly in the headlines. More importantly, Rod had recorded his new solo album *Atlantic Crossing* in America, without the Faces.

Yet, even though the band was clearly disintegrating and there was mistrust and hatred all round, Rod, Mac, Woody and Kenny never quite lost their sense of humour. The posters which proclaimed 'Faces 1975 Fall Tour' were regularly altered by the group to 'Faces 1975 Downfall Tour'.

Minneapolis was the last Faces date in November 1975 and the following month, on 19 December, it was reported that Rod was quitting the group. 'I have only just made up my mind,' ran Rod's official announcement. 'But I'm definitely quitting this time.'

Tony Toon added on behalf of his superstar master: 'Rod no longer feels he can work in a situation where the group's lead guitarist Ron Wood seems to be permanently on loan to the Rolling Stones.' Although the rest of the band must have seen it coming, they were still furious with Rod – especially Mac. 'The way he did it was such a shock,' he says. 'I was naive to it all. I do forgive but I don't forget. The first I knew of it was when I read it on the front page of the *Daily Mirror*. Typical Rod, the reason he had done it that way was that he had tried to one-up Woody. He had got wind that Woody was going to join the Stones and he one-upped him.' Ian McLagan did not speak to Rod Stewart again for another three years, and did not see him for another ten.

Following Rod's announcement, the formal departure of Woody to join the Rolling Stones on a permanent basis signalled the death knell for the Faces. Without Woody, Mac and Kenny knew there was no point in trying to go on.

In all the chaos and confusion of the split, Mac's brand new Hammond organ disappeared. He did not set eyes on it again until the Faces reunion at Wembley in 1986, when he learnt that it had been on permanent loan to Rod Stewart's band. That too began and ended in rancour.

Rod was touring Britain that year and Mac, who since the split had tried to form the Small Faces and was now making a living as a session musician, was particularly keen on a reunion. So he wrote to Rod and the other ex-Faces saying they could make a lot of money from a short tour but that they should make an album together first. 'I even photostatted a dollar bill on the end of the letter so I could get the point across that money could be made. I got a reply from Woody

Spruced up and gleaming Steampacket. (From left) Rod Stewart, Long John Baldry, Julie Driscoll and Brian Auger. *(Rex Features)*

The Jeff Beck Group. Beck, Rod with beard, Mickey Waller, Ronnie Wood, 1968. *(London Features International Ltd)*

Funny Faces in happily alcoholic mood, November 1974. *(London Features International Ltd)*

The Rod Stewart Band, November 1976: Jim Cregan, John Jarvis, Rod Stewart, Gary Grainger, Philip Chen, Billy Peek, Carmine Appice. *(Syndication International)*

Rod warms up with pneumatic assistance. *(Retna Pictures Ltd)*

Faces reunite, with assistance from Bill Wyman, to raise money for ex-Face and multiple sclerosis victim Ronnie Lane, Wembley, July 1985. *(London Features International Ltd)*

Still just good friends. Rod
with Ronnie Wood, 1989.
(Syndication International)

Rock's hottest legs, Rod
Stewart and Tina Turner.
(Retna Pictures Ltd)

Rod in 1975 with essential superstar accessories, legs and limo. Dee Harrington just before Britt Ekland moved in. *(Syndication International)*

Rod and Britt take to the Thames, 1976. *(Syndication International)*

Britt was busy filming in Africa when Rod greeted the girls backstage at London's Olympia in December 1976. From left: Susan George, agony aunt Marje Proops, Julie Ege and Twiggy. *(Syndication International)*

Rod and Alana steal the show at the wedding of lead guitarist Gary Grainger to Barbara Molyneux, 1978. *(Syndication International)*

Hello sailors! Rod and Alana on board the *Ark Royal,* 1978. *(Syndication International)*

Still smiling as divorce looms, 1986. Rod and Alana were daggers drawn but still able to see the funny side. *(Syndication International)*

Happy New Year to 1985 as Rod and Kelly Emberg match gravity-defying hairstyles with Ronnie Wood and Jo Howard. *(Syndication International)*

Rod and beautiful Kelly
Emberg, Camden Palace,
1984. *(Syndication
International)*

Rod and Rachel, the
second Mrs Rod Stewart.
*(London Features
International Ltd)*

but I never got one from Rod,' says Mac, conveniently overlooking the fact that Rod – now truly a superstar – had least to gain from such a venture.

Finally, it was agreed that the Faces would reunite for a handful of numbers at the end of Rod's Wembley gig on 5 July 1986, with Bill Wyman on bass – Ronnie Lane was on stage but in a wheelchair.

'That night we played and did four numbers and the crowd were going crazy wanting more, says Mac. So I said: "Come on, let's do 'Sweet Little Rock and Roller'' ' and he said: "No, I've done it with my band." So I said: "Yeah, that's what I mean. Now let's play it as rock." We went out there and slaughtered it. I felt better after that.

'Now when I see Rod at his birthday parties it's just as though we are doing a gig tomorrow. We have a drink and pull faces.

'The Faces were never given any credit until after we had broken up. A sloppy show was part of our deal. But eventually it got ridiculous. It was "Look at my bum, I'm Rod Stewart!" '

The Faces ethos was very simple: have a good time and become the biggest rock band in the world. They certainly succeeded in the first ambition and for a time came very close to clinching the second. There was a powerful chemistry between the members of the band at their best. Rod's rasping voice was provided with the perfect platform thanks to Ronnie Wood's quality guitar work, Ronnie Lane's melodic bass style, Ian McLagan's inventive keyboard-playing and the reliable rhythms of drummer Kenny Jones.

As they crossed the world leaving a trail of wrecked hotel rooms in their wake the Faces were on an almost permanent high. Before the wrangling it was for Rod the ideal set-up. He did not have the sole responsibility of being the named lead vocalist, yet he could grab a steadily increasing share of the limelight.

With the strong personality of Ronnie Lane to balance Rod's influence, the Faces were remarkably able to enjoy a hedonistic lifestyle of boozing, womanising and good-humoured bad behaviour and still produce some stunning concerts. When the atmosphere soured, Lane left and Wood began guesting with the Rolling Stones, the good times were over.

Chapter Four
Dee Harrington

'If you choose to live with a rock star you have to be prepared to put up with a lot. I didn't know what I was going to have to put up with' – Dee Harrington.

While Rod was building his solo career he had settled into a steady relationship with a lovely, classy blonde girl called Sarah. Although she lived with Rod at his home in Winchmore Hill, Sarah stayed largely in the background as her boyfriend's fame started to spread.

Friends like Rod Sopp and Martin Quittenton remember Sarah with affection. 'She was a very nice girl,' Martin recalls. 'A lot of people were very sad when he did not stay with her permanently.'

Sarah meant enough to Rod for Mickey Waller to find him in tears because he was missing her so much while they were on tour together in the Beck band in America. But the pressures of touring and being away from home so much led to a parting of the ways – and to Dee Harrington.

The very last thing Deirdre Ann Harrington expected to be was belle of the ball the night she tagged along with her best friend Patsy Noble and Patsy's boyfriend Jack Oliver to a party being thrown for Rod Stewart and the Faces in Los Angeles.

It was 29 July 1971 and Dee, as everyone called her, was

in the sprawling city of the angels on America's West Coast to enjoy the holiday of her young life. Bored with the London scene and her job as PA to the manager of a small record company in Westbourne Grove, near the Portobello Road, Dee had decided to head for LA with Patsy almost on a whim. At a farewell party for Jack at London's trendy Speakeasy Club, Jack had blithely suggested 'Why don't you two come over?' Dee and Patsy looked at one another, giggled, and said: 'Yes, why not?'

Next day, so that they could not change their minds, the two girls each put down a deposit for a flight to the USA. They had three months in which to scrape together the remainder or risk losing their deposits. To save a bit extra Dee gave up renting a flat in London and moved back in with her parents in Bourne, Lincolnshire.

As the jet thundered along the runway and headed out over the Atlantic, Dee felt she was literally casting her fate to the wind. She was just twenty-one years old and this was to be a great round-the-world holiday adventure. Los Angeles, she decided, would just be a temporary stop-over. She would find work there and then save up her money to go on to Japan.

Like almost every new arrival in Los Angeles, Dee was wide-eyed at the way everything around her looked straight out of the movies. She almost had to pinch herself. Was she really here in the sunny California that she had heard the Beach Boys sing about so often on the radio while she was growing up? Her sense of awe was complete when she found that Jack's house, where she and Patsy would be staying, was in Hollywood Hills underneath the famous Hollywood sign.

To help out at Jack's house, Dee took on the cooking and Patsy the cleaning. But their first desperate attempts to find more permanent work were failures as they did not have the necessary documents and work permits. They were both beautiful girls but even their efforts to cash in on their looks and become Playboy Bunnies was unsuccessful.

Instead, they ended up with jobs demonstrating shrimp chips in supermarkets, Dee in dreary suburban Crenshaw and Patsy in upmarket Marina Del Rey. But one day was enough. They both returned to Jack's house in the evening complaining their feet were killing them. The next day they phoned up to spin the line that they had had a car accident and wouldn't be returning to work.

What Patsy really wanted to be was a model. On one occasion, Dee went with her to the house of a photographer called Brian Hennessey. As she sat waiting for her friend outside his studio idly thumbing through the Jobs Vacant section of the *Los Angeles Times* Brian suddenly appeared and looked long and hard at her. By now Dee sported a healthy tan and her hair was golden from the Californian sun. She was tall, slim, with spectacularly long legs and she was fresh-faced with a wide, sexy mouth.

Brian liked what he saw and immediately asked Dee if she was interested in posing for some photographs. 'What sort of photographs?' she enquired nervously. Dee had taken a course at Lucy Clayton's in London and had modelled briefly before deciding that modelling was boring. When Brian went on to explain that *Playboy* had commissioned him to take photos for centre-folds, she said 'No, thank you' very firmly until he mentioned that she could expect $3,000 a photo.

'I'd never taken my clothes off before,' she says, 'but at that time, 1971, you didn't have to take very much off for glamour photos. You showed your breasts and that was about the lot, so I wasn't worried.'

As her money was rapidly running out and Brian seemed a nice guy who could be trusted, Dee agreed to some test shots where she would pose topless, nothing more. Brian duly picked her up in his car early one morning and together they drove down to the ocean where Dee slipped off her bikini top and frolicked in the sand for the camera. Back at the house in the Hollywood Hills, Jack announced that he had a friend coming to stay. He was called Kenny Jones and he was the drummer with the Faces pop group who, after the great reception they had received in the US earlier in the year, were currently embarked upon their fourth tour of America.

When Kenny told Dee how much he was missing his wife, she generously cheered him up by cooking him a plate of good old English roast. In return, he invited Jack, Patsy and Dee to a party being thrown for the Faces that same night at a disco called Bumbles. 'I'll put your names on the door,' he promised the girls.

Unknown to Dee at that time, just about every teenage bikini-clad blonde along the beaches of California would have given her best surfboard for an invitation to such a party. Rod's album *Every Picture Tells a Story* had just been released and was on its way to Number One in the charts. Rod and the Faces were three weeks into their fourth US tour. They had taken America by storm and from the moment they had arrived in Los Angeles they had been besieged by devoutly enthusiastic, beautifully tanned girls seeking divine revelation in their beds.

But as Dee thought about what to wear for the party, finally opting for a simple little blue and white dress and white clogs for her feet, she was neither looking for romance nor expecting to be the centre of attention at such a glitzy occasion. She was just thrilled to be going to Bumbles, which was 'the' club in Los Angeles at the time.

Safely inside the disco Dee sipped a drink and sat by the fireplace relaxing until Rod, resplendently attired in a white velvet suit, and the Faces swept in with a noisy flourish followed by a massive entourage of retainers. Soon, they drifted over to talk to Dee and Patsy, whereupon Kenny provided the introductions.

As the party progressed, Dee watched with a mixture of amazement and fascination as a string of girls with bodies that stretched the seams of their outfits to the limit threw themselves unashamedly at Rod all evening, whispering all manner of promises in his ear. But, she noted, he didn't seem to take a particular interest in any of them. Then the first notes of Aretha Franklin's haunting hit 'Spanish Harlem' echoed from the disco speakers and Rod asked Dee for a dance. A pair of clogs was hardly ideal footwear to trip the light fantastic with America's current number one male sex symbol but Dee happily took to the floor with Rod. Envious female eyes sparkled from all directions as the gauche young British girl accepted the invitation that they had all yearned for. When they got chatting, Dee found Rod both friendly and amusing. This was something special indeed.

Horowitz, who had had plenty of opportunity over the years to observe the Stewart libido in action, recalls his protégé's more usual chat-up technique, if it can be called that. 'He'd be in a place like the Dome or maybe Tramp and he'd sit there having a beer or maybe a Bacardi and some leggy blonde would walk in. If it was a girl he didn't know he'd maybe have Tony Toon do his dirty work and send him over to investigate and set things up. But as often as not he'd go over and introduce himself – with a nose like that it was hard to be anonymous. Next thing you know he'd be chatting them up, the Rolls Royce would be summoned, and off they would go.'

With Dee, though, it was different. Big star Rod might have been, but she found him straightforward and down-to-earth. 'I liked him straight away,' she says. 'There was an immediate attraction. He had a good sense of humour, was instantly likeable, and he was just like a regular guy.'

And Rod was not going to forget in a hurry that first time he slipped his arm around Dee's waist and held her close. In an unashamedly romantic gesture, he later bought two copies of 'Spanish Harlem' and gave one to Dee and kept one for himself as a reminder of that first dance they had shared together.

When Rod pulled a little toy Lamborghini from his pocket saying he owned the real thing and that he had had a Marcos before that, Dee made out she knew what they were and looked suitably impressed. 'But,' she admits, 'I hadn't a clue.'

After the party, Rod and Dee wandered for miles talking about music, London, football and what she was doing in LA. They were so completely wrapped up in their conversation that they quite forgot that walking around at night in Los Angeles is not the kind of hobby to pursue if you value your chances of waking up in this world the next morning.

Fortunately, it was a police patrol car that spotted them before any muggers or maniacs. Rod and Dee simply protested that they were British and that they were nearly home anyway. The cops drove on shaking their heads. Crazy English, they muttered.

A taxi took them back to Rod's hotel where they talked and talked in his room until four in the morning. Rod complained of a headache and wanted Dee to stay but, as the well-brought-up daughter of an RAF squadron leader, she was not about to make love to someone she had just met. Unwilling to risk the journey back home on her own and with Rod convincing her he was none too well, Dee worked out a compromise and decided to stay the night. They both got into bed and went to sleep.

According to Dee, they made love for the first time the next morning and when they got dressed Rod put on her white knickers as a symbol of their closeness. Dee was to reveal to the world much later on that Rod wore women's knickers all the time because he liked their softness against his skin.

That day Dee went back to Jack's to pick up her bikini and met Rod, as arranged, round the pool of the Beverly Hills Hotel. He invited her to come to his concert that night at

Long Beach, but first they would go shopping. The limo was summoned to take them to Sunset Boulevard where Dee was astounded to find that a public sighting of Rod was enough to cause a huge traffic jam.

'I'd never seen anything like it,' she recalls. 'All these people started standing up in their cars shouting, "See you tonight at Long Beach, Rod!" It was incredible. Then when we got out and went shopping, we walked and the limo slowly followed us. It was like in the films. I could hardly believe it.'

That night at Long Beach Arena, Dee watched from the wings as Rod and the Faces brought 18,000 youngsters to their feet in an adulatory frenzy, the girls screaming hysterically at Rod's every move. 'I was worried by all the security with guns,' she remembers, 'and the way people behaved backstage shocked me. They were all trying to get close to Rod. He was so popular. After he'd left the stage I followed this mass of people thinking this must lead to where Rod was. I came to a corridor and his room was at the end. I could see him but I was behind twenty other people all in a mad rush trying to get in.

'Then after Rod and the band had changed there were sandwiches and drinks in another room and for the first time I was left having people I didn't know talk to me and they were very strange. Who they were and how they got there I just don't know.'

The next week was a whirlwind for Dee as she and Rod became inseparable lovers. She went to San Francisco with him to watch another concert where she saw still more hysteria every time her new boyfriend so much as moved a muscle. At the post-gig party she was horrified to find a man having an epileptic fit in front of her. He began convulsing before pitching forward and knocking over a lamp as he crashed like a marionette to the floor causing the electric socket to buzz alarmingly. 'Of course, there were hundreds

97

of people doing nothing. I ran off to get a spoon,' says Dee. 'All I could remember was that you had to put a spoon in their mouths to stop them choking. It was all so upsetting.'

Swept along on the rock and roll tidal wave, Dee tried to sort out her emotions when they returned to Los Angeles. She knew she really liked Rod and that he made her feel so special. 'It was quite a physical thing between us but I don't know whether I was falling in love with him,' she says. 'I think I was just wondering: What is all this? But I also remember thinking how my mum would be pleased. She thought I'd marry an American and never come back.'

With Rod's American tour about to finish and his return to England imminent, Dee had some fast thinking to do. Now she had met Rod, did she really want to go to Japan? Was Rod just a holiday fling or was he something more to her? Did she want to stay in Los Angeles? Even more pressing, did she want to appear half-naked in *Playboy* magazine?

She says: 'When we got back to LA, Rod got Brian Hennessey to come round and show him the shots of me topless on a projector and tried to destroy them all. Rod had a love-hate view of the photos. He kind of liked them and yet he didn't. So, much to my relief, I didn't continue with the photos.'

Dee chose to stay on in LA while Rod went home. But soon he was on the phone to her to ask if she was coming back. 'I don't know what to say,' she told him.

Shortly afterwards, in August, Dee's money ran out and Rod was delighted when she told him on the phone that she was returning to England. They agreed to meet in a pub in Lancaster Gate. Dee was sitting waiting for him when Rod walked in and whisked her off to the Serpentine bar to meet a couple of his friends before taking her on to a trendy restaurant in Kensington Church Street. As Dee toyed nervously with the vegetable-shaped salt and pepper pots on their table and gazed at Rod, they both knew that California had been no quick fling. They both came from North London and they could have met up at any time. Yet, for some reason, fate had decreed they travel thousands of miles to find each other. As they looked across the table their minds were made up. 'That was it,' says Dee. 'I moved in with him.'

When she was asked to go back to her old job in Westbourne Grove, Dee readily agreed. She was determined to maintain some sort of independence. In the mornings she would slip out of bed as he lay back on the pillows watching her dress.

'How can you get up and leave me every morning?' Rod moaned.

'It's easy!' Dee teased him.

'I went off to work and he couldn't bear it,' she says.

Before he met Dee, Rod had lived for a time with Sarah in her mother's flat in Wilton Crescent and later in her house in Notting Hill Gate. But he had also used some of his early income to buy a small house in Highgate near the family home. It was just five minutes' walk from his mum and dad and Rod described it as: 'A detached house, like the colonial houses in the States with a verandah at the front.' Baldry was to rent this when Rod moved up the housing ladder to a more spacious, £30,000 home in Stanmore a few miles to the north.

Now Rod was living at the Broad Walk, Winchmore Hill, in North London. It was a four-bedroomed mock Tudor house with two sitting-rooms, one fitted with a thick pile white carpet and wooden panelling, the other lined with beautiful leather-bound books. Outside were manicured lawns and rose bushes. Dee thought it was a lovely house but Rod, who was now reaping the rewards of his recording successes soon put it up for sale and began searching for a new home with the help of a man called Perry Presse who specialised in finding property for the rich men of rock.

Perry would ring up with details of houses that might be suitable and Rod and Dee would pick him up in Rod's big old Rolls Royce and go off to view them. 'But they never seemed suitable for Rod,' Dee recalls. 'He obviously had it in his mind that he wanted a house with a bit more splendour because his accountant had told him to spend £100,000 on a house. But he couldn't find a house for £100,000!'

One day on the way back from the coast, Perry happened to mention that he knew of a house that had just come on to the market that might suit them, although he was not representing it. He told Rod they would pass it on their way back to London, so Rod said he would like to stop and look at it.

Rod was at the wheel as the Rolls glided round a big roundabout near Windsor and Perry pointed out a lodge house and a pair of wrought-iron gates, flanked on either side by two vast white pillars. They drove through the gates and up a drive surrounded by rhododendron bushes. Eventually, they drew up in front of Cranbourne Court, a magnificent Georgian mansion which took even Rod's breath away. 'Yes, I'd like to see that tomorrow, Perry,' said Rod as he turned the Rolls round and drove slowly back down the drive.

Rod and Dee were back next day. Rod loved the house the minute the owner, Lord Bethell, showed them inside. Dee had her reservations as she looked round. It was so big, she thought. The house had thirty-two rooms in all, including eight bathrooms and boasted several exquisite Adam fireplaces. It was set in seventeen acres of grounds and Dee smiled to herself as her rock star lover and the Lord-in-Waiting to the Queen strolled the grounds together. She wondered if Lord Bethell knew who Rod was.

Rod bought Cranbourne Court for £89,000, a princely sum in 1971, but it was a characteristically canny buy – when a valuation was carried out, the fireplaces alone were deemed to be worth £22,000.

They would be able to move in at the end of the year and so, over the next three months, Rod and Dee set about collecting furniture for their new home cramming it into their Winchmore Hill home ready to be taken to Windsor. Dee was impressed by Rod's shrewd good taste on their shopping expeditions and the fact that he knew in his mind exactly what he wanted.

That autumn Rod and the Faces were due back in America for yet another tour, their fifth. Dee flew to New York with Ronnie Wood's wife Chrissie, arriving a day ahead of the band who were due to play their first gig ever at Madison Square Garden. Dee wanted her reunion with Rod to be so perfect that she checked out every single room in the Sherry Netherlands Hotel before choosing a fabulous wood-panelled suite she felt sure Rod would like.

The following evening, 24 November, was Thanksgiving Day. Rod arrived and promptly asked Dee to marry him. It was just three months since he had first set eyes on her. 'It wasn't the trendy thing to get married then but I said yes because we were having a great time, we had a fantastic relationship, I thought he was a fabulous man and we were together as much as we could be,' she says. 'But it was a bit of a shock.'

At that point 'Maggie May' was Number One in both America and Britain and *Every Picture Tells a Story* was still top of the album charts on both sides of the Atlantic. Not even the Beatles or Elvis Presley had achieved that. Rod was the biggest rock star in the world. Not for the first time since she and Rod had fallen in love, Dee thought to herself: 'Why me?'

'I was twenty-two and I never thought I'd get married at twenty-two', she says. 'I turned down the offer of a ring – I didn't want one. But we were engaged.'

The engagement quickly became public knowledge, with the inevitable headlines, and they talked of getting married on New Year's Day. Instead, though, when the moment came, they decided to throw a big party at Cranbourne Court on New Year's Eve and move into the mansion properly the following day. Houseproud Rod figured it would be simpler to have all the guests let their hair down while there was no furniture in the place. And so the happy couple spent their first night together in the mansion sleeping on a mattress.

When the removal van turned up to deliver the furniture they had so lovingly gathered for their new home, Dee was shocked to find that it took up a mere corner of one of the huge rooms. There was so much to do that Dee finally decided to give up her job and devote her energies to the house, for splendid as Cranbourne Court was, it was clear that money would need to be spent on it if it was to be restored to its original glory. Rod's brother Bobby was brought in to oversee the redecoration and over the next two years Rod spent a fortune transforming the old house into a mansion fit for a prince of pop. By the time it was finished it was a remarkable mixture of brazen opulence, exceptional good taste, exquisite elegance and typical Rod.

To give visitors a warm welcome, a large Stewart tartan curtain was draped on the inside of the front door and a scarlet carpet was laid over the huge original black and white chequered stone tiles in the vast hall. After a two-year search, Rod and Dee found a magnificent crystal chandelier to hang from the hall ceiling. Two brass pillar-style lamps, both fully five feet high, stood sentinel at the foot of the sweeping, white-bannistered staircase. On each of two landings above was an eighteenth-century statue of a bare-breasted maiden, recently acquired from Syon Lodge.

Dee chose a McDonald tartan carpet for the snooker room with curtains to match and, for added tartan effect, the square mouldings on the blue-painted ceiling were picked out in a startling red. Above the ornate stone fireplace Rod hung a pub mirror which proclaimed the legend 'Stewart's, Scottish distillers of Finest Whisky'. On the walls were framed photographs of his Scottish footballing heroes in action, notably Denis Law, and his gold discs.

The dining room was painted blue and three Tiffany-style lamps brought from Los Angeles hung low over the specially-made dining table. Surrounding it were eight peacock-tailed dining chairs.

In the music room the shelves groaned under the weight of LPs, books and Rod's hi-fi. A dozen guitars and banjos hung from hooks on the wall and a baby grand piano was installed. When the tuner arrived, he turned out to be blind. Thereafter, since neither Rod nor Dee could play very well, Rod invariably whispered to Dee 'Get him to stay and play.' The blind man would then be slipped a generous tip so that Rod and Dee could listen to his wonderful piano playing throughout the house.

A new wing was added to make way for a space-age kitchen which included a central circular work unit with a breakfast bar made from solid cedar wood, long yellow cylindrical hanging lights and a large yellow mushroom-shaped dome equipped with extractor fans and more lighting.

Perhaps the most tasteful room in the house was the formal sitting-room with its Chinese silk screens, antique furniture and Persian carpets. Leading off it was the much more infor-mal TV room which had a fluffy white carpet and yellow walls covered in French advertising posters. There were deep maroon velvet sofas and a distinctive armchair. Only an environmentally unfriendly coffee table spoiled the room – the legs and struts were made from antler horns. The most ostentatious room, however, had to be the conservatory, a circular folly, its yellow walls stacked high with a collection of glass cases containing stuffed birds, foxes and other animals.

Upstairs, Rod and Dee chose as their bedroom a large bay-windowed room at the back of the house which looked out over a lawn to the classical formal gardens beyond. Above their king-sized bed Rod hung a large Scottish flag – yellow with a red lion.

Two further rooms upstairs were turned over to Rod's model train layout, somewhat expanded since his teenage days. He even had a hole cut through the connecting wall at waist height so that the trains could chuff from one room to the other along a track mounted on a specially constructed stand. Rod spent hours painstakingly sanding, building, glueing and painting various additions to the layout. Expeditions to a shop in Holborn to pick up a packet of plastic animals or models of men digging on the line were one of his great joys.

When he was satisfied that the layout was more or less complete, Rod had an official opening of the line and cracked open a bottle of champagne to toast its success. The pride Rod took in his model railway obviously did not rub off on Dee's cat, Pussy Galore, though. One morning, Rod made an unsavoury discovery in a pile of sand he had lovingly colour-sprayed to look like railway scenery. To his fury, Pussy Galore had left a very messy, malodorous calling card.

While the interior of Cranbourne Court was taking shape, no less attention was being paid to the gardens. The York stone pathway encircling the house was taken up and carefully relaid and outside additions included fountains, paths, lawns, sun dials, rose gardens and rainbow-coloured flower beds. Dee, who had spent some of her youth in a country town in Lincolnshire, particularly enjoyed strolling along a wonderful azalea walkway.

A further £40,000 went on turning the outdoor swimming pool at the side of the house into an indoor pool. Rod had the builders build round and over the existing pool in keeping with the style of the main house. The extension also housed a sauna and solarium and there was a big red spiral staircase which led up towards the staff wing and the corridors that ran the length of the house. When it was all finished Rod could hardly wait for his first dip and watched with mounting excitement as it slowly filled with 32,000 gallons of water from a solitary tap. But suddenly two walls of the pool collapsed as the plaster gave way. All 32,000 gallons had to be drained away again to make way for repairs.

With a housekeeper, an extremely bulky chauffeur called Cyril and brother Bobby living at Cranbourne Court as well as Rod's two collies, Mary Poppins and Sally, Dee was never going to be completely alone when Rod was away on tours. But when he first went away she missed him so much she went out and bought a horse, a bird, a dog and the infamous Pussy Galore all in one day.

The bird was an ornate lorakeet Dee had bought on a shopping expedition to Harrod's. She knew she had to buy him when she spotted him hanging upside down on his perch and he opened an eye and said: 'I saw you first.' From another shop she ordered a large cage to be built for the bird but when she went to pick it up it proved to be too big to go through the door. Obligingly, the shop took the door off its hinges.

Dee named the bird Electric Birdy because he made a noise with his beak that sounded like electricity. 'He really liked me,' she says, 'and put up with Rod. If he screamed a lot, Rod used to lock him in the walk-in-safe. He used to sit on the back of the huge teapot we had and Rod used to try and get him to go in and close the lid – he was only playing, of course.'

Dee's domesticity was complete when Rod had the field fenced off and a stable block built. She bought three horses in all – a Palomino colt called Cheval, a thoroughbred mare called Cara Mia and a mare she bought for Rod called Spotty. Unknown to Dee, Spotty was already in foal and later produced Little Spotty. While Rod played with his train set, Dee was content to go riding in Windsor Park. Rod rode occasionally but decided his Lamborghini was a quicker and more comfortable way of getting from A to B.

If Rod was away Dee busied herself with looking for things for the house. When chauffeur Cyril drove Dee to Harrod's in the Rolls or the Mercedes, she often wondered what people must have thought of her as he held open the car door for her and she would step out in jeans, purple boots from Biba and wearing no make-up, her hair barely combed.

When Cyril was driving her, Dee liked to sit regally in the back and tease him. 'You know, Cyril,' she used to taunt, 'if I was going to employ a chauffeur I'd have this young, really well-dressed, incredibly handsome chauffeur.' But Rod, she knew would never have allowed that.

According to Dee, Rod enjoyed all this domesticity. He loved eating at home and having friends down to the house for a meal. And so, gradually some sort of loose routine entered their lives with Dee getting up every morning to go into the kitchen to make the tea and return with the post and papers. Letters from cranks are an occupational hazard of being a rock star and Rod received his share. 'When we first moved in there used to be this very mad German woman who wrote dreadful letters saying Rod was going to die,' Dee recalls.

For security a ten-foot fence was erected right the way round the house with barbed wire at the top and Rod bought Dee an Alsatian she named after Carlo Ponti, the husband of Sophia Loren whom she so admired. But still the fans some-how managed to get in. One night Dee was awoken by a crashing noise and assumed it was just Rod and his pal Rod Sopp returning worse for wear from a pub crawl. She was so sure it was the two Rods that she even turned on the outside lights for them only to find it was two fans so desperate to see Rod that had they had broken in.

On lazy Sunday afternoons Rod and Dee liked to sit watching television or roasting crumpets on the crackling log fires. Invariably they would see young girls running across the back garden. It was the weekend and some of them had travelled miles for a glimpse of their idol, so Rod and Dee would go out and chat with them, sign autographs and send them home happy.

On the subject of one of the favourite topics of conversation among Stewart-watchers, Dee says, 'How can anyone say he was mean when we went on holiday to Mombasa, flew to Puerto Banus to stay on his boat, and we both had his and hers Rolls Royces and Lamborghinis and a six-door Mercedes? But we were just as happy going down to the pub, as we often did, in our slippers and with the dogs.'

Some of Rod's friends did notice a change in Rod, though, after he acquired Cranbourne Court. Says Martin Quittenton, 'It was possessions and antiques and huge great rooms and it was very difficult to feel natural. I rolled up in a Renault 4 – not that I couldn't afford a bigger car, I wanted a Renault 4 – and there would be a Lamborghini outside. Suddenly it was a different life.

'When Rod wanted to talk to me some faceless person from the office would phone up, a different voice every time, saying Rod says can you do this and can you do that. So I said to him once: "Why don't you phone me any more?" He looked uncomfortable and didn't actually answer. It was fixers in the office and everyone doing things for him and so the personal relationship between Rod and others was bound to change.'

Quittenton also remarks quite shrewdly, 'As for the acquisitiveness, if you are not sure about people, perhaps you have possessions instead because they can't be taken away from you.'

Meanwhile, as the live-in-lover of the world's most celebrated pop star, Dee Harrington was inevitably coming in for a good deal of bitchy envy. It took months for the wives of the other members of the Faces to accept her. A new girl on the scene appeared to be a danger signal. If Rod had fallen for another woman, they worried, it might give their men similar ideas.

Dee was at first horrified by the shameless way the groupies offered their sexual favours. They were so obvious, so brazen, and so determined. But in a way she found it oddly flattering to think that here were all these girls fighting to make it with Rod and yet she was the one in his bed at nights. She was relieved to discover that when groupies somehow tricked their way past security to their hotel room, one call to the management would have them rapidly ejected. However, when Dee did not accompany Rod to gigs she decided she would simply accept that groupies were always going to be part of the rock scene and that it was best to blot them from her mind.

To please Rod Dee dressed in very sexy, skimpy outfits – tight little shorts, tiny tops and figure-hugging halternecks. 'He always liked long legs and short skirts,' Dee says. 'Rod liked me wearing as little as possible and no make-up. But I was young and inexperienced and when we went out I looked at people like Bianca Jagger and thought how glamorous they were. So I'd go back home and try to make myself up and Rod would say: "Take that crap off your face." I always thought I looked a bit dreary except when I wore the huge fantastic colourful feather boa he bought me. It was se-quinned and glistening and I'd wear it over little suede shorts and a tiny top – you couldn't really see I had any clothes on.'

Dee found Rod to be a passionate and ardent lover but she also learned he was capable of moments of great tenderness. He repeatedly told Dee he loved her and was rarely afraid to show his feelings. Jealous trouble-makers would try and label Rod mean because he hadn't bought her a gold Cadillac or a diamond tiara. But Dee would not have wanted them anyway – the roses he personally picked for her from the garden when she was ill meant so much more to her. So too did his admission that he had recorded Jimi Hendrix's 'Angel' just for her.

However, although there was evidently a lot of love between Rod and Dee, the papers were full of rumours that he was seeing other girls. Often the stories were pure fabrication but, while Dee had to put up with all the press rumours of Rod's affairs, Rod could not contain a jealous streak if Dee appeared to be flirting. One night at Tramp, the exclusive Jermyn Street disco frequented by the rich and famous, Rod and Dee were enjoying a night out with the Manchester United football team. While Rod was deep in conversation with his idol Denis Law, Dee proceeded to dance with various members of the team. That was fine by Rod.

Then Ryan O'Neal, the handsome Hollywood actor whose exploits with beautiful women were reputed to run a close second to Warren Beatty's, asked Dee to dance and she accepted. Suddenly Rod's mood changed.

'That was it,' says Dee. 'He bought a pint of beer and came over and threw it all over me. I didn't know what had hit me. I stood up and got hold of his hair and shook him and pounded him. I was crying, hysterical and drenched.'

As they bustled their way up the stairs, they were greeted by another one of Dee's admirers, the designer from Granny Takes a Trip who made all the Faces' stage clothes. Rod's response to his friendly 'Hi' was a punch in the stomach.

Rod was later mortified that he had behaved so badly in front of Denis Law. His idolatry of the Scotland and Manchester United striker was such that when Law visited Rod and Dee at Cranbourne, Rod ordered Dee to faithfully record for posterity every moment of their kickabout in the garden.

But whilst Dee was happy to indulge Rod's footballing fantasies or look after his domestic arrangements, it was not enough. She wanted to be something more than just an appendage to a famous pop star. She talked it over with Rod, taking care to explain to him that she was not dissatisfied with him or with her lot. She simply wanted to *do* something.

'Right from the beginning,' she remembers, 'he had that old-fashioned thing of me being the woman at home. But that wasn't enough for me, although I realise now it must have come over to Rod as though I was saying it didn't matter if he was Number One in the charts, had more money than anyone else, and the biggest house around – I still wasn't happy.'

'I didn't want children or to get married. I didn't want to go out clubbing or behave like Bianca Jagger and be seen out. I must have looked like this miserable, confused female that didn't want to participate and yet he wanted to live the rock star's life. He had to because, although I didn't realise it at the time, he was an industry. He had to have a woman that was very glamorous and it was all to do with living this rock star image and keeping those sales going.

'Before, Rod was just himself with a job and it was great. There was a balance. But then he became enveloped in this great rock star's image. He'd hang out with the Gary Glitters, go to Tramp all the time and be seen, and women wanted to be seen with him. I got the backlash because the newspapers would phone up and ask me if I knew whether Rod was having an affair with Susan Ford, President Ford's daughter, or some other girl. It got so that any girl who spoke to him or sat at the same table as him was assumed to be going to bed with him. I'm sure he was in bed with quite a few of them. But I don't know whether any of these other girls meant anything to him. They never survived very long. I always used to say to the papers: "Well, I'm glad I'm not having a ding-dong with him because I'd never see him – because he's always at home with me!" '

Eventually, though, things came to a head and after a blazing row Dee moved out of Cranbourne Court and went to live at Rod's Highgate townhouse. Rod had bought the house in 1972 to be near to his parents, but he rarely stayed there because neighbours complained about the noise when he and Dee held parties for his footballing pals. It was to be the first of many such departures. For a couple of weeks, Dee worked as a Bunnygirl at London's Playboy Club. During the six weeks Dee and Rod were apart, though, another classy blonde entered Rod's life – actress and model Joanna Lumley.

Rod met the stylish daughter of a high-ranking Army officer at a football presentation evening. Joanna, now at the height of her *Avengers* fame, was there to present Kenny Dalglish with a trophy and Rod had been brought in, because of his well-known enthusiasm for the game, to give Queen's Park Rangers an award as most entertaining team of the year.

There was instant chemistry between the two of them. The intelligent, middle-class actress liked the cheeky, streetwise rock star, even though that first evening she had to share his attentions with Denis Law and company. But Rod felt just a little intimidated by Joanna. She was most certainly not one of those girls you just wander up to and begin a relationship with his oft-used and somewhat unimaginative chat-up line, "Allo, luv. Wanna drink?"

So Rod spent the evening uncharacteristically tongue-tied and left without obtaining the lady's telephone number. The next day, he enlisted the help of Tommy Toon's predecessor as publicist, a diminutive but determined lady called Sally Croft. According to Sally, the conversation went as follows.

Rod: 'Sally, do you know Joanna Lumley?'

Sally: 'Not really.'

Rod: 'Well, I was with her yesterday and I would like her to come out to dinner. Do you know where to find her? Can you find out where she is and talk to her?'

Sally: 'Yes, I can find her and ask her for you, Rod. But Joanna is educated. She is not like one of your usual type of girls. So you are not to try to leap into bed with her on the first date, are you?'

Rod: 'Na.'

Sally: 'If you queer it on the first night you won't see her again.'

The obliging Sally telephoned La Lumley to tell her the famous Rod Stewart requested the pleasure of her company at dinner.

'How very sweet of him,' said Joanna and happily agreed to the date.

Sally organised the meeting and it went ahead. The following day she rang Joanna to find out how it had gone and to ask if Rod had behaved himself. The actress swooned an 'Oh, yes'. Sally asked if she had gone back to Rod's house and Joanna said, 'Yes.'

Says Sally: 'I didn't dare ask any more.'

She could see that Rod and Joanna had really fallen for each other in a big way. Rod was very fond of Joanna's son, Jamie, and admired the actress's independence in bringing up the boy alone and always refusing to name the father.

For her part, Joanna was entranced by Rod's beautiful Windsor home. She gasped visibly at the rambling rose gardens and the tennis courts, at the huge staircase sweeping up to a spacious room lined from top to bottom with cupboards stacked with clothes.

Rod shrugged at her reaction, saying, 'I liked it better when I slept on a mattress and hung all me clothes round the walls.'

Within a week they were talking about marriage. Sally says: 'Joanna moved in for about a week but I don't think she was used to sleeping with that huge flag above her head. It didn't last very long. I think he found Jo too clinging. When he was losing interest in her he made me and Cyril come out to dinner with him and Jo.

'Jo had a hairdo like she had in *The New Avengers*. She had dark hair then. She said, "How do you like my hair, Roddy?" "It's awful," replied Rod, "I don't like it at all." So we had this row over dinner. It was very tense. To cap it all, Rod ordered drinks just for the men and I snorted, "We drink

112

too, you know." He was being so rude. I knew that there was another girl on his mind – obviously she was waiting for him somewhere else. Cyril got as pissed as hell and going home he nearly had us all killed going the wrong way up a one-way street in the Rolls.But then Rod found someone else and that was the end of that.'

Afterwards, Sally recalls having Joanna on the phone at two o'clock in the morning saying, 'Darling, what has happened to Rod? He said he would collect me at eleven o'clock and I'm still waiting. Could you phone him for me, darling? Please phone him.'

In a spirit of sisterly camaraderie, Sally would phone Rod the next day to be greeted by, 'Oh God, I got caught up with some tart somewhere.' Knowing Rod, she would then phone Joanna, explain how unreliable he was and advise her not to take it all too seriously. But the romance inevitably floundered: 'Rod was a bastard to her, he was always arranging to meet and then never turning up. I like Jo but she was out of Rod's class. I advised her to get rid of Rod. And she agreed to dump him. She suddenly said, "Yes, nobody treats me like that," and she dumped him.'

Rod has genuine regrets about the end of the fling with Joanna: 'It lasted about two months. She was a smashing bird and I was very fond of her. She was dead classy and I was dead common and we got on like a house on fire.'

For her part, Joanna says today that she still has a soft spot for Rod although, 'He did not take up that much space in my life any more than I did in his life. It was blown up by the Press into quite a giant thing but it was really a very short term encounter.

'I did like him a lot. It was a fascinating world to drift into. Everyone comes alive at night time frequenting recording studios and clubs, then like owls they go to sleep during the daytime. It was weird.

'I watched how Rod dealt with the fame. It was quite

interesting. I could see that if he behaved quite normally then he was left alone but if he arrived in dark glasses and jumped out of a big car then people started to flock round him. You can almost turn it on by having security men saying stand aside please when no one is taking any notice. Jolly interesting.'

Meanwhile, Sally Croft was doing her bit to ensure that Rod Stewart did get mobbed wherever he went in Britain. Her experience and guidance helped him steer a positive path through the perils of the star-hungry tabloids. Their relationship gradually became more the indulgent aunt and spoilt nephew than public relations person and celebrity. But even for the resourceful Sally Croft it was not an easy job.

Her first visit to Cranbourne Court to discuss terms was not promising. Carlo the Alsatian kept prowling round terrifying the tiny PR lady; amongst the other distractions was Cyril the chauffeur who hungrily ate his way through what looked like a dozen servings of mixed grill from an enormous plate. Dee tried to calm the dog at the top of her voice while Rod shouted at Cyril, who kept snarling: 'I've been up all night so I'm entitled to this.' It was difficult to decide who was shouting louder: Rod at Cyril or Dee at Carlo.

Rod made coffee, escorted the startled Sally into the garden and said bluntly: 'When can you start?' But Sally was flustered and insisted they met for lunch at London's stylish media restaurant San Lorenzo to discuss their working relationship in more detail. Sally arrived first. When Rod eventually turned up she was a little surprised to see that he had scarcely dressed for the occasion. However, she knew enough about the music business to know that rock stars make their own rules. Rod slumped opposite and said, "Allo, luv.'

Sally recalls: 'He was as rough as anything. But he was a star. He still wasn't that well known in Britain but you could tell he was going to be a big name for a long time. He just had this amazing presence and he really wanted to succeed.'

The negotiations settled on a weekly salary for Sally of £20, by no means a generous remuneration even two decades ago. But Sally says: 'I had a job to get him to agree to even £20. And then he insisted the fee was to include all my expenses. "That's the lot," he said. "You're not going to charge me for anything else are you?" ' In return for this, Rod wanted Sally to make sure that his name was never out of the papers.

Rod had selected liver and bacon from the menu and when it arrived he further startled his new employee by picking up the liver and carefully wiping it with his serviette before putting it on his side plate. He repeated the process with his bacon. Sally watched open-mouthed. 'Rod, we are in San Lorenzo,' she stuttered. 'It's the gravy,' replied Rod, oblivious to her social alarm. 'I can't stand gravy.'

When she got under way with her new client Sally soon found that her £20 a week had to cover a very great deal. 'I had to trail out to Windsor with journalists all the time, and pay my own way there and back. Rod would phone me up and ask me to bring me this book or that book down with me. I would bring them but I never got paid. I always felt he was very mean, so mean. He never had any drinks in the house. He would never put his hand in his pocket to buy a bottle of anything.

'So, when I took journalists down we would all go down to the pub and the first thing he would say would be, "Sal, can you pay for this? I've got no money." I was out of pocket all the time. But he was so charming he got away with it. He would just grin at me and joke, "I've got short arms and long pockets, dear." He never used to carry any money. In restaurants I always had to pay, I never saw him write a cheque.'

It was certainly an interesting environment in which to work. Sally would frequently travel out from London for a prearranged interview appointment only to find Rod still in bed. It was among her duties to then bully him out of bed and into the shower before meeting the representative of the press.

One morning, Sally arrived with a journalist to find suitcases parked around the front door. She asked Rod if he was going away only to be told bluntly: 'No, it's Dee. She's leaving.' Not that Rod was ever lonely during Dee's periodic departures. There were many shapely visitors.

Sally Croft recalls: 'There was a pretty little girl I met at the London Weekend Television studios. She was waiting there watching Rod and she looked so pleased with herself. When I asked her why, she said, "You've no idea what's going to happen to me tonight." I said, "What's going to happen to you tonight, dear?" She said, "I'm going to sleep with Rod Stewart." "Oh God," I said. "Well, don't count on sleeping with him tomorrow night as well, dear." She just simpered, "It's going to be wonderful." '

'Rod had an amazing effect on women. He oozes charm. If he wanted a girl he could be so charming he was irresistible.'

Beautiful girls may have come and gone, but Rod had many long-standing male friends, among them Elton John, who spent hours listening to snatches of Rod's new songs and advising on musical ideas. Sally recalls: 'Rod used to send for Elton whenever he was doing a record because Elton was wonderful at saying which notes were wrong or a bit off. He and Rod were very close friends.'

Sally's last memory of Rod Stewart is of rushing to catch him at Heathrow Airport in order to extract her final wages from him in 1972. Says Sally, 'He hadn't paid me for six months so it was quite a lot of money. I knew he was going to America and I was determined to get the money before he left the country because I knew once he got to America I would never get paid. His manager Billy Gaff told me the time of the plane so I just turned up. I was desperate for the money. I said, "Rod, darling, I've come to say goodbye and here's my bill and can you give me your cheque before you

116

get on the plane." And I got it.'

But, in spite of his dalliances and his reluctance to dip into his many millions, Sally Croft remains one of Rod Stewart's greatest admirers. 'Underneath it all, Rod is a really nice person. He just had this roving eye. I don't think he ever stayed with a girl long enough to get to know her but he didn't mean any harm. Nothing bothered him. He was like a feather that just floated along through life.

'Football was about the only thing he ever got excited about. You just couldn't dislike him, however mad he made you.'

Rod's old friend Rod Sopp rejects suggestions that Rod was mean. 'In those days I earned around £10 a week as an insurance clerk. I couldn't afford to go to Tramp, so if we went there it was down to Rod. But in the pub it would be, "It's your go".'

Rod and Dee were back together again by Christmas 1974. It was the last they were to spend together but it was a memorable one. They invited twenty-five people to lunch, including Elton John who arrived in a kilt, bringing with him a present for Rod. Every picture tells a story and Elton's gift to his mate was – a Rembrandt.

They also had a New Year's Eve party for a hundred and fifty people and, as a surprise for Rod, Dee organised a kilted piper to stride through the grounds piping in the New Year. The party went on all night and at eight the next morning Dee, still in her Victorian bustle dress, went out to feed the horses before she and Rod fell into bed exhausted.

The last person to leave, she remembers, was Ronnie Wood's mother. As she was leaving, Rod turned to Dee and thanked her profusely. 'Thank you so much,' he told her. 'It's been so fantastic and it wouldn't have been anything without all that you did.' Dee glowed with happiness.

Early in 1975, the Faces flew off for a two-month tour of the States while Dee chose to stay behind at Cranbourne

Court. Early one morning, Rod phoned and asked Dee to fly out to Los Angeles to be with him. She said she would rather stay at home – she had planned to have the house spring-cleaned before he came back and wanted to oversee the cleaning. Fifteen minutes later, he phoned again and asked her once more to come and join him. This time she did not dither further and the next day she was on a plane out to LA where she was met at the airport by one of Rod's entourage with a Mercedes he said Rod had hired especially for her.

Dee was in high spirits as she drove up to the Beverly Hills Hotel where she and Rod had first become lovers. They had a joyful reunion. However, it soon turned sour when Dee stripped off to take a bath and Rod spotted a scratch on her back. It was caused by Dee sleeping in her jewellery a couple of nights before but Rod would have none of it and continuously accused Dee of having an affair.

A fierce row ensured. After it had subsided, Dee was almost relieved when Rod said he had a 'business meeting' to go to. It would mean she could have some rest after her tiring flight.

But friends who called by persuaded Dee to come out to dinner. Afterwards, she decided on the spur of the moment to drop in at the Troubadour club where she and Rod had been years before. As she pulled up outside, Dee suddenly saw Rod helping a blonde out of a limousine and disappear into the club. Dee's first thought was that it must be Chrissie Wood and she innocently followed them inside. When she caught up with them in the bar, she saw the terrible truth – Rod was with the actress Britt Ekland. There was a deathly silence as the truth dawned. Then Dee turned on her heels and strode out.

Back at the hotel, Dee started to pack. She was seething that Rod had asked her to fly out all the way to LA and that he had then humiliated her like that. Next morning, she was at the airport ready to fly home to England. 'It wasn't Britt

Ekland. I'd just reached a point where I didn't want any more. I had to go, and it was like I'd been given this opportunity to get out.

'Tony Toon was sent in the car to get me back. He was crying in the car, "Please don't go." I told him that this time his job was to stop me getting on that plane but that he wasn't going to succeed.

'After all that, the plane was delayed for four hours and the person in front of me threw up all over the first-class cabin. Other people demanded to get off but I sat there thinking, "I shouldn't be on this plane." I started to worry, then panic that the delay was dragging me back. But then I thought: How can I go back to *that*? That nightmare!'

When the plane finally roared down the runway and nosed through the Los Angeles smog into the bright sunlight, Dee knew she had just flown out of Rod's life. Her love affair with Rod Stewart had begun and ended in Los Angeles. One by one, she noted, the wives of the Faces had gone. 'Sue and Ronnie Lane, Sandie and Ian McLagan, Jan and Kenny Jones, Chrissie and Ronnie Wood – one by one they had all departed. I wasn't Rod's wife but now it was my turn. We had a fantastic three years and there was a lot of love between us for a long time. But I'd learned that you can have everything you could possibly want and yet still be unhappy.'

After the split Dee maintained her dignity but later couldn't resist a snipe at Britt. 'Who can deny that she is a beautiful girl? But I have been told she has got big feet.'

When Rod's new album *Atlantic Crossing* was released in the summer of 1975, the tracks included Rod's own composition 'I Still Love You' and the poignant Danny Whitten song 'I Don't Want to Talk about It'. He later conceded: 'I have to admit that Dee had to put up with an awful lot.'

Twenty years after they first met, Dee is a highly respected manager in the rock business. The walls of her Chiswick flat are lined with gold and silver discs for her efforts in guiding the pop duo Climie Fisher to international success. Ironically, Rod recorded 'My Heart Can't Tell You No', written by her protégé Simon Climie, and took it to Number Four in the US charts in 1989.

Dee Harrington has the last word: 'Apparently, I haven't been completely forgiven for revealing to the press that he wore ladies' underwear.'

Chapter Five
Atlantic Crossing

'I changed everything in 1975. I changed my bird, my house, where I live. I think it's good for everyone to do that now and then – a change of atmosphere, a change of environment. You can't keep on with the same person or the same music all your life' – Rod Stewart.

A move to Los Angeles was always on the cards once Rod had hit the jackpot. He was earning big money but too much of it was being eroded by crippling British taxes. 'I was advised to go and live in America for obvious reasons,' he said. 'I left Britain because I was paying 83 per cent of everything I was earning to the tax man. Giving away 83 per cent of your income is not fair. I was in a position to be able to move – a lot of people can't – and I fell in love with the place.'

The move to America coincided with a switch in record labels. Up until *Atlantic Crossing*, Rod Stewart's solo efforts had been recorded with Mercury. But in a series of complicated legal moves, Rod now effectively switched to Warner Brothers.

He had fulfilled his obligations to Mercury by recording his fifth solo LP *Smiler* in 1974, an insipid album that lacked much of the verve of his previous records. The album contained mainly cover versions and included, as usual, a Dylan number, 'Girl from the North Country', Chuck Berry's 'Sweet

Little Rock and Roller', Sam Cooke's 'Bring It on Home to Me' and an instrumental version of 'I've Grown Accustomed to Her Face'. Elton John played piano on his own composition 'Let Me be Your Car'. The best track was another Stewart-Quittenton number, 'Farewell'.

During the Faces' final tour Rod took record producer Tom Dowd along to a gig and, as Dowd confided to John Pigeon later, what he saw was something quite fantastic. The rapport that Rod and the band had with the audience was extraordinary. However, it was not something that would translate readily on to vinyl.

So when Joe Smith, then head of Warner Brothers, called up Dowd and asked him to work on Rod's next album, *Atlantic Crossing*, Dowd talked with Rod at great length about the sort of songs he wanted to do and whether he would like the Faces to be involved. Dowd was a legendary producer who had worked with many of pop music's greatest luminaries including Otis Redding, Dusty Springfield, Eric Clapton and Aretha Franklin, so when he expressed the view to Rod that the Faces were a limiting factor, he was speaking from a position of authority. He went on to suggest they flew to Alabama to introduce Rod to the much-vaunted Muscle Shoals Rhythm Section.

When they went into the studio and the introductions were made, Rod visibly paled and, taking Dowd by the arm, walked him straight back out of the door. 'That can't be the Muscle Shoals Rhythm Section,' he protested. 'They're all white.' Dowd assured him that it was. Rod was so certain such a soulful rhythm section would be black that still he refused to believe it until Dowd asked the musicians to play for him while Rod stood and listened from outside the door.

Finally convinced, Rod went into the studio and among the tracks he cut there at 10.30 in the morning was 'Sailing', which was to become a monster hit for him in September of 1976. Again, Rod had a slice of luck. Bob Crewe, who used to write and produce the old Four Seasons records, happened to be at the studio when Rod was doing the song and Dowd told him he needed some background vocals to make it sound like a large choir. Crewe immediately volunteered to sing on the track and round up a dozen of his friends to give the song the haunting anthem quality that Dowd was seeking.

Rod intended 'Sailing', written by Gavin Sutherland, to be an anthem for the terraces, and so it proved. Once Rod and his father were at Wembley for an England-Scotland soccer international and at half-time Rod popped off to get a drink. When he came back Rod was disturbed to find his dad crying. He asked him what was wrong and the reply was: 'You should have heard it. The whole of Wembley was singing "Sailing".' The tears were tears of pride.

'Sailing' had a long run in the British charts in 1976, including four weeks at Number One. The following year it went back into the charts again, this time reaching Number Three, thanks to BBC TV choosing the song as their theme tune for a documentary series about the aircraft carrier HMS *Ark Royal*. The television success of 'Sailing' second time around effectively brought Rod to the attention of a whole new range of people who might otherwise have taken little interest in him.

To launch *Atlantic Crossing* Rod, by now ensconced in California, flew with Britt Ekland to Dublin where he threw a lavish press party at a hotel. On the media junket was John Pigeon who remembers that a very good time was had by all – so much so that the whole point of the exercise was almost lost. The aim, obviously, was for everyone to listen to Rod's new album, but someone had thoughtlessly neglected to ensure there was a record player available to play it on. An aide was despatched and came back with the most basic of record players. 'So there we were in Ireland,' recalls Pigeon, 'for an album costing thousands of pounds made with the best session musicians in the best studios with one of the best producers in the world and we were listening to it on this incredibly shoddy piece of equipment. And most of the people were drunk.'

Generously, Rod also had his pal Rod Sopp, his parents and other friends flown over to Dublin to share in the fun. Sopp remembers Rod and his parents enjoying a loud sing-song in the hotel lobby. Once the junket was over, he took Sopp over to Paris where they shared a room for a couple of days. They also went shopping and Sopp was pleased to find that, despite the wealth and fame, Rod had lost none of his old humour. 'We went to look at some antiques,' says Sopp, 'and I remember Rod telling a French woman: "Four grand? I could buy a new one for that!" '

In fact, the Rod Stewart sense of humour has always been very British and down to earth. On another occasion, Rod was staying in an hotel in Australia when he was politely instructed to be on his best behaviour in his suite as the next occupant was to be the Queen. According to Sopp, he therefore proceeded to unfold some of the toilet paper and write on about the eighth sheet in, which he figured was bound to be pulled by Her Majesty, a note which read: 'What are you doing sitting here when you should be writing a speech?'

Atlantic Crossing was very different from anything Rod had done before and made a stark contrast to his records with the Faces. The homespun quality of Rod's previous solo efforts had been replaced by immaculate production, a polished sound that was technically perfect. For the first time there was no Dylan track and the album was divided into a 'Fast Side' which included four new songs from Rod and a 'Slow Side' which attracted most of the attention.

Apart from 'Sailing', there was 'I Don't Want to Talk About It', a plaintive ballad which became a great favourite with fans at Rod's concerts where they knew every word and sang along with him in their thousands. The mandolin was again much in evidence in Rod's self-penned 'I Still Love You'.

Missing from a Rod Stewart solo album for the first time were Woody and Mickey Waller. There was no contribution for the first time, either, from Martin Quittenton, although Rod had asked him to join him in America to work on the album and to tour with the Faces. Martin turned the offer down. He could not see himself fitting in with what went on after the music – heavy drinking and wrecking hotel rooms held no attraction for him whatsoever.

Martin believes Rod's pride was hurt when he turned him down. 'I haven't spoken to Rod since he went off to the US fifteen years ago,' says Martin. 'He had an album to do out there and he wanted the people he knew around him. But because I didn't go to America he took it as a snub. Perhaps it was pride that he couldn't just snap his fingers and I'd jump. I was the one that didn't. I was the one person, perhaps, that he didn't have to put on a show with and I was the one that didn't come.'

Four years after their parting, Martin had a breakdown, went into hospital and subsequently married the nurse who brought him back to health. Today they live in Wales working for wildlife and planting numerous trees on their fifteen acres. His only source of income is the royalties from 'Maggie May', 'You Wear It Well' and other songs he wrote with Rod which generate, he says, between £5,000 and £10,000 a year. 'Rod was very fair with me down to the last letter,' he says. 'But I do wake up at night sometimes wondering what I will do when the royalties stop.'

When Martin was strong enough after coming out of hospital, he went into a studio in Putney and recorded three new songs with Mickey Waller. He had the tapes sent to Rod with a letter explaining what had gone on in the intervening years and asked Rod what he thought of his new songs. 'That was in 1981,' he says, 'but I never did hear anything.'

Although some critics tried to make out that Rod had lost his soul on *Atlantic Crossing*, the fans did not agree. The album quickly went to Number One and stayed in the British LP charts for a staggering eighty-eight weeks.

Rod was still a Face when *Atlantic Crossing* was released and that year they toured together in America to promote the album. It was an unhappy tour in every way, culminating in an appearance in Los Angeles in front of 55,000 fans at Anaheim Stadium where they played a thoroughly ragged set because the truck carrying most of their equipment had failed to arrive on time, having broken down on the freeway. Rod and the boys were all for calling off the gig. But this was LA, the record company stronghold, and they could hardly disappoint all those thousands of fans waiting to see them. There would have been a riot. As Warner Brothers boss Joe Smith said: 'You can't let the fans down. They've paid up to ten bucks to get in to see you. What will they think if you don't appear? It will be a thousand times worse out there.'

Mac's brand new, cut-down white Hammond organ was the only piece of equipment that had arrived and an SOS went out for the rest. 'We went on very late and played very badly,' Mac recalls. 'Each one of us was feeling insecure because everything was different from how it usually was.'

The makeshift amps and mikes continually broke down until Rod, having done his utmost to rouse the audience, realised he was fighting a losing battle with the equipment and angrily hammered the stage with a mike which was refusing to show any sign of life. Mac: 'Rod came over and said, "Fuck this, let's get off." We'd done a short set, maybe an hour, when Rod announced the equipment was rented and he was sorry about the show.'

The performance ended in near farce when Woody, believing Mac's organ was also rented, leaped on top of it and was about to vent his frustration by stomping heavily all over it when Mac blurted out: 'No, Woody! It's mine!'

While Rod was by now living with Britt Ekland in Los Angeles, Billy Gaff and Jimmy Horowitz had taken up residence in nearby Doheny Drive in West Hollywood. It was round the corner from a popular haunt called the Roxy and, since California law decreed no bars were to open between two and six in the morning, Horowitz became accustomed to a knock on the door at 2.15 and finding Rod and friends cheerily demanding that he open up his own drink supply.

'We had a tiny wet bar area with a piano. There were long periods when Rod would turn up every night at the house with his mates and they'd sit around, drink and play the piano. Then, at five in the morning, Rod would summon Toon to bring the car round and they'd all totter off.' Rod had Britt but as ever, he still enjoyed a night out with the boys.

Later, Rod also discovered that Horowitz could cook a very fine curry. It was not easy to find a good curry in LA but Horowitz had taken a special course and threw tandoori parties at his home, to which Rod was regularly invited.

Horowitz: 'Rod used to come and have a meal with us. But, if he was coming to dinner with the management, he expected us to put out the Mouton. One night when he was due for dinner I went to a big wine store and bought as a joke a bottle of Chilean Cabernet Sauvignon that was on special offer for $1.99 and decanted it into a silver case.

'I also had some very good wine put by in case it was really awful and there were any problems with the artiste. But it turned out to be a wonderful wine. For $1.99 this was a real buy, a great wine. Afterwards, I told Rod about the joke, that it was a very cheap wine and that we had merely decanted it. He said: "Yes, it's not a bad wine, is it?" I told him I was going to go back to the wine store the next day to buy some more.

'So I went back to the store and said I wanted to buy a case of the Chilean wine that was on special offer. They told me they had sold out. "How can you be?" I said, "I only came in here yesterday." They said: "Yes, but your friend Rod

127

Stewart came in and bought the lot." He probably went home and had all his friends come by and was serving it in his crystal decanter and telling them it was Mouton or something. He would think that really neat to be able to get away with not having to buy a $10 bottle of wine but buy one for $1.99.

'It was not that he was cheap. He loved the idea of being able to save money and yet he was very generous with big things. He kept upping Billy Gaff's percentage and we're talking about a lot of money here – hundreds of thousands of dollars. But then he'd really try and stick him on a bottle of wine and think that was really funny. Or he'd say, "Let's go out for dinner, Gaff," and he'd choose an expensive restaurant and get there and say: "Oh, I didn't bring any money with me." Sometimes he'd get Tony Toon, who called Rod "her", to call up either me or Billy and say: "Oh, hello, Miss Horowitz. The artiste wants to go to the Dome tonight so I've booked the table for eight o'clock. She expects you to take her." He thought he hadn't been wined and dined enough that month for his percentage.'

'If a record company was taking him out he would look through the wine menu to see what the most expensive bottle was. I remember I was with him in Holland around the time of the Polygram merger and we went out to dinner and he was looking down the wine list to see which was the most expensive bottle of wine to order. He was not a great wine buff but he thought it really funny to find a $200 bottle of wine.'

If Tony Toon always referred to Rod as 'her', Elton John preferred to call him Phyllis because of the famous piece of graffiti at Eel Pie Island. According to Horowitz, Rod called Elton Sharon and then John Reid, Elton's manager, became Beryl and Gaff Bridie. He says, 'I think that's how Rod got a reputation that he was gay or something. But it's plainly not true.'

In 1976, Rod followed up *Atlantic Crossing* with another

massive album-seller, *A Night on the Town*, which also produced three hit singles in America and Britain. The first, 'Tonight's The Night (Gonna be Alright)', stayed at Number One in America for seven weeks – but not without controversy.

'Tonight's the Night' is a song about the seduction of a virgin which some American radio stations felt was too sexually explicit for mainstream consumption, especially the line 'Spread your wings and let me come inside'. When programme-controllers banned it from the airwaves they were besieged by angry fans demanding to hear it. In Britain, the absurd situation arose whereby 'Tonight's the Night' was played by Radio One, the BBC's main pop station, but was banned from BBC television's *Top of the Pops*. It was deemed unsuitable for a family audience, they said. All the heated public discussion about the merits of the song, however, did no harm to record sales.

There was further controversy when 'The Killing of Georgie (Part I and II)' was released as the third single. This was Rod's brilliant, sensitive song about the murder of a young homosexual. Inevitably, it produced a mixed reaction from both the gay and heterosexual communities.

In between these two hotly discussed hits came 'The First Cut is the Deepest', Rod's version of a Cat Stevens song which happily contained nothing to offend anybody. According to Rod's *Storyteller* notes, when they went into the Muscle Shoals studio to record the song it transpired that he was the only person there who appeared to be familiar with it. A frantic call had to be put through to Los Angeles for the record to be bought and then played down the phone while seven musicians crowded round the receiver to listen to it.

A female singer called P. P. Arnold had achieved a minor hit with the song in 1967, but once again Rod showed perfect judgement in picking a song that he felt had been largely overlooked and which suited his voice admirably. In Britain,

Rod's version was issued as the B side of his 1977 chart-topper 'I Don't Want to Talk About It.'

By now Rod was itching to get back on the road after an 18-month lay-off. Although he often found recording a long and frustrating business, he enjoyed getting up in front of his fans. Clearly, he would need a new band and one which would feel comfortable with his earlier material as well as the very different songs that had proved such winners on *Atlantic Crossing* and *A Night on the Town*. After the sour experiences of the final years of the Faces, Rod was determined to choose his new companions with extreme care.

His choice boiled down to six men – Carmine Appice, a drummer he had known from back in his Beck days, guitarists Jim Cregan, Gary Grainger and Billy Peek, Phil Chen on bass and John Jarvis on piano. It says much for Rod's judgement that the musicians he picked became either long-standing friends or prolific songwriting partners or both. Fourteen years, on Rod asked Cregan to be an usher at his wedding to Rachel Hunter.

Rod found Billy Peek while watching television in Denver at two in the morning. He spotted him on the television screen backing Chuck Berry and immediately picked up the phone to call Tom Dowd in Miami – failing to take into account the time difference and that it would then be five o'clock in the morning in Miami. He also forgot that Miami TV stations do not necessarily screen simultaneously the same shows as those in Denver.

Rod's call woke Dowd up. When he drowsily picked up the phone, Dowd heard Rod excitedly telling him he had just seen a red-hot guitarist on the television and that he was just right to play on the new album. What TV show? asked Dowd. Rod didn't know, nor did he know the name of Berry's guitarist.

Next day, Dowd was left with the task of trying to find out the name of a guitarist he had never seen who had been on television in Colorado the night before in a programme that might have been made years before! It turned out that Peek was from St Louis and had been with Berry for seven years. He was duly tracked down.

Jim Cregan, who hailed originally from Dorset, had been in bands such as Blossom Toes and Family before making his mark with Steve Harley and Cockney Rebel, for whom he delivered the stunning acoustic guitar break on the band's 1975 chart-topper '(Come Up and See Me) Make Me Smile'. Rod had already chosen the nucleus of his line-up by the time he saw Cregan with Cockney Rebel in Los Angeles and asked him to join him.

'It was very difficult for me to leave Cockney Rebel,' Cregan points out. 'I liked Steve Harley and working in that band, and we were doing very well at that time. It was not much of a gamble going to work for Rod Stewart but it was still a gamble. Mick Jagger's solo career had floundered and Rod's could have floundered without the Faces. They were such a well-loved band that we might have been looked upon as a nasty little load of upstarts. It turned out not to be that way.'

Cregan fitted in so well and became such a close friend of Rod's that he happily toured with him over a period of twelve years. 'If you are asked to take four of your mates and go round the world first class or in your own Lear jet, have a lot of money in your pocket, have girls follow you wherever you go, and all you've got to do is play rock and roll for two hours each night, you'd say YES PLEASE!' Cregan explains.

Rod called up Phil Chen, who had previously worked with Jimmy James and the Vagabonds, while Chen was in Jamaica working with the legendary Doors, who had recently reformed after the death of Jim Morrison. 'To me Rod was the best singer, the Springsteen of that time,' says Chen. 'I loved all his soul stuff and so I was keen to join.'

John Jarvis had played on Rod's album *A Night on the Town*

and Gary Grainger had been with a group called Strider who had once toured with the Faces, so they were, like Carmine Appice, both already known quantities.

Significantly, Rod's new band included three guitarists, a line-up he had long wanted to employ, who were also capable of providing strong vocal harmonies. In direct contrast to the halcyon days of the Faces, rehearsals did not mean three hours of lubricating the throat with alcohol at the nearest watering hole. When they started, they rehearsed, for four solid months. In addition, there were not to be just sound checks before a gig. At Rod's instigation, they all got together for a little twenty-minute jam session each night just before they went on stage to get the adrenalin going, like a kickabout before a football match.

As Jim Cregan says, 'It was great. You feel that you've done the first three numbers before you actually get on stage, you've got a sweat going, everybody is in a good mood and when you do hit the stage everybody is on fire.'

The band were relieved to find that, although the music was fully rehearsed, there was nothing choreographed about the performance. Rod was not mealy-mouthed about letting the band share the limelight on stage. 'We were never considered to be his backing group,' Cregan stresses. 'We were his band, his mates and we were allowed pretty much a free rein. The only thing he asked was for us to keep out of the way when he swung the microphone stand, otherwise we'd lose a few teeth.'

Unlike the Faces, Rod's new band had not started off on an equal footing with Rod. They were competent musicians but since Rod had hand-picked them personally he was clearly boss from the outset and therefore knew he was unlikely to encounter the ego problems of the Faces that had led to their natural disintegration. The thorough professionalism Rod had witnessed on the making of *Atlantic Crossing* and the general businesslike approach of Americans had instilled a new discipline in him which he determined to carry through on tour.

The Rod Stewart Band's first gig was in Norway on 1 November 1976. Rod was understandably nervous. Despite his huge solo recording success, how would the fans react to Rod Stewart without the Faces? How would he perform without looking round and seeing the familiar grins of Woody, Mac and Kenny? But the roar that engulfed him when he took the stage in loose-fitting red satin trousers, white satin shirt and matching jacket quickly allayed any fears he might have had.

When they all moved on to London and a concert at the vast aircraft-hangar-sized Olympia venue, Rod was given a fantastic scarf-waving welcome from the fans as he ripped through favourites old and new and ended with 'Stay with Me' as an encore which he sang triumphantly from on top of the piano. Moving on to Scotland, the end of the tour was blighted first by Rod losing his voice and then by the police raiding the band's hotel searching for drugs. Several musicians and a secretary were charged and convicted of possession of cannabis. But Rod's dynamic performances, Cregan's dazzling guitar work and the pace and power of the shows set the pattern for Rod's tours for years to come.

Plainly, Rod had lost none of his ability to work an audience. In Amsterdam, the fans lit cigarette lighters and matches, and waved them in time to the beat as they sang along word for word to 'I Don't Want to Talk about It.' 'They sang so loud we couldn't hear ourselves,' recalls Cregan. 'I looked up and saw that Rod had started crying. I couldn't look at him because I was starting to cry as well. The whole band were turning away from each other, all getting choked up. It was bizarre having this whole audience communicating so powerfully they could move a band to tears.

'I had that experience only once ever again, at a great big open-air stadium in Berlin. The seats were very steeply banked and everyone lit candles which appeared to go so far up that you couldn't see where they stopped and the stars began. You had the impression that the stars came right down to the stage. We all had the shivers.'

That unique ability to understand precisely what an audience wants and to use that empathy to best effect puts Rod up with the greats, in the opinion of Jimmy Horowitz. 'Rod's among the Top Twenty all-time great rock and roll artists, in my view. His solo albums are great rock and roll classics and he's done the best shows I've ever seen. The Faces were a great band and he was a wonderful front man for them. He really knew how to put on a show. He's a great, great showman and as he got more confident he got better and better.

'He basically liked the stage to be as simple as possible. He was the first star I noticed who insisted on "flying" all the PA. He had special riggers so that nothing was left on the stage except the back line of the amps. Much of the time they were covered by a curtain, so it looked to be just a stage with musicians on it. There was nothing in front of him – even his own monitors were flown.' With nothing on the stage it meant that Rod could run wherever he wanted and see every part of the audience. It was so simple at a time when everyone else was doing light shows, lasers and explosions. His whole aim was to go out and sing.

'At hard-bitten places like the Garden in New York or the Nassau Coliseum he'd have everybody singing along. On "Tonight's the Night" there's the line "upstairs before the night's too long". The whole crowd would be singing along and he'd stop the band for that one line while he grinned and jerked a fist and forearm into the air! He was like a rock and roll version of Max Miller.'

Phil Chen, who played alongside Rod for five years before parting in not the happiest of circumstances, agrees. 'To me, he's one of the greatest because he was so full of energy. He was a fantastic, incredible performer. He'd really go for it.

He was a true artist and really lived his music. I didn't realise how much soul he had.'

Rod had experienced enough sloppiness and lack of discipline with the Faces to last him a lifetime. With remarkable dedication, he secretly began taking voice lessons in his early thirties from a cantor in Los Angeles who taught him better breathing, how to control his voice and how to do vocal warm-ups and exercises. He did not enjoy doing them but, with the aid of a tape, he religiously put himself through a range of exercises half an hour before he was due to sing to loosen up his face, lips, tongue and throat.

Part of Jim Cregan's job was to know in which key to put Rod's songs – mistakes had occurred in the past where tracks would be cut in the key they had been written in only to find that they were too high for Rod when it came to the chorus. 'I had to know exactly what his best notes were and the highest note that he could possibly hit,' says Cregan. 'Suddenly he was hitting C sharp which was two notes higher and one day he actually hit D, which is unbelievable. Your voice is not supposed to get bigger as you get older, it's actually supposed to get smaller. But he found he had another three notes that he didn't have before. He said it was all down to his teacher. Rod's voice is wonderful. I would say he is the best white male vocalist in the world.

'He has been gifted with this voice whereby no matter what he sings it sounds soulful, even "Mary Had a Little Lamb." I've heard him sing really silly songs when we've been having a pub crawl and when he puts his mind to it he can make anything sound good. It's a wonderful quality, it's a gift he finds surprising. But he is a lot more confident about it and now he recognises it's a natural gift he can enjoy it more.

'As a performer, there is a lovely side of self-deprecation even when he is wiggling his bum at the audience. He doesn't really think it's sexy. It's far more from amusement than for deliberate sexual provocation. Rod knows he is attractive to women but he's not sure of himself to the point where he puts out a belief. Watching him from a few feet away he always seemed to have a smile on his face.'

On tour, Chen noted that Rod was a different man when Britt was not with him. 'Rod was always after the girls,' he says. 'But when Britt was there he just kept looking at the menu without ordering. He was more relaxed when Britt was not around. He has an amazing effect on girls. They go crazy and just want to touch him. In New Zealand we played to one per cent of the country and they really went bonkers.'

According to Chen, who is now a session musician, his spell with Rod came to an end when the band was scattered in different places. Rod thought about getting everyone together to perform just one or two songs for a Billboard award, but 'Everybody was fed up of travelling backwards and forwards,' says Chen. 'Rod's roadie called and said Rod had decided not to do the show and he'll get back to you. I never heard from Rod again, which was a little disappointing when you've worked closely with someone for five years. I called back and he was having a massage and the next time he was playing tennis and all these other flakey excuses. I knew what was happening. I wasn't stupid. Still, I got a lot of credibility playing with Rod. It did me good.'

When Rod embarked on a marathon world tour in 1980–81, Chen was not the only one missing from the line-up. Rod rejigged the group and out went Carmine Appice and Billy Peek as well. New additions such as Kevin Savigar, who had studied classical piano for two years, and Robin Le Mesurier, who had once been guitarist with the Wombles, injected fresh musical ideas into the band which bore fruit both on Rod's new records and on his live performances.

It was the same successful pattern for Rod. He had once again surrounded himself with hand-picked musicians who had multiple qualities besides syncopation and an ability to play totally and utterly together. They were creative enough to spark off Rod's own songwriting talent, they could convincingly deliver the musical goods on stage and in the studio, and they could fit in with and contribute to the camaraderie so essential to a band on long, gruelling tours.

An examination of Rod's albums reveals just what a vital part members of the band played not just as musicians but as co-writers with Rod. Gary Grainger has a co-writing credit on four of the tracks on *Footloose and Fancy Free*, including 'I was Only Joking', which is one of Rod's own personal favourites, and 'Hot Legs.' Grainger has four more on *Blondes Have More Fun*, including 'Ain't Love a Bitch'. Savigar contributed to no less than five tracks on *Every Beat Of My Heart*, two on *Camouflage*, and one on *Body Wishes*. Cregan has four credits on *Body Wishes* and Le Mesurier two, including the instantly catchy 'Sweet Surrender'. But it was drummer Carmine Appice who has the co-writer's credit with Rod on the song that was to change Rod's career in a way that he could scarcely have imagined possible. The song was 'Da Ya Think I'm Sexy' from the 1978 album *Blondes Have More Fun*. It was a phenomenal worldwide hit which topped the charts in no less than eleven countries, including America and Britain, and proved to be one of the fastest-selling singles in Warner Brothers' history. But more than that, it changed for millions of people their perception of Rod Stewart.

'Da Ya Think I'm Sexy' was a startling departure from what most people believed to be Rod's musical roots – this was a bouncy dance number which landed him right in the mainstream of the disco boom. Not only that, anyone who did not listen closely to the words assumed from the title that this was Rod Stewart, the rock star famed for squiring sexy long-legged blondes, at his most vain, arrogant, narcissistic, boastful worst. The critics loathed it and Rod's strutting interpretation in skin-tight leopard-skin pants only made them fill their pens to the hilt with vitriol. The irony was that, although it was such a gigantic international hit, the song temporarily tipped Rod's career off course.

In Rod's often humorous song notes for his compilation *Storyteller* he is deadly serious when he says: 'If I ever wrote a song which put a fly in the ointment or a spanner in the works – it's this one. It was frightening, stirring up so much love and hate at the same time: most of the public loved it; all the critics hated it. I can understand both positions.' He also went on to set the record straight about the popular misconception that the song was sung in the first person by pointing out that he was but a narrator telling a story about a couple and that the song began: 'She sits alone waitin' for suggestions/He's so nervous avoiding all her questions.'

Another twist was added to the 'Da Ya Think I'm Sexy' story when a Brazilian songwriter claimed Rod had stolen part of the song from his compositions 'Taj Mahal', a tribute to the American Blues singer who had named himself after the famous Indian monument. But UNICEF did not complain when Rod donated all royalties to them at a 'Song for UNICEF' concert.

That one record sparked an extraordinary backlash against Rod Stewart and raised a number of questions. Rod's devotees who admired him for his distinctive voice and vivid songs wanted to know why he now seemed more interested in being a preening poser waggling his bottom at them in tight Spandex pants. What had happened to the soulful singer? Where now was the North London boy who was always one of the lads? Why had the rascal of rock fallen so blatantly for the opulent, millionaire lifestyle of magnificent houses, flashy cars and leggy blondes? He had gone Hollywood, hadn't he? Such questions were all the more pertinent for the fact that the Sex Pistols were at this time breaking big with their anarchic brand of street-level, poor-boys rock and were disdainfully holding up two fingers to fame and pop's rich older heroes like Rod Stewart.

The answer, of course, was that Rod was only human after

all, which was the perfectly reasonable justification he put forward when persistently pressed on the point. What, he argued, was he supposed to do when a glamorous woman made a play for him? Run away?

Indeed, if those were the arguments railed against him, then he had 'sold out' some time ago: he had been perfectly consistent in his taste for beautiful blondes since his teenage years; he had been more than ordinarily rich since the success of 'Maggie May'; and, musically speaking, it was *Atlantic Crossing*, with its smooth transatlantic feel, that had marked the greatest departure from the 'old' Rod Stewart. But the fickleness of press reaction is just one of the prices you pay for being an international megastar.

Says Horowitz in Rod's defence, 'Rod's a very, very wealthy man and you can't make that money and not change. It's impossible when you get that rich. People say, 'I'll never change, I'll just be the same humble guy.' But he was not that humble to start with.

'I think he's handled the success pretty well. He deserves it because he's worked at it. For all his failings, he has always taken his work very seriously, worked hard and always given tremendous value for money on his records and performances. He has never short-changed the public. He has always been conscious of his obligation and that people pay hard-earned money at the door. And he has always been very nice to fans. I've never seen him refuse an autograph or be rude to a fan – as long as they aren't rude to him.'

One tragic fan who has experienced at first hand the rarely publicised caring side of Rod Stewart was Londoner Colin Jones who was badly injured when he fell thirty feet from a balcony at a Rod Stewart concert in 1983. The young trainee accountant spent four months in a coma and suffered terrible brain damage. Although Colin, who was twenty-three at the time, won compensation of £625,000 which helps to provide some of the round-the-clock care he needs, his life was wrecked by the appalling accident.

Rod took a particular interest in Colin's plight, visiting his home to offer heartfelt messages of support. He even gave Colin the treasured gold disc he received for his first hit single, 'Maggie May'. At the time Rod said: 'I understand just what Colin's family is going through. It's amazing how much this awful injury must have hit not only Colin's life but his mum and dad's lives, too. That's why I had to come and see him. I wanted to give him something personal. The gold disc means a lot to me. I am sure he will look after it.'

In the same way that the wild behaviour and heavy drinking of the Faces has tended to obscure the fact that they were a tremendous rock band, Rod's reputation as a man with a seemingly insatiable appetite for fast cars and sexy blondes, partly perpetrated by his own formidable PR machine, threatened in the eighties to obscure his talent as songwriter, lyricist and performer.

'He's never really been recognised as a great lyricist,' says Horowitz. 'Nobody's ever really given him the credit for that. But, of course, he has the reputation of being a great rogerer of women. Rumour has it he is very good in bed.'

Jim Cregan: 'Even among musicians his reputation as a songwriter is not really that high. I think if he was more like Elvis Costello and had a bit more of a chip on his shoulder people would study his lyrics with more interest. But because his stage persona and his famous gallivantings around the world are so much more what people are interested in, the other part of him gets overlooked. But he is a great writer.'

When Arnold Steifel took over managing Rod in 1983, they mapped out a long-range plan to restore Rod's credibility as a *bona fide* rock and roll star after the slide that had begun with 'Da Ya Think I'm Sexy'.

'He had a terrible image problem,' Stiefel admitted. 'His image became this glitzy guy with Britt Ekland and beautiful blonde girls who wore fabulous things and drove fabulous cars. I told him that we had to take four to six years to sort of rebuild him without ever admitting to the world that there was any rebuilding to be done.' Stiefel was among those who blame 'Da Ya Think I'm Sexy'. 'It offended and eroded his core male audience,' he said.

The first step on the road to rehabilitation was a new LP, *Foolish Behaviour*, which, despite spawning the hit single 'Passion', did not reach great heights. But Rod's next album, *Tonight I'm Yours*, was a huge improvement which had Rod writing and singing from the gut once more. It produced a hit single, 'Young Turks', a fine song from Rod addressing the subject of teenage pregnancy, and excellent covers of Dylan's 'Just Like a Woman' and Ace's 'How Long'.

By 1988, the rehabilitation was successfully completed beyond anyone's expectations. A US tour originally scheduled for four months was extended to thirteen months, grossing $50 million, and Rod's album *Out of Order* sold over two million copies in the States in the first few months of its release. Kevin Savigar and Jim Cregan again featured strongly on the writing credits – 'Forever Young' is credited to all three.

Rod was back on top and able to admit to his past mistakes. 'In those days I didn't really concentrate on singing,' he conceded. 'I was definitely more interested in showing off the anatomy than in trying to prove my vocal prowess.' The recovery was so complete that Rod felt comfortable enough about 'Da Ya Think I'm Sexy' to include a beefed-up version of the song in his shows – and was pleased to find it went down extremely well with his audiences.

While the planning, the hard work and the discipline was paying off for Rod and his bands, there was always time for play when they were on the road. The hotel destruction that had been par for the course on a Faces tour was largely replaced by jolly japes, jokes, pranks and other relatively harmless mischief – although Rod had to fork out $1,000 after a hotel in Japan suffered a few substantial alterations that the management had not been requiring. In Australia, too, Phil Chen remembers, there was a piano on a hotel landing that various members of the touring party felt should be transferred to the lobby by the quickest possible route – straight through the bannisters.

It seemed that the further away the band were from home, the more mischief they were likely to make. Sax player Jim Zavala had Rod and the band in stitches in Osaka when he gave a new definition to dressing for dinner.

Japanese restaurants often have a gas burner set into the centre of each table with a grill over it on which the food is cooked on the spot. As it can be a messy business, diners are provided with three-quarter-length bibs stretching from neck to knee. As the evening's alcohol intake began to take effect, Rod's merry band were treated to the sight of Zavala leaving the table and returning wearing just his bib and nothing else underneath. Encouraged to dance on the table, Zavala leaped up on top of it quite forgetting the gas grill in the middle. The cheers from his fellow diners changed to gasps as Zavala's joyful semi-naked jig became a tap dance of excruciating pain as the hairs on his calves were burned to a cinder. Everyone agreed they had never seen barbecued legs quite like Zavala's.

It was in Osaka, too, on the 1981 tour, that tour publicist Tony Toon made an extraordinary unscheduled appearance centre-stage right in the middle of the gig. Toon had challenged another member of the touring party to a race around the hotel but had slipped and injured his leg so badly that it had to be put in plaster. Gamely, he decided that nothing would keep him from his duties, so he turned up at the gig in a wheelchair which he parked in the wings.

Right in the middle of a drum solo, Toon suddenly found himself being wheeled on to the stage and abandoned in the spotlight in front of thousands of bemused fans. None too familiar yet with the braking system and the methods of propelling a wheelchair, Toon frantically wrestled with the levers, causing a fair amount of wheel-spin before he managed to trundle sheepishly across the stage to the sanctuary of the wings once more.

In Tokyo, five members of the tour party somehow managed to lose Rod, Jim Cregan and tour manager Pete Buckland when they were all setting out for a disco. Uncertain of the whereabouts of the disco, the latter trio decided there was only one thing to do – find a pub.

Fortified by saki, they staggered out into the street some time later to search for the others. In such unfamiliar surroundings they were now worried that they might lose each other so they decided their best method of progress was to hang on to each other and hokey-cokey their way along the streets with crisp white napkins tied on their heads at four corners to act as identification tags should they become detached from one another.

Such shining night headgear on the Tokyo streets soon led to their discovery by the other five, who promptly tagged on to the back of them and together they performed a hokey-cokey of such saki-fuelled agility that they brought the Tokyo traffic to a standstill.

'Rod's always had a good sense of humour,' says Chen. 'One night he asked Carmine Appice to wear a tuxedo to a party and said we would all be wearing them. He got there and only the waiters were wearing tuxedos – we were in casual clothes.'

Somehow drummers appear the most frequent victims. Chen again: 'With Micky Waller – I think it was the second album at Olympic Studios in London – Rod on one number said, "That's a bit too loud. Let's move you out into the hallway." Then he moved him even further away, then into reception, and then he had him moved into the street. It was like four o'clock in the morning!'

Whenever more than one big-name rock band is touring a country at the same time, there is bound to be rivalry, most of which is good humoured, Occasionally, though, there is an edge to it – as in the time when Sting, who was just about to go on tour in America, took over the private jet that Rod had been using for his own tour. When he first got on the plane and took his seat, Sting was amazed to find a few choice remarks about him had been scrawled indelibly on a table in the plane.

However, the Sting tour party decided they would take revenge. Keith Altham, press representative for the cream of rock stars over twenty years, takes up the story:

'When they got to Los Angeles, they picked a night when they knew Rod would be at one of the Hollywood premières, billed as appearing there in person, and a sort of three-man hit squad with a driver bought black sweaters, black trousers and black balaclavas with eyeholes in them. Then they got a rented car, went down to the docks and bought 150 feet of heavy industrialised chain and some big heavy padlocks. They drove out to Rod's house, charged out of the car and secured the chain around his big electric gates. It took Rod four and a half hours to get into his house that night. He was not amused.'

Rod was amused, however, by Elton John's comic capers. With their shared love of football, the two superstars have been friends and – friendly rivals – for twenty-five years.

'Elton used to be so funny with us,' says Cregan. 'We once hung five giant soccer balls over Olympia when we were playing there and Elton hired a marksman to shoot them all down! Also at Olympia, we had a huge Christmas poster right across the street and Elton hired somebody to go and cut that down. The pranks would go on and on. Dreadful tricks.'

Even though he has ceased to tour with him, Cregan's friendship with Rod has blossomed over the years, to the point where they now see each other two or three times a week when Rod is at home in Los Angeles. They also regularly speak to each other on the phone, write songs together and record together.

In the mid-eighties, when Cregan was feeling extremely homesick for England, he started hosting Sunday lunch parties of roast leg of lamb and roast potatoes for Rod and a group of close English friends. Now it has grown into an institution with Rod and other members of the group taking it in turns to be host. Afterwards there is often a sing-song around the piano with Rod leading the way on anything from Muddy Waters and Otis Redding songs to *My Fair Lady*.

When Cregan got married in 1990, Rod was not only one of the ushers at the wedding but he also footed the bill for the reception for a hundred guests and allowed it to be held in the ballroom of his house. When Rod married Rachel Hunter a few months later, Cregan was an usher to Rod and offered his house for the reception – an offer warmly appreciated by Rod but in the end impractical, as there were so many guests.

But theirs is a friendship that was slow to blossom. 'Rod is a hard man to get to know,' says Cregan. 'It took me three years to get friends enough with him whereby I wouldn't feel uncomfortable in his company if nobody was saying anything. He is quite shy and he is rightly suspicious. Musicians would try to join the group just to give themselves a step up, just to say, "Oh, I played with Rod Stewart".'

As long-term music associate as well as buddy, Cregan has had a unique insight into Rod the songwriter. He says: 'He wears very lightly the responsibility of going off and writing ten or eleven sets of lyrics, which is quite a big job. But I know the responsibility of it scares him so he puts it off and off until the tour is more and more imminent and the record company is screaming and shouting and it's "Time to deliver, Rod". That is the motivation, that's when the talent comes shining through. He works really well under pressure.'

Rod's songwriting formula has barely changed from the days when he collaborated with Martin Quittenton and Ron Wood. 'Usually he gets the music and the melody together first with collaborators like myself or Kevin Savigar,' says Cregan who, being an ace guitarist himself, has a rather more disparaging view than some of Rod's abilities in that quarter. 'He is hopeless on the guitar. He can strum three, maybe five chords – a little Woody Guthrie, a bit of Muddy Waters, a touch of Bob Dylan. He does not have the instrument in his hand when he is writing. He listens and if he has an idea he will sing it. It's a purer way to write because you are not cluttered with any mechanics, it's all in your head.

'But we always have to provide the music first and that gives him the canvas on which to do the lyrics. When he's got it how he wants it to be musically, he then addresses the lyrics and sits with his lyric books, scribbles down the words and his assistant types it up. But without some musical kind of backdrop he doesn't begin. His lyric books will eventually become auction material because he has one for each song with all the notes it in. He has a couple of rows of them, nice leather-bound books, in his house.

'Although he may come up with a title while we're throwing the melody around, he has a title book with a list of two or three pages of titles that he hasn't used yet. Maybe he writes them on a bit of paper and sticks them in his pocket in a restaurant, you never actually notice him doing it. He has a fertile imagination but he is not like other lyricists who are always noting down phrases to use.

'Rod get stories up through his pores. He doesn't read a lot of literature or poetry. He reads a lot – but it's mostly autobiographical and not particularly heavy literature. He pretends sometimes to be very Jack the Lad and invulnerable and that is the persona he has used to get him through his career. Yet the songs give an insight into his real, romantic self. The romantic in him is very often well disguised.

'He is not a quick writer. We wrote 'Red Hot in Black' together and it took us five days. Once again, he wanted to use unusual images. Line one is: 'I met her in a little French cafe, legs like a young giraffe.' Of course, the first problem was what line would you find that goes with 'giraffe'? We wanted to keep the line and in the end we cheated with, 'She was sitting reading Baudelaire, not exactly working class.'

'He takes his writing really seriously. I know because I've been around when he has been sitting down wracking his brains to get just the right phrase and words that not only feel right but sound right.

'I remember sitting in a bar with Rod and his assistant Malcolm Cullimore. The three of us were trying to finish a song that had to be done that night. It was the last song on the record and if we didn't finish, the tour would have to be put back. Basically, we were sweating blood and bullets. We went into the studio and Rod started singing the song. When it came to the blank line, a line appeared and I don't know where from. Rod is a lucky boy.'

Cregan believes the best song he and Rod have written together is 'Never Give Up on a Dream' from *Tonight I'm Yours*, which was inspired by a newspaper report about Terry Fox, the cancer victim who *ran* across Canada.

'Rod turned up with the *Los Angeles Times* under his arm one day and said: "Have you seen about this bloke?" Rod was very touched by the idea and said we should write a song about the guy. We knocked it up in an afternoon. Then Rod got stuck with the lyrics – he said it began to sound as if he was preaching – so he got Bernie Taupin to come in and help out. We dedicated it to Terry Fox and gave a whole big bunch of the royalties to cancer research.'

Rod's songbag is littered with examples of lyrics first entering his head at strange moments. The chorus from 'You're in My Heart,' for instance, came to him while he was standing outside a hotel in Toronto with record producer Tom Dowd. With no tape recorder immediately to hand, Rod sang it to Dowd who faithfully wrote down the music there and then on the back of a cigarette packet.

Similarly, 'Gasoline Alley' came to Rod thanks to a chance remark by a young girl fan outside the Fillmore West in San Francisco. They were chatting and the girl said she must get off home otherwise her mother would think she had been down Gasoline Alley. Rod generally has a tape recorder and a notebook by his bed, as several songs have come to him at night – notably 'Tonight's the Night.'

Cregan hazards a guess that one of Rod's own personal favourites is 'I was Only Joking'. It is an extraordinary baring of the Rod soul which finishes with Rod admonishing himself for pouring his heart out in a song and 'owning up for prosperity so the whole wide world can see'. That line gave everyone a shock when Rod came to sing it in the recording studio.

'He originally meant to say "owning up for posterity . . . ," ' says Cregan. 'Somehow it was either written "prosperity" on his sheet that day or he confused the two words in his head when he was singing, but it turned out to be one of his most honest lines. That really is revealing – I pour my heart out to you for cash! A Freudian slip!'

Chapter Six
Britt Ekland

'If you screw another woman while you're with me, I'll chop off your balls' – Britt Ekland.

Joan Collins was the matchmaker behind Rod Stewart's first great Hollywood love affair. The link with the inevitably blonde and beautiful Britt Ekland began in March 1975. Britt was devastated by the break-up of her long-standing relationship with record producer Lou Adler and Joan Collins knew just the pick-me-up to prescribe.

With her then husband Ron Kass, Joan invited the unhappy Britt to join them for the Rod Stewart concert at the Los Angeles Forum. The prospects of a crashing success from the meeting of two such individual sex symbols did not seem high. Rod was still ostensibly with Dee Harrington. Britt was rich, famous in her own right and unimpressed by celebrity for its own sake. Furthermore, although she knew some of her girlfriends regarded Rod Stewart as hugely attractive, Britt was certainly not overly smitten. In fact, she was reluctant to accept Joan Collins' invitation but Joan insisted and so the meeting which was to change her and Rod's lives took place.

Britt remembers her first sight of Rod on stage: 'I looked into the spotlight and there was this incredible man, so sexy, so animal like.' They were formally introduced at the backstage backslapping that followed the concert. The two drank their champagne and eyed each other with interest. Joan Collins invited Rod to join her party for dinner at the exclusive Hollywood restaurant Luau's where Britt discovered that the private off-stage Rod Stewart was much shyer and quieter than the riotous concert performer. She said afterwards that Rod sat coyly in the restaurant like 'Little Boy Lost', saying hardly a word.

After the meal, they went on to a party at the home of singer turned film star Cher. As the evening progressed, the mutual attraction between the rock star and the actress better known for her lovelife than her theatrical abilities grew and grew. Britt reflected afterwards: 'By the end of the night, I knew that I would have Rod, but I wasn't going to be a one-night groupie. My strategy would be entirely different with Rod than with any other of my lovers. There would be no harm in keeping him waiting, because I figured that Rod needed to respect a woman.'

Britt kept a rein on her emotions. She and Rod met several times without leaping into bed together. After two days they realised, after an intimate dinner together, that they were falling in love. Britt told told Rod she loved him and Rod smiled that he felt just the same way. They happily decided that it was a miracle that two people who had only just met should fall so headlong for each other. Yet still they did not rush into bed. Britt said soon afterwards: 'Rod was touring with his band and staying in a hotel. He didn't want to smuggle me in at night and out again in the morning. He didn't want our love-making to begin like a sordid fly-by-night affair.' Rod was displaying a sincerity and a sensitivity he rarely bothered with on lesser conquests, who were lucky to last a night.

For Britt, after relationships with older men, marriage to Peter Sellers and her long affair with Lou Adler, it was refreshing to be with someone more or less her own age. Britt was just eighteen months older than Rod.

Britt also had enough experience to stay out of Rod's confrontation with Dee Harrington in the Troubador. When Dee caught up with the man in her life, Britt at first thought she was just another groupie after an autograph. But when she heard Dee say in a voice shaking with anguish, 'I am going to take the next plane back to London if you don't want me to stay here with you,' she wisely walked away.

It says a lot for Rod's ability to stay cool in a crisis that when he later joined Britt at their table after finally ditching his girlfriend of five years, Britt noted: 'His composure was remarkably cool. There was not the slightest trace of anxiety.'

Britt knew that she was heading for a serious affair with her newly discovered rock star when they went to a party at singer Joni Mitchell's house a few days later. Bob Dylan and Paul McCartney began a jam session in one of the huge rooms and they invited Rod to join them. He refused, staying firmly by Britt's side. Afterwards he told friends: 'I don't think anyone has ever turned down the chance to jam with Bob Dylan but I was so much in love with Britt.'

The feeling was reciprocated and the couple who became Hollywood's most glamorous partnership swept into an unstoppable physical affair. Years later, Britt was to document her feelings in those heady days at the beginning of their relationship in a book, *True Britt*, which angered Rod almost as much as her financial demands. She wrote: 'Rod admitted that he was in love with me that night; and I could not easily say I felt less about him. As always, I had fallen in love before anyone could even get out their stop watch.

'From that moment on we were inseparable, kissing and cuddling in our new-found passion. We were oblivious to the stares and embarrassment we caused. It mattered little that our first time in bed together yielded no greater reward than that of any other of my experiences. Perfection, however, was ultimately achieved. Very soon we were making love three or four times a day. We were like two pieces of interlocking jigsaw and we matched physically. We were both slender, small-boned and long-legged.'

Britt was much more than just another pretty face to Rod. After his long on-off affair with undemanding Dee, she was a strong-willed mature woman, a partner with a real mind of her own. And for Rod the meeting coincided with a rootless, drifting period which followed his first flush of success. 'For a few years after I became successful and bought the big house in Windsor, all I used to do was go upstairs and play with my model railway,' he said later. 'Sometimes you lose a little bit of sanity and therefore lose the idea of the music you've got. I would be up there for weeks on end, wouldn't make any records, wouldn't write any songs . . . and that's wrong.'

Direction aplenty came from the engaging Miss Ekland. But it was by no means a one-way process. Britt learned from Rod's typically thoughtful band that he usually preferred big-boobed Amazons. She offered to have a 'boob job' to enhance her 'miniature equipment'. Rod declined. Britt said: 'He thought I was perfect as I stood. He liked my teenage-pre-served figure and my long blonde hair. I think the little girl image was different for him and he liked it. He liked me always to dress in virginal white stockings, panties, petticoat, negligée and peel it all off like the leaves of an artichoke. And in bed I wore only Joy, his favourite perfume by Patou. We would make love in all sorts of crazy places. Once, just for the kick of it, we made love on the back seat of my Mercedes which we chose to park in the long, unlit drive of the house belonging to my neighbour Goldie Hawn – whom I'm sure would have been very understanding if she had found out!'

Thus it was a feeling of deep bliss which attended Miss Britt Ekland as she stepped into a three-year love affair which was certainly Rod Stewart's most serious relationship to date. Rod was similarly delighted with the new love. He said: 'With me she can be natural and let herself go a bit. She's like a

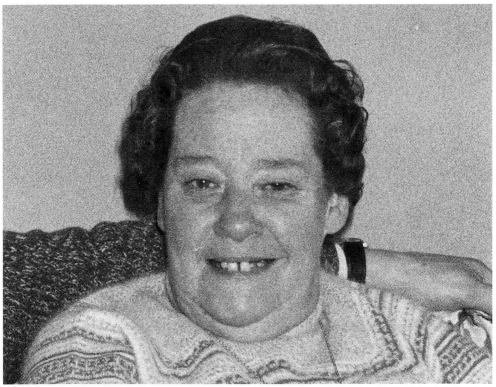

Rod's mum, Mrs Elsie Stewart. *(Syndication International)*

Family man Rod with son Sean and daughter Kimberley. *(London Features International Ltd* (left); *Syndication International* (right))

Rod and Kelly Emberg
with their baby, Ruby
Rachel. *(Syndication
International)*

Rod's long lost daughter
Sarah Thubron.
(Syndication International)

Phallic fun on board
the *Ark Royal,* 1978.
*(Syndication
International)*

Elton makes a grab
for Alana as Liza
Minnelli and Rod
look on, 1983.
*(Syndication
International)*

England 2, Scotland 0,
Hampden Park, 1980. Rod in
deep despair. *(Syndication International)*

Rod and Elton John take a late
fitness test. *(London Features International Ltd)*

Early British mentor John Peel.
(Syndication International)

Rod poses proudly with an outfit
as flamboyant as his car. No one
ever accused him of being subtle.
(London Features International Ltd)

Rock star mansion, mark one: Southgate, north London. *(London Features International Ltd)*

Rock star mansion, mark two: Cranbourne Court, Windsor. *(Syndication International)*

Rock star mansion, mark three: Epping Forest, Essex. *(Syndication International)*

Rock star mansion, American style. With Britt in beloved Carolwood Drive, not quite Beverly Hills. *(London Features International Ltd)*

Rod 'Phyllis' Stewart and Elton 'Sharon' John, 1991. *(Rex Features)*

child all over again. She giggles a lot, which is something she has never done before.

'I've brought all that out in her.' Then he tapped his forehead and said: 'She's good for me here, she stretches me mentally. I'm a changed man. I just don't fancy other birds any more. Britt's everything I want.'

When Britt travelled to England she was delighted to be welcomed by members of Rod's family, even if they occasionally did get her name wrong and call her Dee! She was entranced by Rod's luxurious Windsor home with its elaborate model railway and its paddocks and manicured grounds. She was put off initially by Rod's father's awkwardness with women and his mother's sternness, but Mr and Mrs Stewart soon came to approve of the forceful, independently successful new girlfriend their son had found. Bob Stewart even awarded Britt his greatest personal accolade – he took her breakfast in bed.

The Stewart clan were extraordinarily tight and close-knit. Rod's father busied himself collecting the rents on various British properties the star had shrewdly invested in and, although Rod's mother was confined to a wheelchair with a weak back, she was still a force to be reckoned with. But at Christmas in the small family home in Cambridge owned by Rod's elder brother Don, Britt found herself becoming a real part of the family.

The annual family reunion at the season of goodwill to all men is very important to the Stewarts. As they squashed together for the traditional turkey lunch Britt felt more at home than in the most luxurious of international hotel suites. She was particularly moved when Rod's family also welcomed her children, Victoria and Nicholai. Rod and Britt cheerfully squeezed into a single bed so that they could stay for the celebrations.

Britt was different from most of Rod's previous girlfriends in other ways, too. She made it clear from the start that Rod

Stewart's range of experience was now to be enlarged to encompass a totally new concept – fidelity.

Rod told Britt soon after they met that Dee knew he had other women, but that she didn't mind. Britt made it painfully clear that she did not feel quite the same. 'I looked at him straight between the eyes. "Then that's where I am very different," I said. "I would mind a great deal. In fact if you screw another woman while you're with me, I'll chop off your balls" ' – which left little room for misinterpretation.

Rod appreciated this strong and beautiful woman and her direct approach and he certainly got the message. Asked very early in their relationship if he felt tempted to stray he said, 'Bloody 'ell. Don't talk about it. She'd go mad. She'd take a carving knife to me.'

Britt was as underwhelmed by certain aspects of the rock star lifestyle as she was with the idea of Rod entertaining other lovers. Perhaps the least appealing personality as far as she was concerned was the ubiquitous Tony Toon. Britt was amazed that Rod depended so heavily on the services of the publicist. She found his use of the slickest and cheapest gimmicks to provide a constant stream of stories for the papers, primarily the British tabloids, deeply unattractive.

Britt was appalled when Rod went along with the stunts Toon came up with to make headlines. Tony helped, for instance, to create the worldwide newspaper reaction when Rod allegedly stood up President Ford's daughter Susan on a date. Rod confided to Britt: 'It wasn't true. I didn't stand her up. I just couldn't get back to Washington from my tour in time to take her out,' but he did not mind Tony's rather more imaginative account of events being broadcast far and wide. 'I want the publicity,' said Rod. 'And Tony's only doing his job.'

For Tony Toon the arrival of Britt Ekland was heaven sent. She was beautiful, blonde and brimming with sex appeal, of course, but above all she was newsworthy. Thanks to Toon's deluge of tips and snippets of news about the new twosome, Stewart and Ekland for a time became the hottest celebrity couple on the circuit. The 'Burton and Taylor' of the seventies, according to their assiduous publicist.

Britt wasn't totally averse to life at the centre of the glamorous new relationship. What she missed was some of the sort of glittering jewels that Burton provided for Taylor. 'What I lacked in diamonds – and it became transparently obvious that Rod wasn't going to give me any,' she said, 'I compensated for by wearing the gaudiest of costumes to match those of my new pop hero.'

Yet still they weren't living together. Rod was keen to move the affair on to a more permanent basis but Britt was not in such a hurry. She had two young children to consider. She did not doubt that Rod's so frequently demonstrated expressions of love for her were powerful enough, but could he really accept the kids as well? In fact, Rod genuinely loves children and regarded Britt's pair as a bonus. He insisted to her: 'It's like starting out with a ready-made family and it will be good to have kids around the house. A home isn't a home without kids.'

At last, she agreed and, although marriage was certainly not upon the horizon, the couple made a pledge of loyalty to each other. Rod still held on to his houses in England but, in the summer of 1975, he and Britt decided to start househunting in some of the most exclusive suburbs of Los Angeles for their US home. They eventually settled upon a stylish but neglected twenty-room mansion in Carolwood Drive, one of the leafier locations in not quite Beverly but Holmby Hills. Rod paid three-quarters of a million dollars for the house and paid a further one hundred thousand dollars into 'the Carolwood Account' for Britt to begin renovations.

It was to be a massive job. Wild cats had formed a colony on the terrace and the house had to be fumigated to clear out a huge variety of bugs and insects. Then the real spending began. Britt and Rod found they shared an enthusiasm for Art Nouveau and so soon all manner of stylish fitments and fittings were arriving at Carolwood Drive from all over the world – but at a price. The living-room, which was the size of a basketball court, cost some thirty thousand dollars to equip with dignified wood panelling. Lamps, candelabras and other exotic furnishings arrived from Paris; paintings were purchased at Sotheby's in Los Angeles; crockery, linen and cutlery came from London, New York and Hong Kong. The two and a half acres of grounds were lovingly redesigned.

Some of the couple's shopping trips were featured on a BBC programme which portrayed Britt as pushy and somewhat full of herself. However, after the documentary was screened, Rod chivalrously defended his lady. 'We're desperately in love,' he said. 'Some people think that in the BBC TV documentary Britt came over as a bit of a bitch. But that was the editing of the film. I mean, you can take *Match of the Day* and make it look good or bloody awful. She's not a bitch. She's so bloody helpful. The boys in the band all love her. Whatever happens in the future, I'll never find a better woman.' For Rod, for the moment at any rate, this one was' for real.

Rod's beloved cars, an AC Cobra, an Excalibur and a £26,000 Lamborghini Countach which had been flown out from Italy at a cost of £2,000 competed for room in the garages with Britt's solitary Mercedes. The house even had a guest cottage in the garden for Tony Toon – but then, nothing is perfect. Britt did not mind that. She felt she had never been happier. This was five-star living at its most indulgent. Even when eating alone the glittering twosome donned full evening dress. Rod grumbled a little when he found Britt insisted they adhered to a strict timetable for meals with her children, Victoria then eleven, by her marriage to Peter Sellers and Nicholai, two, from her relationship with Lou Adler. Rod was not keen on routine: 'She insists we all sit down to meals at the same time. I rebel against this regimentation. I hate it. But I put up with it.'

The couple were besotted with each other and with their rapturous new life together. As Britt recalls: 'We made love at all hours of the night and day and we refused to be inconvenienced by guests. Barbecue meals round the pool were always popular but we would not think twice about leaving our guests to chew on their spare ribs and their conjectures while we sought the refuge of our bedroom to make love for maybe the second or third time of the day, trying to set fresh records on the previous day's accomplishments in bed. Our bedroom was a love nest in every sense of the phrase, with blue ribbons softening the brass hardware to convey the cosiness of a child's cot. Rod regarded every orgasm as a testimony of his love for me.'

Rod the romantic loved nothing more than to surprise his new love with a dramatic gesture. Once, while she was working in New York, he flew from Los Angeles to be with her and startled Britt by sneaking up behind her in a chemist's shop and putting his hands over her eyes and saying 'Guess who?' At first she was terrified because she thought she was being mugged but when she calmed down she appreciated the effort.

Although Britt tried to temper some of his loonier traits, she really did appreciate the lively Stewart sense of humour. She encouraged him to stop pulling funny faces every time someone pointed a camera in his direction, but she also said: 'There's a sense of schoolboy naughtiness about him. I can say what I want and be as silly as I want when I am with him.'

Rod has always been an accomplished mickey-taker. When Britt remarked one evening that one of her films was on television that night, he retorted, deadpan: 'Is it a talkie?'

On another occasion, Rod leaped on Concorde to fly from New York to catch up with Britt filming in Paris. Warmly remembering his busking trips, Rod enthusiastically showed his lover all his teenage haunts as well as the more traditional attractions. They wandered the streets hand in hand and kissed on every corner of the city of romance. Later, they drove to the south of France in Rod's exotic Excalibur car exploring quiet, tucked-away villages and distant vineyards on their way. The sentimental journey included a stop for al fresco love-making beneath a stone bridge at sunset, the actress later dreamily recalled.

Theirs was most definitely a worldwide love affair. When Britt had to jet off to the Philippines for the filming of *High Velocity*, Rod came too. Of course, the press were also on their trail, but Rod was an old hand at shaking them off. When he and Britt ate out, Rod would always book their table in the name of Mr and Mrs Cockforth which had the double effect of shaking off the pursuing press and ensuring smiles all round when they arrived.

They could scarcely have been closer. Britt recalled: 'We tried to explore as much of the Philippines as we could. We discovered, three hours' drive out of Manila, a rain forest where we could swim in the hot and cold mineral pools and on one occasion Rod dived in wearing a spare pair of my bikini briefs because he had forgotten to bring his own trunks. Rod was never self-conscious about those kind of things. Very often he chose to wear my cotton panties on stage. Not only were they more comfortable for him, but they were seamless and invisible beneath his skin-tight trousers.' Another addition to the ladies' knickers legend.

Gradually, the two careers were being brought closer together. Rod had to return early from the Philippines to Los Angeles to lay down the tracks of his single 'Sailing'. The song was always very special to Rod: even before it swept to Number One in Britain, the sentimental side of his character found its haunting melody, composed by Gavin Sutherland, so moving it brought tears to his eyes. He thought it was one of the finest tracks he had heard.

When Britt returned to America, the pair joined forces for Rod's promotional tour across America and to Europe. A non-stop round of press conferences became something of an ordeal, especially for Rod. Reporters were much more interested in discussing the couple's domestic arrangements – 'When are you going to marry?' 'Will you have children?' – than they were in Rod's music. Britt handled the intrusive questions much better.

In Chicago, Rod exploded with anger and tore up a journalist's notes because he felt Britt answered the personal queries too frankly and too fully. 'When they ask about our private lives, tell them to get stuffed,' yelled Rod back in the hotel suite. 'It's none of their bloody business.' Britt did not agree and angrily retorted: 'How can you say that when you're throwing a press conference? Once you've asked them, they are entitled to ask any questions they like. If you don't want people to ask about our lives together, then you should have never agreed to the tour.'

Rod was incensed and the couple launched into their first major fight. In her book, Britt recalls: 'Rod grabbed my shoulders and started screaming, "You do as you're damn well told," adding a profusion of expletives. Whack! My face stung as his hand flew. I clenched my fist and sloshed him back as hard as I could. We were all over the bedroom, turning over table lamps and furniture. It was like a Western bar-room brawl and suddenly my black and silver lace dress was ripped from my body. At that point, I burst into tears and collapsed on to the bed. Rod quivered with self-reproach and fell limply beside me, and began to cry himself.'

The intense public scrutiny was taking its toll. Rod was full of the most profuse apologies once he had calmed down. He even bought Britt an exclusive new Ted Lapidus gown to replace the one he had torn. As she drily records: 'For Rod, that was a gesture of overwhelming proportions. He paid nearly four hundred dollars for the dress and it took him some time to recover. The only other present he gave me through our entire relationship was a diamond bracelet.'

If the relentless media interest in their relationship was one significant pressure threatening the couple's long-term happiness, then Rod's traditionally Scottish view on spending money was another.

Britt tried not to react at what she considered examples of penny-pinching meanness – she knew Rod had come from a family background where cash was always short – but her feeling of irritation at Rod's reluctance to be parted from his money gradually grew.

Their telephone bills were a regular nightmare. Britt would write to query the bill to buy Rod time to pluck up the enthusiasm to settle the account, but it did not always work. Once, all three of their lines were cut off and only reconnected upon payment of an extra two hundred and forty dollars. Rod badgered Britt to buy her groceries at the cheapest store in town. He even told Tony Toon to warn her to cut down on spending. Britt paid Rod a hundred dollars a month for the upkeep of her two children, but she resented being criticised for spending money on wining and dining his frequently visiting friends, who always seemed so thirsty and hungry.

One of Britt's most marked influences on Rod's life was on his style of dress. They both enjoyed the thirties films of Fred Astaire and Ginger Rogers and Britt bought several antique dresses of the period. She took him to the Hollywood memorabilia store, Harold's Place, to find him an authentic thirties straw boater. The hat was worn with great flair on the cover of Rod's 1976 album *A Night on the Town*. However, later Rod was to bitterly regret the headwear.

Yet, if a promotional tour with Rod was fraught with emotional problems for Britt, it was a picnic compared to life on the road with the Faces – still his band at the time. The entourage numbered some thirty-odd people, most of them, in Britt's view, extremely odd. And the process of transporting musicians, equipment, technicians, lighting crew, managers, stars and all was a bewildering new experience for Britt. To her, hotel rooms were refuges in which to sleep or rest, or even to stay on holiday. She had not previously seen them as places to attack.

Perhaps her earliest introduction into the raw unbridled animalism that is a rock group on tour occurred in beautiful Hawaii. It was August 1975 and Rod Stewart and the Faces were one third of their way through a massive tour of sixty cities in three months. The band had played two highly successful concerts on the island and Rod and Britt were staying in the premier suite of the luxurious Kalahala Hilton.

Britt was busy packing while Rod and friends were enjoying a last beer on the beach. As time drifted past the normal check-out hour of noon, the next occupants of the suite arrived in reception. Australian singer Helen Reddy and her manager and husband Jeff Wald were not impressed by the offer of alternative accommodation while Mr Stewart and Miss Ekland made their exit.

The volatile Mr Wald decided to take matters into his own hands. Rapping on the door of his favourite suite he confronted a bemused Britt. Britt recalls: 'When I answered the door a small abusive man started ordering me to get out of the suite. He just terrified me and I was so scared that I called the switchboard to have Rod paged.'

Rod and assorted roadies and Faces rushed back from the beach to deal with the situation in their own decisive way. Rod snarled a single word instruction – 'Destroy!' – and the opulent hotel room was transformed into a war zone within seconds. Britt stood and stared open-mouthed with astonishment as the wiring in the television set was attacked, towels were stuffed down the toilets, telephones were ripped from their sockets and the bed had several vital screws removed.

161

Meanwhile, downstairs, more trouble had started. Opinions differ as to who shoved whom first, but what appears to have happened is a flyweight contest between Faces keyboard player Ian McLagan and the now incensed Mr Wald. Unfortunately for him, Mr Wald fell against a wall and dislodged an indifferent reproduction of John Constable's ubiquitous 'Hay Wain', which cracked him smartly on the side of the head. A free and frank exchange of views followed, with several of the Faces expressing forceful opinions on what could happen to Mr Wald should he decide to continue the fracas. The hotel management called the police. Wald decided to have McLagan charged with assault. McLagan filed counter charges.

Gradually tempers cooled and Rod Stewart, satisfied with the alterations to the suite, commented: 'The next time they ask us to leave, maybe they'll be more courteous.' With that he led his party from the hotel. Billy Gaff handed a representative of the hotel's management some two thousand dollars and the incident was closed.

Britt was flabbergasted. She found the encounter even more extraordinary in retrospect when she and Rod returned to the same hotel some months later to be greeted by flowers and fruit in the suite and not a mention of the previous excitement.

Yet, as the tour progressed, Britt was to become even more bewildered. Rod Stewart had always attracted a particularly attractive and inventive breed of groupie. Girls – often rich and beautiful girls – seemed to regard Rod as some sort of sexual Messiah to be grabbed and squealed at whenever the opportunity arose. Anti-groupie security was tight, particularly when the lady in the star's life was in evidence, but one night in West Virginia a stunning and somewhat stunned blonde got to Rod and Britt's bedroom door. Britt remembers: 'I thought it was one of the guards and when I opened the door she almost brushed past me. Her eyes were glazed as she cried, "Where's Rod? I'm going to screw him." ' Britt decided this was one function of room service she was going to refuse and angrily slammed the door on that particular female.

However, she could not shut groupies completely out of Rod's and her lives. Endless telephone calls from girls telling her to get the hell out of Rod's life and threatening to give her cocaine with broken glass in it steadily disillusioned Britt Ekland about the glamour and fun of life on the road with a rock band. Yet more disturbing to her were the raunchy letters the young females would write to Rod. Some actually addressed their letters to Britt with instructions for her to describe Rod's anatomy in detail. 'Draw it for us,' one letter urged.

Britt had to cope with odd behaviour from other quarters. She was particularly puzzled by Rod's reaction to a request from Rolling Stones Mick Jagger and Keith Richard. When Mick and Bianca dropped in to see Rod before a New York concert he was frosty and off-hand. Soon afterwards, Rod made his triumphant return to London with his enormously successful series of concerts at Olympia – they became the hottest tickets in town. Even stars were buying them on the black market. Jagger and Richard asked for passes but Rod ruled they should be kept out. He even ordered extra security guards at all doors. This broke all rock business codes. Britt reckons that, for the first time in his life, Tony Toon was speechless. Britt decided that deep down her rock-singing lover was simply jealous of old rival Jagger, still widely acknowledged as the world's top rock star. But the clamp-down on security continued – at one point, security men even stopped Britt entering with Rod's own parents.

Rod and the Faces finally split just before Christmas 1975. Britt insists that she was not involved in the decision.

Rod surprised Britt by asking her to come into the recording studio to do a voice-over in French to the final line of

'Tonight's the Night'. Initially she thought he wanted her to sing. She reacted honestly: 'I can't sing. I've got a lousy voice.'

'You won't have to sing, you'll just talk to the music,' assured Rod. Then he darkly hinted that if Britt did not join in he might ask the beautiful Stevie Nicks of Fleetwood Mac to do it. That convinced Britt to agree. How suitable a Swedish actress of thirty-four is for the part of a sobbing young French virgin who is about to be deflowered is debatable, but in any case her anguished muttering of *'Mon Dieu'* can't have done much harm. The record was yet another worldwide success and the track was featured on the bestselling *A Night on the Town* album.

'What I was saying,' said Britt afterwards, 'is, "Hold me tight. Put your arms round me. I'm a little frightened. I love you so much!" '

'No she isn't,' interrupted Rod. 'She's saying, "Get your trousers off, Jock." '

Britt's recording debut was not a financial success for her, however. 'I didn't get a dime from the multi-million dollar royalties and I didn't ask for one. I did it all for love.'

No one could accuse Britt Ekland of holding out for cerebral movie roles, but she did want to work again. After a period of being the other half of a rock star, her agent persuaded her to take a role in *Slavers*, a movie set, predictably enough, against the background of the slave trade which was to be made on location in what was then known as Southern Rhodesia. She did not enjoy the separation from Rod and, because of the sanctions that then applied to Rhodesia, telephone calls were hard to connect. When she did manage to get through, she appealed to Rod to send her a romantic message.

The response rattled through on the telex within hours. It read: 'Dear Britt. Here is the romantic message you wanted. Tired of wanking. Please come home, Soddy.'

Soddy was Britt's pet name for Rod while he called Britt

Poop or Poopy. It just suited him, she felt, because, well, he always was a bit of a sod.

Britt went on to make another action adventure, *King Solomon's Treasures*, in Swaziland before heading home with a present for Rod of a $1200 lion's head and skin. 'It's like having another member of the family in our house,' said Rod. The dead creature was spread out on the carpet of the rented flat in Portland Place, central London, that the couple took over briefly from Rudolf Nureyev.

The relationship seemed idyllic. All it needed to complete the blissful picture, it appeared, was a glittering showbiz wedding and the patter of tiny feet. And for a time it looked likely that a happy ending had been written into the script of the Hollywood love story. But Britt already had two children by different fathers. Thoroughly modern and fiercely independent as she was, she could not bring herself to consider having another child without a husband to stand by her. Rod understood and proposed as their jet flew towards Britt's homeland of Sweden. Soon the newspapers were full of quotes detailing Rod's plans to get married and have children with Britt.

But not all the publicity was so positive. Rod's glitzy lifestyle had long encouraged criticism, particularly in the trade press, that he was losing his roots and selling out to commercialism, with a consequently disastrous effect upon his music. Now he was accused of being completely overwhelmed by the influence of this famous film star who was endangering his whole career.

Rod reacted dramatically. He gave a press conference at which he insisted that Britt had no such influence, that he had no intention of marrying. 'She is not the right woman for me. I have no plans to marry her.'

Not surprisingly, the effect on their relationship was devastating. Britt broke down as she tackled Rod with the cruel words. He weakly tried to play down the remarks, saying that it was simply how he had felt that day. Tony Toon was instantly summoned to fix up a new interview to give Rod the opportunity to deliver a complete retraction. 'I should not have said these foolish things,' he said. 'Britt is the only woman in the world for me and one day we will marry.'

Of course, he simply succeeded in a refocussing of the media spotlight on the love affair. In such a situation a story linking Rod with Susan George was just what the newspapers needed. Britt and Rod met the shapely Susan at a Los Angeles dinner party and as Britt chatted to Queen's Freddie Mercury Rod talked with Susan George.

When Britt decided that it was time to go home she chose not to interrupt Rod's conversation, simply whispering that she was taking the car and leaving. Back at the house she began to wonder. As she put it: 'Maybe Rod fancied Susan, I fretted. She had big boobs and most of Rod's earlier women had big boobs. What if he slept with her?'

After two hours, Rod returned home and the lively discussion surrounding his *tête à tête* with Susan George developed into a fracas. Britt blacked her eye as she cracked her head on the bedpost and Rod rushed to get some ice cubes to keep down the swelling. The evening was concluded by an emotional reconciliation. As Britt put it: 'We made love and the incident was closed.'

Except not quite. The newspapers had to deliver their side of the story, which somewhat more imaginatively suggested that the dinner party had been enlivened by Britt hurling a glass of champagne over Rod and accusing him of an affair with Susan George. Tony Toon was questioned over his role in this version of events but proclaimed his innocence. Susan George said categorically: 'Any talk of a romance with Rod is a load of rubbish. I was merely talking to him about tax problems and he asked me to say hello to his mother when I got to England.' Rod's love life was always able, with the aid of a skilfully heated quote, to edge earthquakes off the front pages.

In February 1977, as Rod and Britt celebrated their third Valentine's Day together during Rod's tour of Australia, he paid generous public tributes at a press gathering to the strong-willed nature of his lover. 'Before I met Britt I was drifting. I was getting to the point of not caring. But she gave me back my self-confidence. Before, I never gave women the time of day. I was terrible to some of them, treating them with utter contempt.' And he added with words that were to come back to haunt him: 'But I could never do that to Britt – I would hate to see her hurt.'

There was yet more speculation about the strength of the romance after Britt was reported to have hired a locksmith to gain entry to the Portland Place flat in the hope of finding Rod closeted with Susan George. Britt insisted she had paid a locksmith some £40 to get into their flat, after she had returned from Munich and Rod was in Scotland with the keys.

With Rod devoting more time to his music and his new band, Britt found herself thinking more and more about their relationship. When he found time to take a cruise on the *QE2* with her they were blissfully happy together. They appeared for all the world like young honeymooners to other passengers. Rod even felt inspired to write two songs on board. He also found time to pace the decks late at night musing on a favourite preoccupation of his, the *Titanic* disaster. In his black velvet cloak lined with red silk he must have felt himself in tune with the doomed liner.

But although the cruise provided a cheery respite for the lovers, their relationship was itself heading towards a few treacherous icebergs. By June 1977, after the couple had been living together for two years, Britt was examining her future.

Her trusted agent Maggie Abbott counselled about continuing life in the goldfish bowl. She felt the affair was heading nowhere. At one time Britt's feeling for Rod were so strong that she would have instantly dismissed such advice. Instead, she decided that perhaps all they needed was a break from each other. She planned a trip home to Sweden and the picturesque seafront house in Smadalaro that had once belonged to her grandfather. When she told Rod she was taking the children and going away for a while, he agreed the holiday would do her good.

Rod was right. The hot Swedish summer was a peaceful and happy time for Britt, Nicholai and Victoria. When Rod rang she felt she was talking to a stranger. When she returned to Los Angeles at the end of July she found him looking weary and exhausted. He was working hard in the studio, but he did delight Britt with the words of a new song he had written for her. 'You're in my heart, you're in my soul . . . you'll be my breath till I grow old . . . you're my lover . . . you're my best friend' was just what she wanted to hear.

But a meeting with old flame George Hamilton, then married to a beautiful blonde by the name of Alana Hamilton, was to shatter that happy return. Britt had enjoyed a fling with the engaging Mr Hamilton in the South of France years ago and the two were still friends.

Britt was at a Hollywood party given by film producer Alan Carr and was busy apologising for Rod's absence when what George Hamilton said completely stunned her.

'Fancy Rod going out with Liz. I never thought you two would bust up,' he smiled, and Britt's life was tossed up into the air. The expression on her face told Hamilton she knew nothing of Elizabeth Treadwell, the curvy Californian socialite who was enjoying a fling with the man she thought was confining his favours only to herself.

The recriminations were long and painful. Britt, never one to duck an issue, insisted Rod make his choice there and then. Reluctantly, she gave him a week to do it. He moved out of the Carolwood house and Britt was left alone with her pain. Sadly, she was told that Liz Treadwell was not the only one. Rod had been seen with a succession of other women, including American model Bebe Buell, an on-off girlfriend for some time while Britt was on the scene, until Rod let it be known publicly that their affair was over. Unfortunately he had neglected to explain the situation to Bebe and she was not amused. The girl, who has also had relationships with singers Todd Rudgren and Elvis Costello, regards her fling with Rod as the unhappiest section of her rock star hat trick. 'Rod Stewart is a dangerous person as far as I'm concerned if you're a woman. Because even if you go out with him once, it's plastered everywhere, and for some weird reason, he's always used it as a method of getting attention . . . I think he's fucking abused the shit when it comes to using people at that level.'

The affair with Liz Treadwell, though, had added poignancy for Rod. It happened while he was in the studio recording *Foot Loose and Fancy Free*, on which one of the tracks was 'If Loving You is Wrong, I Don't Want to be Right'. Rod admitted later: 'That really fitted into what was happening. I was seeing Liz Treadwell, but Britt didn't know. The whole track was done live in the studio. Liz was there and I'm singing, "If loving you is wrong, I don't want to be right . . ." You couldn't help but sing it with guts. That was the last track we recorded.'

The feelings Britt felt for Rod Stewart melted away like a snowball on Malibu beach. She swiftly acquired those essential Hollywood break-up accessories, a psychiatrist and a lawyer. She expensively examined her innermost thoughts at this terrible time in her life and even more expensively issued Rod with a twelve and a half million dollar lawsuit. The following months were painful for both Rod and Britt.

Britt's version of events is that at first Billy Gaff came to plead Rod's case but she insisted on discussing the situation with Rod himself. They reconciled, they split apart. Her father jetted in to lend support. She lost twenty pounds in weight. They reconciled again and then more news of Rod with fresh affairs split them up again.

Britt herself had a fling with a young actor during the making of an undistinguished TV movie called *The Great Wallendas*, based on the lives of a famous circus family. Then she returned to Rod, but they were unable to recapture their old magic. Britt blamed Rod: 'Rod was back into the whole groupie thing and he really thought that I would accept it all without so much as raising an eyebrow. One night he came home so drunk that Tony Toon had to drag him across the floor to the bed.'

Britt changed psychiatrists but she knew in her heart that she really had to change men. In desperation, she turned to ex-lover Lou Adler, who generously put a house at her disposal. With sadness in her heart, she moved out of Carolwood.

Britt records the miserable farewell. 'Rod lingered around the house that morning and he asked, "Are you really going?" I tried not to look at him for fear I would burst into tears. "There's no option is there?" Rod did not answer. He took sanctuary in his room. There were no goodbyes.'

Both the size of the lawsuit and the intimate details of their life together revealed in Britt's book wounded Rod Stewart. Although the financial acrimony between the two was settled out of court, Britt's version was very much in the public eye. The cash demand was 'A big shock to me,' said Rod. 'I lost a lot of faith in women. Not only that, but also having my so-called life story written by so many women I've been out with. It's happened four times now.

'Three women I've been out with, Dee Harrington, Britt Ekland and Bebe Buell in the British papers – and then some secretary who used to work for me sold her story to the papers. I'm sure Britt regrets it now, but I did lose faith in women a little during that period.'

Rod was anxious to get the Britt Ekland period out of his hair, epitomised in his mind by the boater picture on the cover of *A Night on the Town*. On a 1975 television documentary reflecting back on his life and music, Rod said: 'Nowadays I am just improving my persona. I wouldn't have changed anything apart from THAT album cover, where I was wearing a straw boater. I don't think that was me. That was a bad period of my life.'

Later he grumbled: 'I've lost all the songs about drinking pina coladas under a parasol. I was just listening to Ekland all the time having stupid album covers done. The music was overlooked for a few years there.' Rod blamed Britt for his foray into fatuity during the mid-seventies, which he came to feel was his most negative period: 'The image was being built for me and I just let it happen until it ran away with itself. It was stupid, posing all the time. I deserved the criticism I got and I certainly did get some. We're all allowed to make mistakes, though, and I've come through the other end of the tunnel.'

As he told a press conference: 'A lot of the criticism was absolutely correct. I had left what I started out to do – to be a rock 'n' roll singer. I was in love and I did a lot of foolish things.'

But was it all Britt's fault?

'Well, a great deal of it,' said Rod. 'Also, I closed myself off and didn't go out and listen to music the way I do now.'

Fans recall that the *Night on the Town* boater really seemed to bother Rod. On the tour after the release of the LP, the official logo was a drawing of him putting his fist through the somewhat stagey headwear. The boater had seriously embarrassed the singer.

He said: 'It was Britt's idea to wear the straw boater on the cover while holding a glass of champagne, which is just not me. I think that album cover is the most embarrassing thing I've ever done in my life. So shortly afterwards, when I'd fallen out of love with Britt, I looked at it and said, "My God, Stewart, what have you done now, lad?" So that's why we came out with that tour logo.'

Rod refused to agree that he ever really 'went Hollywood'. He said later: 'The whole thing about "going Hollywood" has been blown out of all proportion. First, I live nowhere near Beverly Hills. I live in Holmby Hills, which is a Los Angeles address. And I don't go out with film stars the way I'm supposed to. OK, I live next door to Gregory Peck, but I just say hello to him and he's the only one I know. I don't go to ritzy parties. If I did I'd admit it.'

But Britt did have an enormous influence on Rod. She was perhaps the first really worldly woman with whom he had shared a long relationship. While Rod never felt fully at ease in the movie world, always preferring musicians to actors for playmates, Britt did open his eyes to many of the finer things in life, from French antiques to Continental films.

And he might not have attended so many 'ritzy parties' if it weren't for Britt, but he was not exactly one for staying in anyway. Another ex-girlfriend describes him as the 'least domestic person' she has ever known. All he wants to do is go out. Rod did hit the social scene when he was living in Hollywood but he has always hit every available social scene. Rod didn't regard it as going Hollywood, most of the time he was just going out.

Chapter Seven
Alana Hamilton

'Marriage is closer than it has ever been. I am in love with Alana, and she is not an ugly girl' – Rod Stewart

Alana Hamilton appeared to have all the qualifications to be Rod Stewart's ideal woman. She was blonde and beautiful, of course, and, at five feet eleven inches, with the requisite long and shapely legs, she easily measured up to Rod's unwavering physical standards. But Alana was much more than just another pretty face. She possessed a mind and a determination which was to have an enormous impact on the life of Mr Rod Stewart.

Yet there was nothing in their first meeting at a Hollywood party in March 1978 that predicated a marriage and children for the rock world's most dedicated bachelor. They were introduced at a star-studded party by Rod's close friend, actor David Jannsen, better known as *The Fugitive*, and his wife Dani, who were doing some nifty matchmaking after Rod's break-up with Britt.

'It wasn't really an instant thing,' said Rod. 'At first I thought she was just another blonde that I should bed, but it wasn't quite as straightforward as that.'

The next day, when Rod instructed his faithful aide Tony Toon to ring and arrange a dinner date with the former wife of actor George Hamilton the response was cool. 'What's wrong with Rod ringing me himself?' said Alana.

Toon was startled to find that the lady was by no means bowled over by the suggestion that she meet the famous rock star for dinner. She wasn't even sure she could make it. But if she heard the invitation from Rod's own lips she just might. Not for the last time, Rod complied.

Because the statuesque Texan model, former wife of actor George Hamilton and stylish lady about Hollywood was most certainly not inclined to become just another decorative bimbo notched on the bedpost of the libidinous Mr Stewart. Although she was single when they first met, she had never considered the singer as a possible suitor. She told friends afterwards that Rod Stewart was the last person she would have thought of dating: 'Given a list of a hundred men, his name would be last on the list. Besides, he has a funny-looking nose.'

In fact, her reaction to her first encounter with the famed Rod Stewart was even less promising. 'I didn't really like him,' she said. 'I had this sort of image of him. I thought he'd be cocky and that we'd never have anything in common.' But then she noted that Rod kept staring at her and realised there could be more to the spiky-haired singer than a string of hit records and a wild reputation.

As it turned out, their first impressions were both wrong. Having agreed to meet for dinner, the alluring Alana refused to sleep with Rod – for all of forty-eight hours. Rod realised she was no run-of-the-mill one night stand and Alana was struck by the attractive and amusing man underneath the brash exterior. It was to be a relationship which dramatically changed both their lives.

But in those early months together they were just like any other pair of new lovers. Rod adored Alana's accent: 'She's from Texas. And I'd never had a girl from Texas . . . I'm lying again, probably just a couple. Anyway, it took me a couple of days and many clever wordings before I got her between the sheets. I'm extremely happy I've found a nice lady at last.'

Alana Collins was born in the tiny Texan town of Nacogdoches and got her unusual name because her mother had a crush on Alan Ladd at the time. Alana stood out at school where most of the other girls were called something like Mary Lou or Billy Jo and she hated her name because nobody could pronounce it. Even compared with Rod's down-to-earth origins, Alana's family were very poor. Her mother and father separated soon after she was born and Alana was brought up by her granny and her uncle on their small farm in a rural outpost.

As a child she helped planting vegetables and feeding the chickens. She can remember existing for days on potato soup until Granny's pension cheque came in and then the family would walk the three miles to the grocery store. They bought their food in huge sacks which her grandmother later used to fashion little dresses for Alana. Her mother worked in Houston and came back every few weeks. Alana used her height and her beauty and her remarkable self-belief to climb out of the poverty trap via success as a model. But she never regretted her harsh childhood.

Always very religious from an early age, Alana is a member of the Church of Religious Science and draws great strength from prayer. 'I've been going to church and praying for years. I'm very religious. I've prayed for almost everything I've wanted in life and most of the time I've gotten it.

'My religion teaches you that you control your life by your thoughts. You are master of your own fate. I believe in that totally.' But reports of her devotions were frequently garbled – a source of considerable irritation. 'The way it was printed made it sound as if I was practising some kind of voodoo,' she said.

Rod loved Alana's vibrant energy and her sense of fun. He said she was the first girl he had found with the same sense of humour as him. David and Dani Jannsen had thought Rod and Alana would be perfect for each other and Rod agreed they had been right. But in their first whirlwind of mutual attraction they almost wore each other out. The two jet-setters were both thirty-three when they met and were initially consumed with a determination to compete with each other. They went out every single evening into the nightlife of Los Angeles for six weeks to show how life was one long entertainment and then, both exhausted, sat down and agreed to stay in.

Rod recalls: 'We said to each other, "Who are we trying to impress?" The answer was each other. That was really the turning point. Then we went through all those little tests. We knew we were great together in LA but we both knew that we might hate each other away from there, living in a hotel together. Dirty socks and all that. And we went through all that and it was still great. We knew that we were made for each other.'

Rod and Alana had much in common. They were both blond and neither had ever been jilted. Alana always insisted she had been the one to end her relationships and Rod said: 'I've never lost either. No one has ever left me. The trouble is, I love a girl with spunk who can stand up for herself. Alana's independence is what I like.'

The couple did not rush to move in together. Even eight months after they first got together, Rod was still in Carolwood Drive and Alana had her own home in Beverly Hills. Rod said: 'She has her own house and lives there. I stay at mine. We made that decision at the beginning. We swop around. She sometimes stays over at my house, or I go over to hers. It's good that we don't live together. Britt and I made a big mistake about that. You should keep it separate and independent.'

One of Rod and Alana's favourite pastimes was to go shopping together. They found they had almost identical taste in clothes, although Rod did concede that some of their matching outfits were a shade bizarre. Alana said: 'Rod likes me looking slinky and sexy. He adores me in mini-skirts and high thin heels. I like more feminine clothes – a party style with lace and frills. Basically, though, he likes me in anything as long as I don't look too old-ladyish. And if I buy really raunchy jackets and coats I have to be careful – because he'll have them off me as quick as a flash and wear them himself!'

By the autumn of 1978 Rod was hard at work on the European legs of an ambitious world tour and concerned about his first British concerts for two years. He was anxious about the reception, keen to be seen as the old Rod, rather than what he knew had come to be known as the 'Hollywood' version. As the tour got underway, Rod confided: 'When I was with Britt I was pretending to be something I'm not. She brought out a posh, phoney side in me. I lost a lot of friends by going around with her. Now it's back to square one.' But someone must have liked him still – the British leg was sold out, he had a Number One single, 'Da Ya Think I'm Sexy', and an album at Number Three, *Blondes Have More Fun*.

When the tour began in Manchester, Rod realised he need not have worried. The 12,000 tickets for the four shows sold out in just four hours and the wave of adulation that swept from the audience to the stage as the band struck the first few chords almost overwhelmed him. He said afterwards: 'You don't know what it's like to have an audience respond like that. I was so moved that tears filled my eyes and I cried momentarily. I lost my voice and couldn't remember the words of a song I've been doing for years. When we did "Maggie May" and "Sailing" the fans were singing and we were playing. I don't know who was entertaining who most. They knew all the words. I felt so humble, my fans are the best in the world.'

Also on the road was Alana. Before she met Rod Stewart she had only been to one rock concert. After watching her new lover's remarkable live performances, she was, like so many people, hooked. And she was a voice of reason in the hectic male-dominated world of a travelling rock band. She insisted that Rod took his vitamin pills and cut down on his alcohol intake. Rod relished the attention: 'Marriage is closer than it has ever been,' he said. 'I really am in love with her. And she is not an ugly girl.'

The couple found time to pay their respects to the doomed aircraft-carrier *Ark Royal* in Plymouth docks where she awaited her final voyage to the scrapyard. Rod was the first to admit that he owed her something for the huge success of 'Sailing'. 'She helped to build my reputation and I desperately wanted to visit her before she was scrapped,' he said. 'The song is still a showstopper at my concerts and every time I sing it in the future it will give me a very special feeling.'

When the Stewart family met Alana, they were somewhat taken aback by the forceful former model. Rod's father was even less impressed when he kept reading that the couple were 'trying for a baby'. 'You're not even married,' he yelled down the phone at his famous son.

Rod seems to have found his triumphant return to Britain inspirational in all sorts of ways. Because, just nine months after he opened his sell-out homeland success, Alana gave birth to their daughter Kimberley, in July 1979.

But on one subject, at least, Alana agreed with Rod's father. She wanted his baby all right, but only if they were married first. They organised a very low-key wedding away from the prying cameras of the press in Los Angeles in April 1979. The ceremony was conducted by the Reverend Jackie Eastland, a minister in the Church of Religious Science. Rod was impressed by the Reverend Jackie's insights into their future, though less impressed when she was dubbed his 'personal psychic' by the British press. Rod credited the Reverend Jackie with predicting a medical problem for his friend Elton John and began to share some of Alana's convictions.

Rod's father joked that he was too young to get married at thirty-four and his mother caught him by the arm and whispered: 'Make sure you keep your trousers on in the future. Be a good boy.'

Rod bought Alana a beautiful Art Deco ring of diamonds set in onyx, which she decided was an impractical idea for a wedding ring, so, when Kimberley was born, Rod gave her another, a twist of emeralds and diamonds set in gold.

Two months before Kimberley's birth Rod was keen to point out that he had not been pushed into marriage simply by the pregnancy. He knew after a month with Alana that they would be together for life. He explained at the time: 'I never said that, "I'll try to be faithful now that I'm a married man." I did say, "For the first time in my life I will be faithful to one woman – my wife. I am really glad we got married. I have never been happier and for the first time in a long time I am leading a normal life. We keep on getting happier the more we get to know each other.'

The birth was a very emotional time for Rod. 'I was there when she was born. Now that was something else. An amazing experience. I didn't hold Alana's hand – she was far too busy shouting and getting on with it . . . When she was actually born. Well, it's probably nearly as good as Scotland beating England. A once-in-a-lifetime thing. And thank God she hadn't got my hooter.'

When asked if Kimberley would be spoiled, Rod recalled his own indulged childhood: 'Well, I was spoiled rotten and I've turned out OK. No, she'll get anything she wants out of me. I haven't thought about her growing up yet but I like to think I'm fairly liberal. That may all change when she gets to fifteen or so, of course.'

Rod and Alana calculated afterwards that their unborn baby kicked her way through forty-three Rod Stewart concerts around the world while still in the womb, and heard forty-three renditions of 'Maggie May'. No wonder that by the time she was sixteen months old her doting dad was giving the toddler piano lessons and remarking on her amazing aptitude. Why, she even seemed happy to sit captivated by a video of one of dad's concerts. 'Without wishing to sound like a doting father – and I don't really care if I am a doting father – you just try and get a kid this young to sit still and watch TV for an hour,' he said. 'All these songs had registered with her. They were in her subconscious. It was absolutely amazing.'

Rod had one of his rare public flare-ups when he, Alana and baby Kimberley disembarked from the *QE2* at Southampton on 1 October. He angrily refused to be photographed with his little daughter. Afterwards he snorted that he was not remotely ashamed of her: 'It's just that kids are not very pretty at that age and we had already decided to wait a bit before she was photographed. Anyway I hate those dumb pictures of fathers holding babies and smiling like melons. They look so stupid.'

Rod and Alana were astonished when Kimberley was born a girl. All the tests had indicated that Alana was expecting a boy and they had planned to call him Roderick Christian. Rod had even joked about flying Alana over to Scotland so the youngster would qualify to play soccer for his beloved national side. Fortunately, he did not bother.

When young Kimberley arrived, they were at first stumped for a name. After two days they came up with Kimberley from a book of names – no other significance. Her full name is Alana Kimberley.

'I don't feel tied down by being a father,' said Rod. 'I'm a happy man. I know sex and sexy things surround us wherever I go. I have always had a weakness for long-legged blondes but since I'm married to the best I'm not going to be interested any more in testing for any other fish in the sea. We have never been happier together than we are now.

He was sincere when he said, 'It's a hundred times better than I ever thought possible and I just look forward to it going on getting better. My reputation as a killer with women precedes me wherever I go, even now that I am a married man. But I plan on standing by the vows I made when I got married. I know my hell-raising nights are over, as far as others are concerned. Now it is just Alana and me that raise the hell with each other.'

Alana was happy too, shrugging off reports of her husband's previous philandering: 'I could not care less about what he did in the past. I have never been jealous. Those things written about him by women he knew! I don't know what has happened to good taste in this world. It reaches the point where nothing is sacred.'

She could not comprehend the tales of Rod having boisterous fights with Britt. For her and Rod, she said, their lowest point was half an hour of sulking after they could not agree on a colour scheme for the house. 'I am fairly good natured, and the only time Rod gets into a bad mood is when he's not working.'

Unlike Britt, she didn't make the mistake of getting involved in the musical side of his business: 'I can't carry a tune in a bucket. If I sang one of Rod's own songs he wouldn't be able to recognise it. At home, Rod makes up little songs on the spur of the moment, which he sings to the baby.'

Rod worked hard at his marriage with Alana. Friends report a real determination to make the relationship a success. However, one lingering irritation remained in his life in sunny Los Angeles. He missed Britain. He missed the seasons, the newspapers, the pubs and the pals. But he got a blast of a sound that really reminded him of home when an old friend, comedian Jonathan Moore, gave an unscheduled bagpipe performance on Christmas morning 1980. Rod woke to the familiar sound, threw open the bedroom windows and roared with laughter when he realised Jonathan had sneaked into the grounds to serenade him.

In their early days, the Stewarts' life together was very simple. They went to few parties, entertained only occasionally – even though a magnificent ballroom was added to the house. Alana's only rival for Rod's affections was his beloved weekend football game with his Los Angeles Exiles side – an enthusiasm she most certainly did not share. However, they did exercise together at regular keep fit classes. Although, as Alana put it at the time: 'Rod enjoys it, but it's torture for me. I only exercise because I feel I ought to.'

When she had finished breast-feeding and they got more organised at home, Alana tried to please her man in the kitchen as well as elsewhere. She bought English recipe books and attempted his favourite steak and kidney pie. But for Christmas she insisted on a traditional Texas-style dinner of roast chicken, black-eyed peas, sweet potatoes and banana pudding. No wonder Rod also used to work out on an exercise bicycle in the evening as well.

The years have always been kind to the singer. Although he has enjoyed a drink, he also knows when to stop. 'I might go crazy for five or six nights in a row and then I'll say, "This is it", because I look in the mirror and there's a big spot coming on the end of me nose so I decide to stop. Or worse still, if me hair won't stand up, then I know that something is wrong!'

Rod's late-night drinking sessions were now supplemented by vegetable juices. 'Really, all you need is lung power,' said Rod. 'The most important thing is that I don't smoke.'

And so, Rod's determination to stay fit helped more than just his football. It also enabled his concert routines to reach remarkable athletic heights. The energy levels at Rod Stewart concerts were always higher than at those of his contemporaries. As they moved into their mid-thirties, the gap grew.

The buzz of live performing always required him to make an extra effort. The first few weeks of a tour would see Rod lose seven or eight pounds. Alana was much more of a country music fan than Rod. 'She tries to kid on but she don't really like rock 'n' roll,' said Rod. 'She likes watching me perform but she likes the slow songs, the romantic ones. I think that most women do. I like making the fast ones – fast and furious.'

Rod Stewart was never going to join the many casualties of the rock business. While the early deaths of stars like Keith Moon, Elvis Presley and Led Zeppelin's John Bonham all saddened Rod, his solid family background always set him apart from those rockers who move out of the fast lane only to overtake. After Bonham died, Rod said glumly: 'I had a sneaking feeling about Bonham, that he was pushing it just a bit too much and not being fit enough to carry it off.'

The shadow of Britt Ekland occasionally passed across Alana's ideal view of her new life. After Britt's autobiography came out with its frank, although largely positive, view of Rod Stewart, Alana threw up her hands in horror. 'I really do think,' she trilled, 'that this kiss-and-tell syndrome is disgusting. It's appalling. I mean, I swear to God that if I was starving in the streets and someone offered me a million pounds, I wouldn't write such a book. I just honestly don't understand how you can write intimate details about someone you once cared for.'

Alana was particularly angered by Britt's complaints about Rod's meanness with money, suggesting the multi-millionaire was so careful with his money that he used to grumble about the grocery bills. Alana was aghast: 'When I moved in [to the same Carolwood Drive home Rod had shared with Britt] I went mad when I saw the grocery bills. I said, "Rod, this has got to stop," and he said, "Oh, is it expensive?" He didn't even know. Sure he's conscientious about money but I've never known a less stingy man. He gives me an unlimited budget. If he was mean with Britt, maybe it was because he didn't want to spend money on her. A lot of men are like that with their girlfriends. With their wives, it's a different story.'

Alana found it hard to be generous, however, when it

183

came to Rod's previous life. She simply loathed people who assumed that Rod was nothing more than an insolent womaniser. All right, so he went out with a lot of women, she would say. But then he was a good-looking man. And all men like to sow their wild oats. Alana described all Rod's previous girlfriends as 'old sluts' and felt that Rod just wasn't ready to settle down until he met her. She believed that he was waiting until the right person came along and that he knew he would never marry Britt. Alana said, 'Today he believes in the sanctity of marriage as much as I do. I basically think that if a man is happy at home and in love with the person he is with, I don't think he wants to go and pop into bed with any little groupie who comes along.'

She and Rod certainly threw themselves into the family-building business with enthusiasm. Their second child, a son to be called Sean Roderick, was born in September 1980, only a little over a year after Kimberley was born. Rod had just returned to California from the Bahamas where he had been on a 'song-writing' trip with Richard Harris, an old friend.

The next night, at their beach retreat just up the coast from Malibu, Alana's labour pains started. As her contractions increased, so did Rod's speed in his Lamborghini as he drove at up to 90 mph towards the hospital. Alana was screaming, 'I'm going to have it in the car!' and Rod had not a clue what to do. He might have watched Kimberley's birth, but he dreaded the thought of having to deliver his second child himself, particularly in the cramped passenger compartment of an Italian sports car designed for speed rather than its potential adaptability into a maternity ward.

The next thing Rod heard above Alana's yells was the wailing siren of a police car. He skidded to a halt and, being British, leaped out and moved towards the policemen – definitely not the thing to do in gun-happy California. The cops both jumped out and shouted 'Freeze!' to the anxious rock star. Happily, the law officers were Rod Stewart fans, even though, as he observed afterwards, they must have been ten years younger than him.

The guns were quickly exchanged for autograph books. Then Rod explained the urgency of his problem and then the Highway Patrol really came into their own. They swept Rod and Alana to the waiting ward at top speed. Just as well as it turned out, for young Sean Roderick arrived a mere fifteen minutes after they did.

In fact, it was a difficult birth and Sean made his entrance to the world via a Caesarean operation which prevented Rod witnessing the second marvel of his life. However, Rod is credited with the ultimate footballer's reaction to the birth of a son: 'I'm over the moon.' Later, he noted: 'Kimberley looks just like Alana but Sean is more like me though. He's got a real big hooter there, a real Stewart hooter. I think when he's old enough I'll do what my dad did to me. He always put a tennis ball at my feet, you know. I'll try that tactic, but if he turns out to be a chess player who likes classical music, then I shall support him all the way. He's got a very intelligent look on his face, which worries me. I don't really think he's cut out to be a rock and roller. That comes from his mother. She's got an IQ of 148. It doesn't come from me. I was a secondary modern school idiot.'

Sean was very welcome, but by no means planned. Rod and Alana did not intend to have a second baby so soon. As she put it: 'No one in their right mind wants to have two babies in nappies at the same time.' They decided not to extend the family any more for a while. Alana said: 'I'd like to have a rest. I've spent the last two years being pregnant and it's hard work.'

Alana was convinced Rod would be an ideal father when she saw how well he got on with her son Ashley from her marriage to George Hamilton. Ashley was only three when Rod and Alana first fell in love and initially he was jealous of the strange spiky-haired rival for his mother's affections.

But Alana watched how Rod's zany sense of humour and dogged persistence gradually made a friend of the young child. By the time he was six, Ashley was putting on his own private rock 'n' roll concerts in his bedroom, singing along to Rod's song 'Hot Legs'. Only Rod was allowed to watch.

Razor wire tops the high wall surrounding Rod's Carolwood Drive mansion. Security is a fact of life in the swisher parts of Los Angeles. But Rod was most worried when the children were very small. The fans never bothered him and he would cheerfully chat at the gates and sign autographs but he said: 'We've got some nutters who try to get over the fence. When you've got three kids you can't afford to take chances.'

Soon after Sean's birth, Rod left to start his next tour. Alana had to stay behind in America for their longest separation since meeting – all of three weeks. There was the inevitable press speculation. Said Alana: 'We were both very lonely then. But I had just had the Caesarean with Sean and was still breast-feeding. I just couldn't have gone on tour. Unfortunately, now we've been together for a while, people are looking for cracks in our relationship. But I trust Rod. If you are going to get worried about what sort of women groupies can be, and that your husband has to go away, then you shouldn't marry someone in Rod's profession.'

All the same, Alana bridled a little at what she felt was a double standard. She understood Rod's need to go to a night club to unwind after a concert, but she knew that if she went to a club without him, Rod most certainly would not approve. 'A few years ago, I would have felt tied down,' she said. 'But now I find my children more interesting than anyone I could meet in a nightclub.'

Rod loved being a father from the very start and played for hours with both children. 'I don't know what I did with my life before I had children,' he said with a grin as he arrived in London in November 1980 for another successful concert tour. His new album, *Foolish Behaviour*, included a song dedicated to his daughter, 'My Girl', as well as the thoughtful 'Oh God, I Wish I was Home Tonight'. Although the tour was another towering sell-out success, it was a crucial time for Rod after all the flak he had taken for 'selling out', so he was more nervous than he had been since his early days. About two hours before the show began he found himself shaking and on the second night he even forgot the words of 'Maggie May'. As the tour went on, though, he eased back into his familiar confident style.

At the time, Rod considered *Foolish Behaviour* to be his finest work to date. Its subsequent success gave him a feeling of real personal satisfaction. 'We can't be at the top for ever, but if this was all taken away from me, just give me the wife, kids and guitar and I could do it all again. I know I could, it's in there.'

As he approached thirty-six, Rod sensibly began to qualify his statements about his inability to imagine himself rock 'n' rolling into his forties. He said: 'You know, it would have been very easy for McCartney to have retired five years ago, but there's this old die-hard thing in him that still has so much music to make. Well, it's the same with me. It's what I've done all my life and I'm not about to give it up when I know deep down that the best music I've ever had is on this album.

'When it starts tapering off and I'm not pleasing myself any more – and there has got to be a turning point – that's when I'll change.'

He wrote all the tracks on the album and the flow of inspiration was never stronger. He even included a song about killing your wife. 'I know I'm going to get some stick over that,' said Rod.

After their three weeks apart Alana flew in to London and installed herself with the children and their nannies at the Dorchester Hotel in central London as a sort of tour base camp. Alana went along to some of the concerts but more often than not she waited with the family back at the hotel for her husband to jet in on his days off from rushing around Europe.

Rod felt he was living a double life. He adored the children. He even changed their nappies once each so he could at least say he'd done it and the sentimental side of his nature could not resist their babyish hugs and cute adoring faces. Yet, in a way, he was captive to a career that forced him to stay young. Rod was beginning to feel more mature. He loved Alana for her strength and even for her jealous possessive qualities. Rod wanted to prove to the world and to himself that after five years of philandering, of playing the jet-setting, super-stud pop star, he could settle into this new role of happy, family man. As he said at the time: 'It's very confusing. For the first time in my life, I find that I have two personalities and that I am split down the middle. Half of me is the family man and the other half is the 35-year-old who will not grow up. I know deep down that it is time that I grew up. After all, you can't be in rock for the rest of your life, but I am trapped in a business that refuses to let you grow up.'

His friends remember a quieter, more thoughtful Rod Stewart on tour. Rod insisted that he had come to realise that taking out an endless stream of different women was pretty unimportant, even if it had been enjoyable. The children had quite an effect on the singer: 'It's amazing when you go home and they put their arms around you or tug at your trousers and look at you with their open, honest faces. It's a remarkable experience to me. Now I have to prove to myself that I can stick with one woman. I've had years of running through one woman after another. Now I want to make a relationship work.'

Alana was the driving force behind the Stewart purchase of a luxury $2 million Malibu beach house. She found the eleven-bedroom beachside mansion while Rod was away on tour and fell in love with it. Rod telephoned his agreement and Alana clinched the deal. The house is built on huge wooden pilings lifting it high above the Pacific waves that lap right underneath at the highest of tides. Sitting out on the twenty-foot high deck Rod composed some of his most memorable songs, for which he found the sun and the sea great inspiration.

The house was also a favourite weekend place for the three children. They loved to leave the smog of Los Angeles, go down to the beach and have their famous parents to themselves. Years later, Rod said: 'Kimberley and Sean spent a lot of time at the beach house. I've got such fond memories of those two tiny things crawling around on the big rug in front of the fireplace. The kids loved the place. Sean used to call the Ocean "Daddy's pool". It was so beautiful and romantic for Alana and me down there. But we had some wild parties as well when the place really came alive.'

Rod's old rivalry with Mick Jagger was often in his mind when he compared lifestyles. Rod considered Jagger's relationship with Bianca to be very much an 'open marriage'. He and Alana, he maintained, had a much more traditional view of the marriage vows. And Jagger irritated Rod with some published criticisms of the Carolwood Drive house. Britt had helped Rod develop a love of antiques and he was very proud of his collection of lamps. When it came to beautiful objects that were likely to appreciate in value, Rod always insisted that he positively enjoyed spending some of his millions. He said: 'I'd rather put my money into antiques than have it all in the bloody bank. I've got nothing in the bank. I just spend it on things that I enjoy seeing around me. I've got no time for people who pretend they haven't made any money out of this business.

'Jagger's one who tries to make out he's come in from the street. He had a go at me about my collection of lamps in an interview. They all come round here, drink my booze and then go away and knock me! Why pretend all your life? Why not be honest? I think people admire those who are honest. I am wealthy – relatively wealthy – and I enjoy it. People are so embarrassed about being successful. That's one of the things I love about Elton. He has made a lot of money, he is also quite prepared to share it with people. He is probably the kindest guy I've ever met in my life. I respect him for that, he's a marvellous man, I love him. I've got no time for pretenders.'

On the American leg of the tour Rod and Alana took time out to visit her tiny home town of Nacogdoches. He wanted to see where she came from, but the return visit was painful for Alana because to her the house seemed so small.

Of course, the publication of Britt's book *True Britt* at this time was a brutal blow to Rod. He claimed to have stolen a copy on the way through Heathrow towards a concert in Brussels, though aides quickly insisted that they had paid for the copy after Rod had picked it up. He snorted angrily at the suggestion that he had not liked Britt's children and at the patronising references to his family. And he firmly rejected the idea that he wanted to be the permanent centre of attention. As Rod remembered, it was Britt who went bananas if she was not featured in every photograph at every reception. But he laughed at Britt's description of the two of them having similarly shaped bodies and long legs. Uncharitably, Rod said: 'Britt says in this book that she has long legs. That's not on. She has horrible legs and her bottom wasn't that good either.'

But he was genuinely hurt by the book because he had been hopelessly in love with the lady for a long time and he recalled many marvellous moments together. He said: 'It's just sad to me that someone so close could write these things. But then, I wouldn't like to get hurt the way I hurt her.'

An even more disturbing reminder of previous loves was

the arrival on Rod's Los Angeles doorstep in 1981 of 18-year-old Sarah Thubron, his illegitimate daughter from a teenage romance with an art student. It was hardly the happy reunion Sarah had hoped for. A newspaper had paid for her flight and she turned up with a photographer. Rod leaned heavily on Alana for support. He said afterwards: 'It was all so wrong, and it was so awkward with my other little daughter and my son sitting there when this girl came in after all these years. It is a part of my life that has gone now. She can't expect to just step back into my life again. Perhaps she should never have been told. Perhaps that would have been the best thing for her.'

For Sarah, the meeting was even more upsetting. She had been adopted as a baby and brought up by Brigadier Gerald Thubron and his wife Eve in a quiet country village in the south of England. She did not know who her father was until she was eighteen when her grandmother told her that he was someone very famous. 'When I asked my adoptive parents, they told me my father was Rod Stewart. At first I did not believe it,' says Sarah, who now works as a children's nanny in Sussex.

She remembers her first meeting with her father as a complete disaster. 'And for that I blame Alana. Before I could see Rod I had to be vetted by Alana and his lawyer. The lawyer was all right but she thought I was a threat to her and her kids. I took an instant dislike. She was off-hand and didn't even look nice. She was too tall. I got the impression that she wanted to make sure I was not after any of his money.

'When I finally got to see Rod it was all very embarrassing. There were lots of people around the recording studio. There was no emotion. At one point, I walked out in tears. I thought he would be fatherly and hug me like a father should. I felt more like a fan than a daughter. Alana did not want us to be on our own together. Bitchy is too strong a word to describe her, maybe she was just a little bit jealous. She told me I was

191

something from his past and could not expect to walk into his life.'

Sarah's bitter disappointment at her first encounter with her natural father meant that she was to wait until Alana was off the scene before contacting him again.

Gradually the rock 'n' roll lifestyle began to pall for Alana. When Rod got together with rock writer Robert Palmer, they burnt the midnight oil talking about his music for once rather than 'Britt fucking Ekland', as he colourfully put it.

Palmer recalls one incident when Alana turned in early, soon after midnight, saying: 'You're not going to stay up all night are you, Rod?'

'Oh, no dear, we'll just listen to some music for an hour or two,' replied Rod with as much innocence as he could summon.

'I want you to know that when we got back to Los Angeles after our last encounter with you, Rod came down with the flu and was as sick as a dog,' said Alana drily to Robert.

'Good night, dear,' said Rod, bringing out a much-prized Jimmy Reed tape. Their session ended shortly after six a.m.

The spectre of the formidable Miss Ekland raised itself in person when Britt encountered the Stewarts at a Hollywood party. Accounts differ, as they say, to exactly what happened. Alana recalls Britt brazenly coming up to Rod, sitting on his knee and kissing her former lover. She therefore decided that her predecessor needed cooling off and poured champagne down the back of her dress to conclude the clinch. Britt describes the champagne incident as 'untrue, but very imaginative'.

On tour, Alana had a profound effect on Rod's behaviour – he was the model of good husbandly behaviour. However, as soon as she was off the scene, Rod, Jim Cregan, Kevin Savigar and company would indulge in just the sort of boys'-night-out behaviour that Alana had thought had been left behind. The male rock bonding was something she found hard to come to terms with.

'Tora, Tora, Tora, Out with the Boys', Rod's irresistible rocker from *Tonight I'm Yours*, celebrates the wild macho feeling that has always stayed close to his heart. 'My wife hates that track,' he said. 'She asks me, "Why do you stay out drinkin' with the boys in the band until three in the morning, after you've been with 'em in the studio all day?" She's got a point there. I really enjoy her company, too, and I'm really working at the marriage. But I really think that if you're gonna make rock 'n' roll, you've got to live the lifestyle.'

Rod has always felt at his most relaxed talking about male subjects with male friends. Whether it is the finer details of an historic Scottish goal or the even finer details of a shapely passing female, he felt there were some conversations you simply cannot have with ladies present. Rod was sorry that Alana never quite understood that.

Rod also began to resent that Alana could never quite bring herself to accept his mates. He opened his house and his life to her more glitzy Beverly Hills celebrity acquaintances but Alana never wanted to get friendly with Rod's more ordinary down-to-earth musical or football-playing pals.

Early in their relationship, Rod and Alana were totally besotted with each other; they would spend twenty-four hours a day together. But gradually Rod wanted to spend more and more time doing the thing he had always enjoyed, being one of the lads. Alana felt threatened and insecure. She knew she was being possessive but she wanted life to stay the same as it had been when they first met. She got furious and ranted and raved at him when he spent all day Sundays playing football. She felt it should be a day for her and the family.

She said afterwards: 'Suddenly I found myself with three children and a lot of responsibility. I was no longer the sort of fun, party girl Rod was used to. He didn't realise that once you've got children you have to raise them. I resented his drinking and playing football with the boys. Instead of sitting down and saying, "We love each other, let's work it out," we just wanted each other to bend to our will.'

The total communication they had enjoyed in their early days together also began to break down. Alana would sulk. Rod would go drinking with the boys. As Los Angeles legend goes, she sometimes tracked him down in bars, once angrily pouring a drink over his head and another time telephoning the bar in which Rod had allegedly been telling friends he was putting on his tin hat and going back home into battle.

Forceful, opinionated Alana gradually grew tired of being confined to the role of housewife. In spite of Rod's millions and the endless opulence which surrounded her life, by the time young Sean was two she was itching to get back to work. It was important to Alana to earn some of her own money. She had started work at fourteen behind the counter of a Texan Woolworth's and she liked being financially independent. A former successful model, her switch into acting had just been getting underway with a role in an action movie called the *The Ravagers*, starring Richard Harris, when she had been swept off her feet into motherhood on the birth of Kimberley.

Alana's previous husband, George Hamilton, had always made it clear that he did not want a working wife. Rod minded less. Alana insisted, though: 'I would not leave my husband and children to go on location, so whatever I do will have to be close to home.' But she was rejected for several roles before landing a small part in the Goldie Hawn movie *Swinging Shift* in which she played a gum-chewing girl from Texas who arrived in Hollywood determined to make a name for herself. At least that was not difficult for her to imagine.

As well as wanting her own money, Rod increasingly found Alana determined to have her own way in arguments. She was never prepared to bite her tongue. However, she was always honest about her forthright approach to life. 'If I have a gripe I have to get it into the open,' she said. 'I'm a believer in being honest.' So when Rod broke with his long-serving manager Billy Gaff and his faithful headline-maker Tony Toon, Alana was not surprised to get the blame. A flurry of bad publicity followed, along with the graffiti attack on the walls of the Carolwood house which announced 'Alana Piranha' to passing motorists. She shrugged and denied telling Rod to fire Gaff and Toon. She said that while Rod was surrounded by people telling him he was wonderful she always told the truth. Rod had to get used to her honesty, she insisted.

She said at the time: 'I wish I could take the credit for Billy Gaff's departure. But I can't. I never get involved in Rod's business. I kept my mouth shut. I thought, "I'm the wife, I'm not going to stick my two cents in." But if it happened again I would stick my two cents in. When Rod told me he was going to fire Billy I said, 'Are you sure?' Billy wouldn't take any of Rod's calls. In the end, Rod sent him a telegram firing him.'

Rod insisted publicly that it was his decision to ease the old guard out of his entourage and put Alana's manager Arnold Stiefel in charge of his own affairs. He was also angered by the graffiti. 'She is not a bloody piranha,' he said. Billy Gaff denied all knowledge of the giant insult on Rod's walls but cheekily added that he was considering holding a party for all the people who might have done it. Except he couldn't find a hotel big enough.

Despite Rod's and Alana's best efforts to repel all boarders, however, by 1981 the marriage was already having its problems. They both desperately wanted it to work and prove all the cynics wrong, so they went to marriage guidance counsellors for advice. But the couple were coming more and more into conflict over the children. Rod kept hankering to return to live in Britain: at times he tired of the endless sunshine, saying that on the few occasions it did rain in Southern California he would rush out in the downpour until he was soaked. Nor did he want Sean and Kimberley to become totally American. Even Alana agreed that some Californian youngsters with their private phone lines and their foul language gave cause for alarm.

The couple's sincere efforts to make their relationship work were not helped, though, by the fact that Alana was clearly not at all popular with many of Rod's male friends. Jimmy Horowitz, Gaff's partner, says: 'I never got on very well with Alana. She was a very odd choice for Rod. She thought she was the Queen of Beverly Hills. I think she liked Rod because he was one of the top ten big rock and roll stars in the world but she wasn't very comfortable with musicians.'

And Alana's humble upbringing never prevented her from insisting on absolutely the very best of service, usually at the top of her extremely loud voice. 'Rod is a pretty easy-going guy,' recalls Horowitz. 'As long as he can stick somebody for a bottle of wine, he's happy. Alana used to complain all the time, very loudly and very vocally, and make terrible scenes so a lot of hotels at the end wouldn't take their reservations.'

Alana's demands did not stop there. 'I remember we were flying back from New York to Los Angeles with them one time. I was at the airport with them,' said Horowitz. 'They had decided to go at the last minute and they were flying first class. Alana was really angry because first class in a 747 is split into two halves by the spiral staircase and she wanted the four seats all together in the front sections, for her, Rod, one of the babies and the nanny. I couldn't get them, they were sold, but I managed to get them four seats behind. Alana was trying to get the people to move. There was one guy there she wanted to move who was executive vice-president of Chrysler or something who didn't give a fuck about Rod Stewart or Alana. He had his seat and he was not going to move.

'She was causing all kinds of a ruckus. They had to call the supervisor. In the end it got sorted out. But some time later I saw the airline computer come up with Rod and Alana's name followed by the initials DP, which stand for difficult passenger.'

Difficult passenger was an understatement the night Alana refused to accompany Rod on a rare chance to ride on a red double-decker bus in Los Angeles. Horowitz again: 'They had done five nights at the Forum in Los Angeles. Rod likes to be one of the boys and instead of all going down in limos they went in a London bus. Alana didn't take too kindly to it. She had some big row with Rod and the band. She was going to go home in the limo but the limo had already left and they were on the bus. She said, "I'm not going back to Beverly Hills in this," and she stormed off the bus in the middle of Inglewood, the darker part of town. Apparently, she was walking along in her sprayed-on trousers when the police picked her up and said, "Hey, you shouldn't be walking along here at night." '

Alana clashed with Billy Gaff and Jimmy Horowitz on more than one occasion. She liked to take charge of Rod's social life. Horowitz recalls: 'I wasn't even on this tour but there was going to be a big after-tour party which was going to be held in a private room at the Dome. So I got a call from Tony Toon saying would I like to come, and Billy – but on his own. Now Billy's the manager. The tour manager, Pete Buckland, wasn't invited. Most of the key people weren't invited. Me and my wife Carol and Billy were, but no partner. Alana was the one organising. I thought this was really bad.'

Horowitz's secretary at the time he was running Riva Records was one May Pang. In their busy office in New York they became used to some peculiar demands from the star and his wife in Los Angeles.

Alana's dependence on the advice of her psychic became particularly wearing. Horowitz recalls: 'We had to give them the numbers of every flight they took and then Alana had to see if the numbers were right and if they could fly on that flight.'

All hotel rooms also had to be checked out in advance to ensure the vibes were suitable for the strong-willed Mrs Stewart. Horowitz remembers trudging through one of New York's snow storms with May Pang to run a rule over yet another hotel room. 'It was really miserable. We walked for miles to find this hotel to see it if was good enough for Alana. Suddenly the thought hit us: "If this psychic is any good why doesn't she just take a look in her crystal ball and vet the rooms from California?" That made us laugh a lot, but we didn't say that to Rod.'

But even worse for Horowitz was the night Alana had him thrown out of the house by armed guards, which perhaps helps to explain the strength of his antipathy to the lady. 'I never really forgave her for that,' he said. 'I was in New York and Rod was having a really big party at home and Billy rang and said, "I'm in London, Rod wants someone from the company to be at the party, you'll have to go. Fly to Los Angeles for the party or Rod will be disappointed."

'So I flew in on a Saturday night and my crazy friend Jonathan, the guy who played the bagpipes on Rod's lawn, picked me up at the airport. He's a good friend of Rod's, so I said to him, "Why don't you come along to the party with me? Rod will love to see you." There's always a lot of security at these parties and I don't normally bring people, but it was just a party for Rod not a sit-down dinner. So we went in there and he wasn't on the list but we were ushered in. And then Alana saw Jonathan and me together. She knew he wasn't on the list so she ordered the armed guards over to throw us out. Rod said to me, "You can stay." I said, "Fuck off, Rod. I'm not staying. I flew three thousand miles to come here out of courtesy." I was so annoyed. This was not like Rod. This was purely Alana. She didn't like Jonathan because he is not a big star in Beverly Hills. Everyone was so embarrassed. I was totally mortified.'

Appearances were always important to Alana, but even that razor-sharp mind did not always prevent her from sounding silly. In the depths of the winter she arrived in London sporting a fox fur coat and announced: "I don't believe in wearing animal furs, and I would never wear a seal fur or anything made from an endangered species.

'I feel guilty but the trouble is that I catch cold easy and they told me the English winter had arrived, so I took it from its secret hideaway. I console myself that the fox was dead before I bought it.'

But Alana could not always get her own way. When she arrived at the St Peter's Basilica in Rome in a split leather mini-skirt cut short to show off her long legs the guards decided she was not suitably dressed and turned her away. 'We are on hallowed ground, madam, and you are not decorous,' she was told. For once Alana accepted the ruling with not too bad a grace: 'I didn't really think my skirt was that short, but I guess they have their codes. They were turning a lot of tourists away. Anyway, they were all very polite about it. We are moving on now. When I come back I'll make sure I wear a longer dress.'

Protocol upset Alana nearer to home when she and Rod were separated by nationality at a Hollywood dinner in honour of the Queen in March 1983. With other British celebrities Rod was a top table guest while Alana was forced to fume along with other non-Britons just out of the limelight. What no doubt rubbed salt into the wound was that Rod delighted in telling all concerned just how upset his wife was by the snub.

The summer of 1983 saw the rumours about the marriage

fuelled to boiling point. Rod was working hard on yet another tour in Europe and Alana took on another film in America. For little Sean and Kimberley, it must have been a mystifying life of nannies, first-class travel, top hotels and constant media attention. In June, they made a brief appearance on stage at London's Earl's Court during yet another sell-out concert by their father and on the other side of the Atlantic they visited Alana's relatives in a suburb of Palm Beach, Florida. Rod and Alana were unquestionably living increasingly separate lives.

Rod hated being apart from his children and phoned them regularly. At first, little Kimberley refused to talk to her father because she was so angry that he had gone away. Eventually, though, when she came on the line the rugged rocker and his beloved four-year-old sobbed transatlantically to each other.

By September 1983 Rod was being sighted in England with the traditional 'mystery blonde', although denials were formally issued from both London and Los Angeles. The biggest public nail in the coffin of the glittering marriage came from Rod's ever-loving ever-indulgent mother Elsie. Asked about the chances of a split, she said frankly to *Daily Express* showbiz editor Garth Pearce: 'I am not sad. I didn't want them to split up but I could never understand why he married her in the first place. After all the lovely girls he had seen and been with. Oh blast!

'Still, he's gone and done it now and that is it. There was always an atmosphere while Alana was around. She is not a sociable sort of girl who will sit down and chat with you. In fact, she doesn't say anything at all. Rod is completely different on his own. He relaxes and we can all get together properly like we used to. My husband wished Rod had married a girl from Scotland. He'd have been a lot better off.'

Alana was shocked and hurt by Elsie's comments. She thought she had got on reasonably well with Rod's parents and suggested that Elsie was suffering from a problem that mothers face who cannot accept that their little boys are growing up when they reach thirty-eight years old. 'Maybe I'll feel exactly the same way when my children grow up and get married,' she said rather more charitably.

While Rod was still in England, Alana moved out of Carolwood Drive and down to the beach house at Malibu, taking the children with her, but said it was simply to get away from the heat. Then she moved back to Carolwood, but she did frankly admit: 'There have been some bad times. Sometimes things get us both down. I'm waiting for Rod to come home so we can talk this over. There are long separations and all the travelling and me with the kids. Sometimes I get very unhappy.'

On Saturday 10 September 1983, Rod went with Elton John to watch Watford play Notts County in an English soccer match. As the inevitable reporters badgered him for a comment on the state of his marriage, the usually cool celebrity snarled: 'Go away. I don't want to say anything.'

A final Christmas attempt at reconciliation failed. And after the parting came the recriminations. In January, reporters found Alana at a Hollywood party to celebrate the end of filming the TV movie *Masquerade*, in which she had a small guest role. Happily for the headline seekers, she announced: 'I've had just enough beer to say what I think about Rod Stewart. As far as I'm concerned the marriage is over. If he wants to go out with a series of mindless moronic young models rather than being with me and the children, I don't think I'm losing anything. I'm well aware of the other women in Rod's life, and if that's the way he wants to go then it's his loss. He's lost a wife and two kids. All I've lost is someone who can't grow up.'

Rod was publicly angry at Alana's allegations after the break-up but inwardly very hurt. He knew that some of the things that she was saying were true. After his split with Britt

201

he had sounded off about his rejection of the Hollywood lifestyle but his life with Alana had been dominated by Tinsel Town. He enjoyed his days out playing soccer with his mates and his nights out drinking with them much more than being one half of a glittering showbiz couple. He had very much wanted his marriage to work but Alana had simply wanted the sort of commitment that Rod could not bring himself to make.

Chapter Eight
Enter Younger Blondes

'I never face them and make a clean break. I'm a bit lily-livered when it comes to that. I just wait until I'm found out, which always happens in the end' – Rod Stewart.

Rod Stewart was crouching on his knees helping to cultivate a Pennsylvanian garden when he realised he must have fallen in love again.

With the agony of his split from Alana fading month by month, Rod had met a 25-year-old model called Kelly Emberg at the preview of a forgettable film called *Portfolio*. Not altogether surprisingly, she had all the physical qualities Rod has always looked for in a woman. She was tall. She was blonde. And she was beautiful. Rod was taken aback by her looks but as they chatted at the party following the screening it was Kelly's easy-going, relaxed approach to life that turned the rock star on. Decades of being the groupies' target and the focus of determined attention by international beauties like Britt and and Alana had helped to make Rod wary.

So, although the sparkle in Kelly's eye and the girlish giggle in her voice got the exhausted hormones sparking back into action, Rod was very cautious. It was only when he went to Kelly's home in Pennsylvania that he realised the strength of his feeling. He was hooked.

'I went to stay at her place in the country and ended up

on my knees in the pouring rain, digging holes and putting plants in. To my surprise, I found I thoroughly enjoyed it,' said Rod.

On his own admission Rod always needed a woman. In the early days of his relationship with Kelly, he said frankly: 'It's much too early to talk about the possibility of marrying Kelly, but I do want to get married again eventually. I always need a woman in my life. I'm lost without a woman. I'm totally dependent on a woman. And it's not just a sexual thing any more. It used to be, but not any more. I need someone who can be a friend as well.

'I don't want to end up at fifty as some lonely old bachelor. I want a home and a wife to go back to. And I also want more children. Armies of them.'

When his marriage to Alana finally broke down at the end of 1983 Rod decided to move out of the Carolwood mansion and rent a small house in the Hollywood Hills just off Sunset Boulevard. Taking time to lick his marital wounds, Rod found he was much more at peace with himself than he had been for several years.

He said: 'Now I'm separated, I live very simply in a small place. It's just two bedrooms, one little living room, a toilet and a pool, and it's great. I've had servants all around me for the last ten years and it was really starting to get on my nerves. Now I'm doing it all myself – even the housework – and I'm enjoying myself more than I have in quite a while. I used to live up there where the rich and famous live when I was married. Now I live with the regular people. I guess I've got back to the streets – or as near as I'm ever going to get back to the streets. Because when you literally come from the streets, you're not in too much bloody hurry to get back.'

Rod came to realise that he had long been seduced by a lifestyle of conspicuous consumption. While Alana was still driving the children around in his black Rolls-Royce Corniche, Rod trimmed down his collection of cars and put a hold for a time on the shrewd buying of his beloved Art Nouveau treasures.

He did not regret the flamboyant displays of wealth, for a time at least; he just grew out of it. 'I think it's a period you go through,' said Rod. 'And I think that anyone who has earned the sort of money I've earned will sometimes do the same. You want to experience as much of life as you can, and some of that is having material possessions. But I've completely grown out of it now. I've sold the yacht, and I'm down to just two cars now, and I'm going to sell one of those because I never drive it. In the end you get everything in perspective, and all those things weren't making me happy. It took a long time for me to find out that big houses, fast cars etcetera are not necessarily the answer. And I think I've learned my lesson.'

Getting down to your last Porsche Carrera is not exactly life on the poverty line, but for Rod it was an important and significant change. Alana may not have succeeded in getting him to take his adult responsibilities seriously during their marriage, but the break-up had certainly had its effect. By the summer of 1984 the friends who expected Rod to return instantly to his old philandering ways were to be surprised.

As Rod and his band toured Canada, for instance, an intriguing and stunningly attractive pair of females tagged on to the party. The boys in the band could not decide who was the more attractive – the shapely 33-year-old mother or her slender 16-year-old daughter. And they were both demonstrably available to the star of the show. But even this tantalising twosome could not tempt Rod.

Rod knew that gorgeous girls were throwing themselves even harder in his direction than ever before, but he just did not want to know. 'It's ridiculous, the way the girls are behaving on this tour,' said Rod. 'It's worse than ever. The lines on the face must have helped. But nowadays it gives me great satisfaction to say, "No thanks. I don't want to know."

'It's a bit of an internal struggle sometimes, and I might lie in bed alone wondering what I am missing. But when I wake up next morning I pat myself on the back and think, "Good boy".

'I love women. I have a great appreciation of them and I'm not denying that in the past I've made the most of my opportunities But how many times do you need to prove over and over again that you can have whoever you want? When you do that all the time you only prove that you're lacking something in yourself. So I think I owe it to myself, as well as to my girlfriend Kelly to say "No".'

After Britt's much-resented rebuilding of his image and Alana's relentless social climbing, the easy-going Kelly was just what Rod wanted. 'Kelly is a very good influence on me,' said Rod. 'She doesn't want to dominate me, but at the same time she wants respect. She doesn't want me playing around. And I really don't want to any more. She can trust me. I'm not the same person I was. Despite what Alana says, I don't want to carry on doing what I was doing at twenty-five. What I'm looking for now is one loyal person by my side. I'm at the stage where I want to prove to myself that I really do want just one woman. And Kelly is enabling me to do just that. She's got me.'

Kelly was, like Alana, from Texas, but when she and Rod met she was living in a luxury Manhattan apartment and was earning over $4,000 a day as a top New York model, so at least Rod knew she was not after his money.

'She's a slightly unsophisticated country girl at heart, which is lovely,' said Rod. 'After what I went through with Britt and Alana, it's nice to have someone who is the complete opposite in that respect. She is quite different from Alana in most ways. Alana could be a bit snooty and put people's backs up but Kelly is the kind of girl who wins everybody over.'

Kelly was certainly more of a hit with Rod's family than Alana. She joined the rowdy Stewart clan at the annual England *v* Scotland soccer match and both his mother and father took to the unpretentious model who made their son try his hand at gardening.

But Rod still had to formally disentangle himself from wife Alana, who was still living with Sean and Kimberley in Carolwood Drive. It was going to be a complex business. For the first time in his colourful love life, Rod was facing the break-up of a marriage, with two children involved, and all the added legal complications that that entailed. Rod winced at the unpleasant publicity but accepted its inevitability. He always found breaking up, like the song goes, so very hard to do. Rod could never face the lady in question and discuss a diplomatic departure. Every time he ended a relationship he inspired angry headlines.

As Rod said after the split with Alana: 'I think it's the way we break up that upsets me. I never face them and make a clean break. I'm a bit lily-livered when it comes to that. I just wait until I'm found out, which always happens in the end.'

Rod often regretted the way he left his lovers, if not the decision itself. He knew how much he had hurt Dee and Joanna and Britt and Alana but he could not help it. He tried to explain: 'I'd like to change the way I handled some personal relationships. I wish I wasn't so cowardly when it comes to dealing with people, but it comes from shyness and from not wanting to hurt people. I have been rotten to women, but not intentionally. I never wanted to hurt any woman, or anybody. From the outside it may look as if I hate women but I don't. I need a woman by my side. I need a woman to bounce off. They give me so many things.'

Alana's public washing of their dirty linen annoyed Rod and he was incensed by her version of their split. He angrily insisted that he had not simply abandoned his family to go running off after yet another model. He had met

207

Kelly Emberg *after* he split with Alana.

Rod insisted that his marriage to Alana had been in trouble for a long time. 'I married the wrong person,' he said simply. 'We were miles apart, really. I think nine out of ten men have to be pushed into marriage and I was no different. I tried to worm my way out of it but I don't regret it now. Look what I've got out of it – two wonderful kids.'

The biggest problem between Rod and Alana had been what Rod came to regard as his wife's snobbish attitude towards his friends. He said almost a year after the break-up: 'I accepted all her friends, the wealthy and famous in Beverly Hills, and welcomed them in my house with open arms. But she would never do the same for the boys in my band, the guys I play football with, and the ordinary people among my friends who don't happen to be rich and famous. There were many other things but that was the biggest breakdown in our marriage.'

Rod was deeply upset at allegations that he did not care about his children. In fact, it was the complete opposite. As far as Kimberley was concerned, he later admitted, she was helplessly spoiled. 'I'm to blame. I've spoiled her, but she is my first one and she is beautiful.' Alana, Sean and Kimberley still lived in the Carolwood Drive house while Rod still lived up Sunset Boulevard in his more humble rented house. Most days he would collect Sean and Kimberley from school and take them home for splashing games in the pool.

Rod said: 'I pick them up from school, bring them to the house and make lunch for them myself. I really love my kids so much, and I spend as much time with them as possible. We make meals together, and I teach them how to slice up the cheese and bread and I even clean up after them. And now Sean has fallen in love with football, so he makes me put on my Scotland jersey and then we kick a ball around the yard. That's the wonderful thing about being a parent – there is so much to teach them and show them. And they really pick up fast. And when I'm away, I make sure I speak to them every day on the telephone.

'Alana hasn't bothered to mention that we were seeing marriage guidance counsellors for two years. They were very helpful in trying to rekindle the spark, but it was too late. I never thought it would be this traumatic for me, but it is. There's not an hour goes by when I don't think about it and worry about my kids and whether I'm letting them down.'

The public image, fostered deliberately for so long by Tony Toon, of Rod Stewart the ruthless seducer of an endless stream of blondes, was one that Rod felt had got way out of control. 'I'm not the womaniser I am supposed to be,' he said. 'I might have gone off the rails a bit when I moved to Hollywood. I did neglect my music, but the music is still very important to me. I am a musician. I'm not just a sex machine. I know I've written some good songs which have made people happy. I would like to be remembered for that, not how many women I've bedded.'

And to Alana's accusations of dalliances with 19-year-old bimbos, Rod retorted: 'It is her who is going out with every guy she wants to, and me who is sticking to one girl. Kelly is the only girl I've been out with since Alana and I split up. I'd love to have had all the girls I'm supposed to have had. The idea that I was always cheating on my wife while we were still together is rubbish. And Alana knows that.'

Rod was angry when Alana took Sean and Kimberley to a child psychologist because they were so 'disturbed' by the break-up. He said: 'All that happened was that Kimberley had one or two bad dreams and Sean got a bit naughty and starting saying "I hate you" when he wasn't allowed to have his own way. Most parents would regard it as quite normal, but in California people rush off to a child psychologist at £50 a session.'

Alana accused Rod of being a forgetful father, of meaning well with the children but spending too little time with them.

She described him as a lost soul, confused, lonely and very sad. 'Rod's trouble,' said Alana, 'is that he has never grown up . . . and he never will.'

But although their parting was public and painful, Rod and Alana were still united in their determination to protect the children. Rod insisted that, inspite of everything, he did not dislike Alana: 'I don't think you ever dislike someone you've really loved. And deep down, whatever she says about me, I think Alana still loves me. Without a doubt. She would never be so vindictive as to cut me off from the kids. She knows how important it is that they should have a father's influence.'

Rod knew that the end of his marriage to Alana also meant the end of his dreams of having Sean and Kimberley educated in England. 'But I still hope they don't grow up to be Beverly Hills kids, never playing on the street, and never doing any of the things I did when I was growing up. I think it will be a pity if they miss out on that completely, but I'm afraid they probably will.'

Rod was so anxious to see as much as possible of his children that he planned to bring them along on part of his next tour. To head off Alana's objections, he went to his own child psychologist who advised that so long as the trip did not interfere with their schooling it was good for the young-sters to be with their father.

Rod planned their excursion to fit in with their holidays. He said: 'Now it's just a matter of getting permission from the ex-wife.' He felt he and Alana had come through their most difficult time and said they were 'good friends. But she's a bit overprotective with the kids, and she thinks there'll be thousands of women hanging around my hotel rooms. Of course, it won't be anything like that. I'd let the kids sleep in the same room as me. They can come in with their nanny and all their toys and set up Stewart camp.' Alana agreed and Rod was delighted to risk his hard-won reputation as one of rock's wildest hellraisers by bringing along two wide-eyed youngsters on the road.

Rod always tried to put his family first and although he had no plans to marry Kelly she became perhaps the closest of all the ladies in his life to his mum and dad. Kelly helped, for instance, Rod to organise the eightieth birthday party for his wheelchair-bound mother Elsie in January 1986. More than a hundred guests were invited to the Firs, a banqueting centre in Palmer's Green, North London, when Rod decided to mark his mum's big day.

This was a far cry from the usual champagne and smoked salmon showbiz functions that usually confront Rod. No celebrities or hangers-on were invited, just family and close friends, dining on Hungarian pancakes, made with chopped egg, tomato and spinach, followed by roast beef and Yorkshire pudding. For desert was served Coupe Jamaique – pineapple with rum and raisin ice cream. There was sherry and Martini and red and white wine. The occasion was a real family success, climaxing in a Cockney knees-up to a four-piece band. Rod relaxed in the bosom of his family, and Kelly enjoyed every minute.

Kelly was also a hit with Rod's troubled eldest daughter, Sarah. Poor Sarah was so upset by the frosty reception she was given by the haughty Alana that she did not see her father again until the marriage was over. Sarah said: 'There was no way that I could get together with him again whilst Alana was on the scene. But once she was gone I contacted him again. He said he was pleased to hear from me and we met in a London hotel.

'Kelly Emberg was with him and she was really great. She accepted me straight away and she was really nice. We all went shopping and he bought some clothes. I suppose he would have bought me something if I had asked, but I didn't bother.'

Sarah saw her father again after she went to one of Rod's

London concerts and the party afterwards where she met Kimberley and Sean properly. 'I saw him quite a lot that year,' said Sarah. 'And he even bought me a birthday present – a bracelet and a box of chocolates – although I had to remind him the night before.'

As he moved into his forties the legal wrangles over the divorce went on but Rod took great care not to let them sour feeling between himself and Alana and the children. 'It's really nothing to do with Alana and me now. It's the lawyers who just can't agree,' he shrugged as he arrived in Britain in May 1986 to rehearse for his first British concerts for three years. For the man who was supposed never to want to grow up, Rod was curiously at ease with middle age. Everything Joan Collins had done for the older woman, he could achieve for the older man, he thought. 'Anyway, I think we men do get better the older we get. Everyone keeps asking me about turning forty as if suddenly I should have cobwebs covering me. I like middle age right now. It's like a silly novelty. My knees haven't started to click like Cliff Richard's. I've never felt so good in my life or looked so good, so I'm loving every minute of it. I'm probably the oldest swinger in town.'

It was never easy for Kelly. When she went with Rod to the Malibu beach house she was confronted by a note pinned to the main wardrobe. A bitter farewell message from Alana, it read: 'Attention all sluts. Hands off my clothes. Signed, the soon-to-be-ex-mistress of this house.'

Alana still used the house with the children and Kelly had to put up with pictures of happy family scenes featuring Rod's wife beaming at her. Rod used to rush down before taking Kelly and remove some of the snaps, but Kelly still got upset at many of the memories involving Rod's previous love that the house held. Rod's bedroom was home for his huge brass four-poster bed surrounded by floral curtains. He loved to tell visitors: 'That bed has had a few rough and tumbles in its time. I call it the midnight trampoline.'

In spite of the difficult circumstances, even Alana conceded that Kelly got on well with Sean and Kimberley and she was grateful to her for that. Alana said: 'At first it really hurt me that Rod was able to find someone so quickly, but then I realised it was just his pattern. He needed to find a woman immediately because he hates being alone. I'm not jealous of Kelly Emberg, because our break-up had nothing to do with her.

'It had to do with problems we should have worked on, and if it hadn't been her it would have been some other blonde. I haven't met her, not because I've tried to avoid her, but it just hasn't happened. I know she's sweet to my kids when she's around them and that's very important to me.'

Alana felt that the fifteen-year age difference between Rod and Kelly was important to him, but she did not think Rod was happy with Kelly. And when she heard of Rod's brief romance with English actress Kelly Le Brock, the strong-willed star of Gene Wilder's hit 1984 movie *The Woman in Red*, she was delighted: 'I was actually pleased when Rod had an affair with Kelly Le Brock and I thought they might end up together. She's much more the kind of girl I could see Rod with than Kelly Emberg.'

But while Rod and Kelly accepted that they had to take turns with Alana and the children at Malibu, the fabulous Carolwood home became the centre of Rod's complex divorce settlement with Alana. This was a marriage that had been a great deal easier to start than it was to finish. It was March 1987 before the agreement was finalised. Rod was to buy a luxury $5 million, 15-roomed home in the swish Los Angeles suburb of Brentwood for Alana and the children and he was also to provide a generous cash sum and future regular payments. In return, he was to get the Carolwood Drive house back.

Although Alana criticised the decor she had inherited from Britt, she was sorry to leave Carolwood. Living on the same street as Gregory Peck, Barbara Streisand and Burt Reynolds carried the sort of cachet that was important to Alana. And it was the first home Sean and Kimberley had ever had. She said: 'The children love the house because they were born here, it was their home and they'd never known anything else. They just didn't want to go. Sean's a real home bird and whenever he is away he can't wait to get back to his dog, his skateboard and his bike. But the more I talked about moving the more he and Kimberley came to accept it.'

The idea of making Kelly Emberg the second Mrs Rod Stewart certainly started to enter the singer's mind. Particularly in December 1987, when their daughter Ruby Rachel was born. But Rod was still very cautious of marriage after the painful split with Alana and their long-drawn-out divorce. He had such a good relationship with Kelly as it was that he was reluctant to change anything.

When modelling assignments took her away from him he groaned: 'I have withdrawal symptoms. I miss her so much.' But he would always push the subject of marriage further forward into the future. 'I believe in marriage, because I come from a big family. I want to have more children – as many as I can – so that when I'm eighty I have lots of kids around me. I want to be able to commit myself to one person in marriage for the rest of my life. That's the hardest thing, when you get married you have to say, "Can I grow old with this person?" The one thing Alana and I didn't do was sit down and talk about what we wanted out of the marriage, which is what I would do if I got married again.'

When Ruby was a baby Kelly was forced to take some time off from modelling and the three of them spent some of their happiest moments at the Malibu house. The rhythm of the ocean and the distance from busy Los Angeles helped to isolate them from the rest of the world.

Rod has always had a special feeling for the elegant beach-side home. It houses much of his valuable collection of Art

Nouveau lamps and furniture which he started collecting even before he knew what they were. It was Britt Ekland who tutored the rock star in the elegant style and encouraged him to invest some of his massive income in art.

Rod might criticise Britt's discretion, but he has always been grateful to her for her advice on this score: 'She advised me well and it's probably the best investment I've ever made. My pieces are now worth a fortune.

'Collecting Art Nouveau became a real passion with me. I read a lot about it and searched through tiny, hidden-away shops in one country after another. I could become quite a dealer now if I wanted to. I think what first attracted me to it was that in the early days you never found it in anyone's house. Later it became a cult thing. When I married Alana she became interested in it as well and then Kelly really got into it. It's a very feminine style, with sensuous lines, and I think that's why so many women like it.'

No one could accuse Rod of exactly growing old gracefully, but as he eased into his mid-forties the rocker seemed to be at peace with the world. He spent two or three hours a day playing with his beloved model railways. Although he joked about his appearance – 'When I see myself in the mirror in the morning, it's a horrible sight' – he still kept up the football which helped him to stay fit and consequently made him look years younger than his real age.

'You can't thrash your body as much as you could when you were younger. If I want to sing five times a week I have to get eight or nine hours of sleep each night. That cuts down a lot on my frivolity. Every other morning I have to get up and take the kids to school and I have to be up at seven a.m. They don't want their father smelling of alcohol with bags under his eyes, so I cut back on it a lot.'

As the eighties came to a close, Rod put down the secret of his long success to 'more luck than anything. Attitude is the most important thing. I like a good time. If I want to go out and take my trousers down in public I will do that until I'm eighty. I'm going to annoy all the rock critics and keep singing until I haven't a breath in my lungs.'

Rod's success as both singer and songwriter is beyond doubt. By 1990 the Rod Stewart songbag totalled more than one hundred and he was showing no signs of slowing down. The release of *Storyteller: The Complete Anthology 1964–1990* served as a reminder of Rod's achievements both as a gifted, prolific songwriter and as a singer whose records consistently made the charts. *Storyteller* also served to pinpoint the sharp contrast between the folky flavour of his early recordings and the artfully produced, classy songs of the eighties.

Rod moved into the Nineties with confidence having notched up yet another Top Ten hit towards the end of 1989 with his version of a Tom Waits composition, 'Downtown Train'. Exactly a year later he was up in the Top Five with a duet with Tina Turner on 'It Takes Two'.

All dates for Rod's British tour in 1991 were quickly sold out and further proof of his undimished popularity was the instant chart entry at number 20 of the latest in a long line of hit singles, 'Rhythm of My Heart'. The single peaked at number three and the new album, *Vagabond Heart*, reached number two in the LP charts.

Chapter Nine
Rachel Hunter

'He might have a naughty sense of humour, but deep down he's a real softy' – Rachel Hunter.

When Rachel Hunter was born in New Zealand on 8 September 1968, Rod Stewart was twenty-two years old and was starting to attract an excited female following in America as lead singer with the Jeff Beck Group.

Rachel was just three when Rod was falling in love with Dee Harrington and creating pop history by topping the charts in America and Britain with 'Maggie May'.

Rod was forty-five, more than twice Rachel's age, when they were introduced to each other at a nightclub in Los Angeles in September 1990. He was not looking for a new lover, although he was perhaps a little bored with sensible Kelly, but one glance at Rachel was enough for Rod to know she was exactly his type. Standing before him was a creature of exceptional beauty with a smile like a Pacific sunrise and legs so long they seemed unsure when to stop. The little girl whose parents had grown up listening to Rod Stewart records had blossomed into a stunning young woman. She was six feet tall, with eyes like African violets and a splash of reddish-blonde hair which tumbled around her shoulders. There was a fresh-faced, girlish quality about Rachel's looks, but the endless flood of photographs of her posing in swimsuits and skimpy underwear revealed a ripe young body that was undeniably all woman.

Rachel had embarked on a modelling career after being spotted at just sixteen by Lacey Ford and brought over to New York to join her mother Eileen's world-famous model agency, Ford Models Inc. Rachel swiftly proved popular with photographers, but the agency were struck not just by Rachel's looks but by her bubbly personality and her constant good humour. By the time she met Rod, Rachel was a *Vogue* cover girl able to command £6,000 a day and as such was enjoying minor celebrity status.

For two years Rachel had been living with heavy metal rock guitarist Kip Winger while Rod appeared to be edging closer to marriage with Kelly Emberg, whose daughter Ruby was now four.

Rod told British chat show host Michael Aspel and ten million viewers: 'I'm a lot closer to marriage than Mick Jagger.' As it turned out, Rod was to marry just weeks before his old rock rival Jagger tied the knot with his long-time girlfriend Jerry Hall. But to the surprise of almost everyone, Rod's bride was not Kelly but Rachel Hunter.

Rachel's impact on Rod was instant. At the nightclub on their first meeting Rod succeeded in attracting Rachel's attention when he took to the dance floor and imitated an exercise routine she had demonstrated in a video. 'I suppose that was when the first sparks of romance started,' she said. 'Soon I began to see how kind and considerate he is. He might have a naughty sense of humour but deep down he's a real softy.'

Very soon they were head over heels in love. Rachel abruptly left Winger and Kelly, deeply upset but realising her seven-year affair with Rod was finally and irretrievably over, moved away quietly to set up home with Ruby Rachel at Manhattan Beach, a stylish residential area hugging the Pacific Ocean right on the edge of Los Angeles. Her new house, she said, could fit inside the ballroom of his Carolwood mansion.

As news broke of Rod's new love affair, it appeared for all the world that Rachel was simply a newer, younger version of all the girls that had gone before. She was, it seemed, just another of Rod's leggy model girls. But Rachel was different, and not just because her endless legs made her an inch or two taller than the famous new beau at her side.

Despite, or perhaps because of, her youth Rod felt Rachel was somebody special. He could not fault her looks but there was also a spark of vitality, a sense of energy and fun about her that Rod found simply irresistible. They had known each other little more than six weeks when Rod suddenly asked her to marry him while they shared a tuna sandwich together on a picnic in a Los Angeles park. Rachel swallowed hard, joyfully accepted, and Rod slipped a sapphire and diamond engagement ring on her finger.

Soon Rod was excitedly on the phone to members of his family to tell them the good news. Of special importance was a call to his 60-year-old brother Don. 'Are you sitting down?' he asked when Don picked up the phone. 'I'm getting married and I want you to be best man.'

The family were naturally surprised that Rod and Rachel were to wed so soon. They knew Rod had split up from Kelly, but they were taken aback at this new turn of events. Rod had absolutely no doubts. 'I realised,' he said, 'that this was the woman I wanted to spend the rest of my life with.'

Rachel was fully aware that she was marrying a man who was old enough to be her father. Indeed, her actual father, Wayne, an airline worker, was just a year older than Rod. But she said: 'Rod's a fine man and has made me so happy. He has taken me higher than I've ever been.'

The whirlwind affair with Rachel coincided with a hectic period in Rod's career. He was in the middle of recording a new album in Los Angeles and was planning a long and

219

arduous world tour for the following year.

Now, suddenly, he was in love and getting married as well. The pressure to continue recording meant that Rod had to hurry away to the studio immediately after attending a wedding rehearsal at the chapel on Rodeo Drive.

It was never destined to be a conventional wedding right from the moment Rod and Rachel sent out 250 invitations to family and friends asking them to the Presbyterian Chapel in Beverly Hills, Los Angeles, on 15 December 1990, and a 'piss-up' afterwards at the Four Seasons Hotel. 'Are you sitting down?' said the invitation, 'Rachel Hunter and Rod Stewart invite you to be a guest at their wedding.'

Neither was it ever likely to be a strictly formal church ceremony from the moment Rachel swept up the aisle to join her husband-to-be at the altar, slipped an arm around his waist, then ran her hand over rock's most famous bottom and pinched it in full view of the assembled congregation who broke into spontaneous applause.

Rachel had arrived some thirty-five minutes late and Rod, resplendent in a formal morning suit save for a stud in his collar rather than a tie, fidgeted nervously and was clearly relieved when she finally stood beaming at his side.

It was ten days before Christmas and the chapel had been seasonally decorated, the pews festooned with branches of Christmas conifers and white ribbon. Among Rachel's eight attendants were Rod's daughter eleven-year-old Kimberley. The chapel rang to the singing from a children's choir and kilted pipers greeted Rod and Rachel as they left the chapel with a stirring rendering of 'Scotland the Brave' and 'When the Saints Go Marching In'.

Omitted from the ceremony was the request for the intervention of anyone who knew any just cause or impediment why Rod and Rachel should not lawfully be joined together in matrimony (legal under Californian law) and Rachel opted to cherish her husband rather than obey him.

A double-decker London bus and three coaches decorated with huge white bouquets conveyed the majority of the guests the two miles to the reception which was never likely to bow to convention once a football had been produced and the groom and his son had proceeded to enjoy a kickabout on the plush, beige, patterned carpet.

The three-foot-tall wedding cake was shaped like the Houses of Parliament and Big Ben with a giant kiwi perched on the roof in celebration of the bride's national origin.

Amid all the merriment, Rod briefly slipped away to a separate bar to talk football with members of his soccer team, the Exiles. Some had been ushers, jokingly arriving at the chapel for the ceremony wearing dark glasses and carrying white canes. 'The blind leading the blind,' Rod explained.

Rod's wedding was certainly not a star-studded affair. Instead, the singer and his young bride preferred a real family-and-friends occasion. Rod thoughtfully included his faithful fan club organiser John Gray among his nearest and dearest. The mild-mannered statistician from the Department of Transport in London has dedicated most of his spare time in recent years to running Rod's international appreciation society and editing the excellent *Smiler* magazine which has subscribers in some thirty-seven countries worldwide.

'I was amazed to be asked,' says John. 'It was the trip of a lifetime. I was made so welcome by Rod and his family. And it was great to see people like Ian McLagan from the Faces and Long John Baldry.

'Rachel made a lovely bride. She is even more beautiful in real life than in photographs. Her father had been quoted in the newspapers that Rod would have to look after her or he would have him to answer to. At the wedding, Rod's brother Don, who was best man, referred to that in his speech and said that he would have him to contend with as well.

'Rod just sat there beaming all the time. He really enjoyed himself. And when it came to his speech he certainly seemed delighted. He said, "I feel like a dog with two dicks." '

However, the marriage was but a few hours old when Rod encountered bizarre teething problems of his new bride's making. Rachel, in high spirits, gathered up the folds of her ivory calf-length wedding dress and hoisted them almost to her hip before slumping back in a chair and high-kicking a leg at Rod, thereby revealing a tantalising expanse of her bare thigh, white stockings and suspenders, and a white frilly garter.

Rod feigned embarrassment, then sank to his knees in front of Rachel and seized the garter between his teeth. Roared on by the guests, he began to tug it down Rachel's shapely thigh, over her knee and down to her ankle like a playful puppy pulling at a lead.

Finally, to tumultuous cheers, Rod tugged it over his giggling bride's white satin court shoes and rose to his feet with a broad grin and the garter hanging from his mouth. He further savoured the achievement by waltzing Rachel round the room with his prize still clamped triumphantly between his teeth. Mrs Rod Stewart the Second simply threw back her pretty blonde head and laughed.

Kelly Emberg and daughter Ruby pointedly and tactfully stayed away from the wedding. Embarrassingly for all concerned, Rod and Rachel had found themselves sitting just a few tables away from Kelly a week before the wedding when they all attended the opening of a new Beverly Hills nightspot owned by London club-owner Peter Stringfellow. Kelly wore a brave smile – and a tiny figure-hugging mini-dress with a deep plunging neckline.

However, just as Rod was preparing for his £250,000 wedding, Kelly's lawyers served him with a massive palimony suit for almost that figure per year. Kelly claimed £240,000 as annual income to keep her and Ruby in the style they had previously enjoyed. And the suit was served on the day of his stag night.

She insisted: 'Rod is capable of paying for raising a child commensurate with a man of his means. Throughout our relationship Ruby and I were never deprived of anything we wanted.'

Kelly backed up her claims for £20,000 per month with a detailed list of expenses which included £1,205 per month for food and £385 for Ruby's clothes. But she agreed that Rod had already paid for furniture and a nanny and allowed her to use credit cards for other items.

The wrangle looks set to enrich a lot of Los Angeles lawyers before it is settled, but perhaps most upsetting for Rod was Kelly's insistence that she was requesting the court for sole physical and legal custody of Ruby.

Sadly for Rod, his mother Elsie, suffering as she was from multiple sclerosis, felt unable to travel to Los Angeles to see her youngest son get married. But it was the best possible Christmas present when he brought his new bride over to London to see her.

Also absent from the festivities were two of Rod's closest friends, Elton John and Ron Wood. Woody was recuperating from a car crash and Elton sent an apology and a £10 gift token from Boots the Chemists with a note urging the happy couple to buy something new for their home that was signed E of Windsor.

Spending their first Christmas together in England gave Rachel an opportunity to become acquainted with Rod's fabulous new home in Epping. The mansion in Carolwood Drive had been put on the market for £8 million. It had been home to Britt, Alana and Kelly, but now with the wisdom and energy of youth Rachel persuaded Rod to lay to rest a few ghosts and help in the search for a new home for them both.

They saw in the New Year together at a party at a London hotel and then flew off to New Zealand to visit Rachel's mother Janine at the family home in Brown's Bay, north of Auckland.

For Rachel, the New Year held the prospect either of trailing round after her husband on his massive world tour or seeing very little of him. She decided to reschedule her modelling arrangements and go with him.

For Rod, 1991 was to be the year of the new start. In 1990 he had been deeply shaken by the death of his father. Eighty-six when he died, Bob Stewart's passing in September had been deeply felt by all members of the family. Although it was by no means a surprise – Bob had not been in the best of health for some time – Rod in particular was profoundly shocked.

Although he clowned around and teased his parents, Rod remained respectful of his father's views until the end. He knew his father was embarrassed by some of the more lurid reports of his not-so-private life and that in turn irritated Rod. However, he never forgot the sacrifices his parents had made to give their youngest son the very best they could afford. And Rod's father of course was the full-blooded Scot he always aspired to be himself. Although he lived in London for most of his life, Bob Stewart never lost his rasping Scottish accent. Rod is a sometimes uncomfortable cross between a Cockney and a Scot. Friends say he can never quite decide precisely which identity to choose.

Rod is intensely proud of his family. Indeed he once announced: 'We're directly related to the Royal Stuarts, you know. My dad's brother did all the studying just before he died. The spelling was changed by Mary Queen of Scots' mother because there was no "e" in the Celtic vocabulary.'

But in the cash and celebrity-conscious society of the United States, Rod has become the sort of aristocrat the Americans understand best, a famous millionaire.

'I prefer the American class system,' says Rod. 'In England, so much is based on the way you speak: it's very false. You're not considered intelligent if you're a Cockney. I'm not saying we're all brain surgeons, but we have heads on our shoulders, us Cockneys.' But even making that point his confusion came across, for he continued: 'There I go again. One minute it's my Scottish heritage and the next I'm a London Cockney.'

Close friends noticed signs of a new maturity following Rod's trip to London for his father's funeral. He had already met and fallen for Rachel before his father died, but the assurance with which he swept into a new marriage with his first full-scale church ceremony suggested he was no longer looking over his shoulder for paternal approval.

Rod was forty-six in January 1991, but his physical fitness and air of youthful enthusiasm make him appear years younger. So, when he announced after the wedding that he was planning to start a family with his beautiful new bride, no one doubted his resolve.

In spite of the age difference and the groom's somewhat colourful track record, this looks like one rock marriage which could just surprise the cynics and stay happy.

Discography

Singles

WITH LONG JOHN BALDRY
You'll Be Mine / Up Above My Head (1964, United Artists –
   Rod featured on B side only)

WITH SHOTGUN EXPRESS
I Could Feel the Whole World Turn Around / Curtains (instrumental) (1966, Columbia)

WITH JEFF BECK GROUP
Tallyman (instrumental) / Rock My Plimsoul (1967, Columbia)
Love Is Blue (instrumental) / I've Been Drinking (1968, Col-
   umbia)

WITH PYTHON LEE JACKSON
In a Broken Dream / Doing Fine (1970, Youngblood)

WITH THE FACES
Flying / Three Button Hand Me Down (1970, Warner Brothers)
Had Me a Real Good Time / Rear Wheel Skid (1970, Warner
   Brothers)
Stay with Me / Debris (1972 Warner Brothers)

Cindy Incidentally / Skewiff (Mend the Fuse) (1973, Warner Brothers)

Pool Hall Richard / I Wish It Would Rain (1973, Warner Brothers)

Cindy Incidentally / Memphis / Stay with Me / Pool Hall Richard (1974, Warner Brothers)

You Can Make Me Dance Sing or Anything / As Long as You Tell Him (1974, Warner Brothers)

Memphis / You Can Make Me Dance Sing or Anything / Stay with Me / Cindy Incidentally (1977, Riva)

WITH THE ATLANTIC CROSSING DRUM AND PIPE BAND
Skye Boat Song / Skye Boat Song (instrumental) (1976, Riva)

Solo Singles

Good Morning Little Schoolgirl / I'm Gonna Move to the Outskirts of Town (1964, Decca)

The Day Will Come / Why Does It Go On? (1965, Columbia)

Shake / I Just Got Some (1966, Columbia)

Little Miss Understood / So Much To Say (1968, Immediate)

It's All Over Now / Jo's Lament (1970, Vertigo)

Handbags and Gladrags / Man of Constant Sorrow (1970, Mercury)

Maggie May / Reason to Believe (1971, Mercury)

You Wear it Well / Lost Paraguyos (1972, Mercury)

Angel / What Made Milwaukee Famous (Has Made a Loser Out of Me) (1972, Mercury)

Oh No Not My Baby / Jodie (1973, Mercury)

Farewell / Bring It on Home to Me (1974, Mercury)

It's All Over Now / Handbags and Gladrags (1975, Mercury)

Sailing / Stone Cold Sober (1975, Warner Brothers)

This Old Heart of Mine / All in the Name of Rock 'n' Roll (1975, Riva)

Tonight's the Night / The Ball Trap (1976, Riva)

The Killing of Georgie / Fool for You (1976, Riva)

Sailing / Stone Cold Sober (1976, Riva) (re-released in UK when Sailing was adopted as theme tune for the BBC TV series Sailor)

Get Back / Trade Winds (1976, Riva)

Maggie May / You Wear it Well / Twistin' the Night Away (1976, Mercury)

First Cut is the Deepest / I Don't Want to Talk about It (1977, Riva)

You're in My Heart/ You Really Got a Nerve (1977, Riva)

Hot Legs / I was Only Joking (1978, Riva)

Ole Ola / I'd Walk a Million Miles for One of Your Goals (1978, Riva)

Da Ya Think I'm Sexy / Dirty Weekend (1978, Riva)

Ain't Love a Bitch / Scarred and Scared (1979, Riva)

The Best Days of My Life / Blondes (Have More Fun) (1979, Riva)

(If Loving You is Wrong) I Don't Want to be Right / Last Summer (1980, Riva)

Passion / Better Off Dead (1980, Riva)

My Girl / She Won't Dance with Me (1980, Riva)

Oh God I Wish I was Home Tonight / Somebody Special (1981, Riva)

Tonight I'm Yours / Sonny (1981, Riva)

Young Turks / Tora, Tora, Tora (Out with the Boys) (1981, Riva)

How Long? / Jealous (1982, Riva)

Baby Jane / Ready Now (1983, Warner Brothers)

What am I Gonna Do? (I'm So in Love with You) / Dancin' Alone (1983, Warner Brothers)

Infatuation / Three Time Loser (1984, Warner Brothers)

Some Guys Have All the Luck / I was Only Joking (1984, Warner Brothers)

Love Touch / Heart is on the Line (1986, Warner Brothers)

Every Beat of My Heart / Trouble (1986, Warner Brothers)

Another Heartache / You're in My Heart (1986, Warner Brothers)
Lost in You / Almost Illegal (1988, Warner Brothers)
Forever Young / Days of Rage (1988, Warner Brothers)
Downtown Train / The Killing of Georgie (1989, Warner Brothers)
Rhythm of My Heart (1991, Warner Brothers)

Albums

(Compilations and Greatest Hits Albums are Not Included. Original compositions are listed).

WITH STEAMPACKET
The First Supergroup (1988, Charly Records)
Can I Get a Witness? / The In-Crowd / Baby Take Me / Baby Baby / Back at the Chicken Shack / Cry Me a River / Oh Baby / Don't You Do it / Holy Smoke / Lord Remember Me

WITH JEFF BECK
Truth (1968, Columbia)
Shapes of Things / Let Me Move You / Morning Dew / You Shook Me / Ol' Man River / Greensleeves (instrumental) / Rock My Plimsoul / Beck's Bolero (instrumental) / Blues De Luxe / Ain't Superstitious
Beck-Ola (1969, Columbia)
All Shook Up / Spanish Boots (Beck-Stewart-Wood) / Girl from Mill Valley (instrumental) / Jailhouse Rock / Plynth (Water Down the Drain) (Hopkins-Wood-Stewart) / The Hangman's Knee (Hopkins-Beck-Newman-Stewart-Wood) / Rice Pudding (instrumental)

WITH THE FACES
First Step (1970, Warner Brothers)
Wicked Messenger / Devotion / Shake, Shudder, Shiver /

Stone / Around the Plynth (Stewart-Wood) / Flying / Pineapple and the Monkey / Nobody Knows / Looking Out the Window / Three Button Hand Me Down (Stewart-McLagan)

Long Player (1971, Warner Brothers)

Bad 'n' Ruin (Stewart-McLagan) / Tell Everyone / Sweet Lady Mary (Wood-Stewart-Lane) / Richmond / Maybe I'm Amazed / Had Me a Real Good Time (Wood-Stewart-Lane) / On the Beach / I Feel So Good / Jerusalem

A Nod's as Good as a Wink . . . To a Blind Horse (1972, Warner Brothers)

Miss Judy's Farm (Wood-Stewart) / You're So Rude / Love Lived Here (Wood-Stewart-Lane) / Last Orders Please / Stay with Me (Wood-Stewart) / Debris / Memphis / Too Bad (Wood-Stewart) / That's All You Need (Wood-Stewart)

Ooh La La (1973, Warner Brothers)

Silicone Grown (Stewart-Wood) / Cindy Incidentally (Wood-Stewart-McLagan) / Flags and Banners (Lane-Stewart) / My Fault (Wood-Stewart-McLagan) / Borstal Boys (McLagan-Wood-Stewart) / Fly in the Ointment / I'm on the Late Side (Stewart-Lane) / Glad and Sorry / Just Another Honky / Ooh La La

Coast to Coast/Overture and Beginners: Live Album (1974, Mercury)

It's All Over Now / Cut Across Shorty / Too Bad / Every Picture Tells a Story / Angel / Stay with Me / Wish It Would Rain / I'd Rather Go Blind / Borstal Boys / Amazing Grace / Jealous Guy

Solo Albums

(Compilations and greatest hit albums are not included. Rod Stewart compositions are listed.)

An Old Raincoat Won't Ever Let You Down (1970, Mercury)
Street Fighting Man / Man of Constant Sorrow / Blind Prayer (Stewart) / Handbags and Gladrags / An Old Raincoat Won't Ever Let You Down (Stewart) / I Wouldn't Ever Change a Thing (Stewart) / Cindy's Lament (Stewart) / Dirty Old Town
Gasoline Alley (1970, Mercury)
Gasoline Alley (Stewart-Wood) / It's All Over Now / Only a Hobo / My Way of Giving / Country Comfort / Cut Across Shorty / Lady Day (Stewart) / Jo's Lament (Stewart) / I Don't Want to Discuss It
Every Picture Tells a Story (1971, Mercury)
Every Picture Tells a Story (Stewart-Wood) / Seems Like a Long Time / That's All Right / Tomorrow is a Long Time / Maggie May (Stewart-Quittenton) / Mandolin Wind (Stewart) / (I Know) I'm Losing You / Reason to Believe
Never a Dull Moment (1972, Mercury)
True Blue (Stewart-Wood) / Lost Paraguyos (Stewart-Wood) / Mama You Been on My Mind / Italian Girls (Stewart-Wood) / Angel / Interludings (instrumental) / You Wear it Well (Stewart-Quittenton) / I'd Rather Go Blind / Twistin' the Night Away
Smiler (1974, Mercury)
Sweet Little Rock 'n' Roller / Lochinvar (instrumental) / Farewell (Stewart-Quittenton) / Sailor (Stewart-Wood) / Bring It on Home to Me / You Send Me / Let Me be Your Car / A Natural Man / Dixie Toot (Stewart-Wood) / Hard Road / I've Grown Accustomed to Her Face (instrumental) / Girl from the North Country / Mine for Me

Atlantic Crossing (1975, Warner Brothers)
I Don't Want to Talk about It / It's Not the Spotlight / This Old Heart of Mine / Still Love You (Stewart) / Sailing / Three Time Loser (Stewart) / Alright for an Hour (Stewart-Davis) / All in the Name of Rock 'n' Roll (Stewart) / Drift Away / Stone Cold Sober (Stewart-Cropper)

A Night on the Town (1976, Riva)
The Ball Trap (Stewart) / Pretty Flamingo / Big Bayou / The Wild Side of Life / Trade Winds / Tonight's the Night (Stewart) / First Cut is the Deepest / Fool for You (Stewart) / The Killing of Georgie (Parts 1 and 2) (Stewart)

Foot Loose and Fancy Free (1977, Riva)
Hot Legs (Stewart-Grainger) / You're Insane (Stewart-Chen) / You're in My Heart (The Final Acclaim) (Stewart) / Born Loose (Stewart-Grainger-Cregan) / You Keep Me Hangin' On / If Lovin' You is Wrong I Don't Want to be Right / You Got a Nerve (Stewart-Grainger) / I was Only Joking (Stewart-Grainger)

Blondes Have More Fun (1978, Riva)
Da Ya Think I'm Sexy? (Stewart-Appice) / Dirty Weekend (Stewart-Grainger) / Ain't Love a Bitch (Stewart-Grainger) / The Best Days of My Life (Stewart-Cregan) / Is That the Thanks I Get? (Stewart-Cregan) / Attractive Female Wanted (Stewart-Grainger) / Blondes Have More Fun (Stewart-Cregan) / Last Summer (Stewart-Chen) / Standing in the Shadows of Love / Scarred and Scared (Stewart-Grainger)

Foolish Behaviour (1980, Riva)
Better Off Dead (Stewart-Chen-Savigar-Cregan-Grainger-Appice) / Foolish Behaviour (Stewart-Chen-Savigar-Cregan-Appice) / My Girl (Stewart-Chen-Savigar-Cregan-Grainger-Appice) / She Won't Dance with Me (Stewart-J. Ben) / Gi' Me Wings (Stewart-Chen-Savigar-Cregan-Grainger) / So Soon We Change (Stewart-Chen-Savigar-Cregan-Grainger) / Somebody Special (Stewart-Harley-Chen-Savigar-Cregan-Grainger) / Passion (Stewart-Chen-Savigar-Cregan-Grainger) / Say It

Ain't True (Stewart-Chen-Savigar-Cregan-Grainger) / Oh God I Wish I was Home Tonight (Stewart-Chen-Savigar-Cregan-Grainger)

Tonight I'm Yours (1981, Riva)

Tonight I'm Yours (Don't Hurt Me) (Stewart-Cregan-Savigar) / How Long / Tora, Tora, Tora (Out with the Boys) (Stewart) / Tear It Up / Only a Boy (Stewart-Cregan-Savigar) / Just Like a Woman / Jealous (Stewart-Davis-Johnson-Appice) / Sonny (Stewart-Taupin-Savigar-Cregan) / Young Turks (Stewart-Appice-Savigar-Hitchings) / Never Give Up on a Dream (Taupin-Stewart-Cregan)

Absolutely Live (1982, Warner Brothers)

The Stripper / Tonight I'm Yours (Don't Hurt Me) / Sweet Little Rock and Roller / Hot Legs / Tonight's the Night (Gonna be Alright) / The Great Pretender / Passion / She Won't Dance with Me / Little Queenie / You're in My Heart (The Final Acclaim) / Rock My Plimsoul / Young Turks / Guess I'll Always Love You / Gasoline Alley / Maggie May / Tear It Up / Da Ya Think I'm Sexy? / Sailing / I Don't Want to Talk about It / Stay with Me

Body Wishes (1983, Warner Brothers)

Dancin' Alone (Stewart-Le Mesurier) / Baby Jane (Stewart-Davis) / Move Me (Stewart-Brock-Davis-Stocker-Savigar) / Body Wishes (Stewart-Cregan-Savigar-Le Mesurier) / Sweet Surrender (Stewart-Le Mesurier) / What Am I Gonna Do? (I'm So In Love With You) (Stewart-Davis-Brock) / Ghetto Blaster (Stewart-Cregan-Savigar) / Ready Now (Stewart-Stocker) / Strangers Again (Stewart-Cregan-Savigar) / Satisfied (Stewart-Taupin-Cregan-Savigar)

Camouflage (1985, Warner Brothers)

Infatuation (Stewart-Hitchings-R. Robinson) / All Right Now / Some Guys Have All the Luck / Can We Still be Friends? / Bad for You (Stewart-Savigar-Cregan) / Heart is on the Line (Stewart-J. Davis) / Camouflage (Stewart-Savigar-Omartian) / Trouble (Stewart-Omartian)

Every Beat of My Heart (1986, Warner Brothers)
Here to Eternity (Stewart-Savigar) / Another Heartache (Adams-Vallance-Stewart-Wayne) / A Night Like This (Stewart) / Who's Gonna Take Me Home? (The Rise and Fall of a Budding Gigolo) (Stewart-Savigar-Davis) / Red Hot in Black (Stewart-Cregan-Savigar) / Love Touch (Theme from Legal Eagles) / In My Own Crazy Way (Miller-Seals-Setser-Stewart) / Every Beat of My Heart (Stewart-Savigar) / Ten Days of Rain (Stewart-Savigar-Brock) / In My Life
Out of Order (1988, Warner Brothers)
Lost in You (Stewart-Taylor) / The Wild Horse (Stewart-Taylor) / Lethal Dose of Love (Stewart-Taylor) / Forever Young (Stewart-Cregan-Savigar) / My Heart Can't Tell Me No / Dynamite (Stewart-Taylor) / Nobody Knows You When You're Down and Out / Crazy About Her (Stewart-Hitchings-Cregan) / Try a Little Tenderness / When I was Your Man (Stewart-Savigar)
Storyteller (1989, Warner Brothers)
Good Morning Little Schoolgirl / Can I Get a Witness / Shake / So Much to Say / Little Miss Understood / I've been Drinking / I ain't Superstitious / Shapes of Things / In a Broken Dream / Street Fighting Man / Handbags and Gladrags / Gasoline Alley / Cut Across Shorty / Country Comforts / It's All Over Now / Sweet Lady Mary / Had Me a Real Good Time / Maggie May / Mandolin Wind / (I Know) I'm Losing You / Reason to Believe / Every Picture Tells a Story / Stay with Me / True Blue / Angel / You Wear It Well / I'd Rather Go Blind / Twistin' the Night Away / What Made Milwaukee Famous / Oh No Not My Baby / Pinball Wizard / Sweet Little Rock 'n' Roller / Let Me be Your Car / You Can Make Me Dance, Sing or Anything / Sailing / I Don't Want to Talk about It / Stone Cold Sober / To Love Somebody / Tonight's the Night / The First Cut is the Deepest / The Killing of Georgie (Parts 1 and 2) / Get Back / Hot Legs / I was Only Joking / You're in My Heart / Da Ya Think I'm Sexy / Passion / Oh God I Wish I was

Home Tonight / Tonight I'm Yours / Young Turks / Baby Jane / What am I Gonna Do? (I'm So in Love with You) / People Get Ready / Some Guys Have All the Luck / Infatuation / Love Touch / Every Beat of My Heart / Lost in You / My Heart Can't Tell You No / Dynamite / Crazy about Her / Forever Young / I Don't Want to Talk About It / This Old Heart of Mine / Downtown Train

Vagabond Heart (1991, Warner Brothers)

Rhythm of My Heart / Rebel Heart (Stewart-Golub-Kentis-Rojas) / Broken Arrow / It Takes Two / When a Man's in Love (Stewart-Kentis-Golub-Rojas) / You are Everything / The Mowtown Song / Go Out Dancing (Stewart-Golub-Kentis) / No Holding Back (Stewart-Savigar-Cregan) / Have I Told You Lately? / Moment of Glory (Stewart-Kentis-Golub-Rojas) / Downtown Train / If Only (Stewart-Savigar-Cregan)

Chart Positions
of Solo Works

Solo Singles

Date	Title	Position
1964	Good Morning Little Schoolgirl	–
1965	The Day will Come	–
1966	Shake	–
1967	Little Miss Understood	–
1970	It's All Over Now	–
1971	Maggie May	1
1972	You Wear It Well	1
1972	Angel	4
1973	Oh No Not My Baby	6
1974	Farewell	7
1974	You Can Make Me Dance, Sing, or Anything (with the Faces)	12
1975	This Old Heart of Mine	4
1976	Sailing	1
1976	Tonight's the Night	5
1976	The Killing of Georgie (Parts 1 and 2)	2
1976	Get Back	11

Date (cont)	Title	Position
1977	First Cut is the Deepest	1
1977	You're in My Heart	3
1978	Hot Legs	5
1978	Ole Ola	4
1978	Da Ya Think I'm Sexy?	1
1979	Ain't Love a Bitch	11
1979	The Best Days of My Life	63
1980	If Loving You is Wrong	23
1980	Passion	17
1980	My Girl	32
1981	Tonight I'm Yours	8
1981	Young Turks	11
1982	How Long?	41
1983	Baby Jane	1
1983	What am I Gonna Do?	3
1983	Sweet Surrender	23
1984	Infatuation	27
1984	Some Guys Have All the Luck	15
1986	Love Touch	27
1986	Every Beat of My Heart	5
1986	Another Heartache	54
1988	Lost in You	21
1988	Forever Young	–
1989	My Heart Can't Tell You No	49
1990	Downtown Train	10
1990	It Takes Two (with Tina Turner)	5
1991	Rhythm of My Heart	3

Solo Albums

Compilations, retrospectives and re-issues are not included.

Date	Title	Position
1970	An Old Raincoat won't Ever Let You Down	–
1970	Gasoline Alley	62
1971	Every Picture Tells a Story	1
1972	Never a Dull Moment	1
1974	Smiler	1
1975	Atlantic Crossing	1
1976	A Night on the Town	1
1977	Footloose and Fancy Free	3
1978	Blondes Have More Fun	3
1980	Foolish Behaviour	4
1981	Tonight I'm Yours	8
1982	Absolutely Live	35
1983	Body Wishes	5
1984	Camouflage	8
1988	Out of Order	11
1989	Storyteller	–
1991	Vagabond Heart	2

Index